Accidental Archaeologist

||||| Memoirs of
Jesse D. Jennings

FOREWORD BY
C. Melvin Aikens

University of Utah Press
Salt Lake City

Frontispiece: Portrait by Alvin Gittins, 1975. Jesse D. Jennings in front of a cut through the Sudden Shelter site.

CATALOGING·IN·PUBLICATION DATA

Jennings, Jesse David, 1909–
    Accidental archaeologist : memoirs of Jesse D. Jennings / Foreword by C. Melvin Aikens.
       p.   cm.
    ISBN 0-87480-452-3
    1. Jennings, Jesse David, 1909–   . 2 Anthropologists—United States—Biography. 3. Archaeologists—United States—Biography.   4. Indians of North America—Antiquities. I. Title.
GN21.J46A3 1994
930.1′092—dc20   94-9300

Dedicated to

Jane Chase Jennings,

my wife of nearly sixty years.
Her unwavering love, support, and
tolerance have steadied and strengthened me
through hard times and good times,
successes and failures, ever since we met in
North Carolina in 1934.

CONTENTS

FOREWORD

JESSE D. JENNINGS is one of the most distinguished and influential founders of North American archaeology as it is known and practiced today, and this memoir offers a glimpse of the field's crucial growth period as reflected in the real-life experience of a leading protagonist. Jennings arrived at the University of Chicago in 1929 with a bachelor's degree from a small and now long-defunct Baptist college in Hot Springs, New Mexico. Having grown up in a dirt-poor farming family, Jennings was by then long-accustomed to earning his own way, and he put himself through Chicago during the early and mid-1930s with a succession of jobs as a construction laborer, busboy, hospital orderly, campus policeman, and archaeological fieldworker, with time out teaching high school for two years in Hope, New Mexico. The Chicago faculty and distinguished visitors of the time included Robert Redfield, H. R. Radcliffe-Brown, Fay-Cooper Cole, Edward Sapir, and Wilton Krogman, among others, with Redfield occupying a special place in Jennings's memory. Some of Jennings's fellow students were Donald Collier, Fred Eggan, Robert Braidwood, Madeline Kneberg, James Griffin, Kalervo Oberg, Philleo Nash, Alexander Spoehr, Georg Neumann, and John Embree, to mention a few comrades who later became well known. During the 1930s and 1940s (interrupted by service as a naval officer during World War II) Jennings worked in the Midwest, Southeast, and Mississippi Valley for the WPA and National Park Service, interacting with such colleagues as Thorne Deuel, Charles Fairbanks, David DeJarnette, Stuart Neitzel, Frank Setzler, John Corbett, George Quimby, Robert Wauchope, William Webb, Gordon Willey, James Ford, Philip Phillips, and Albert Spaulding. These years also included stints in Guatemala, the Plains, and the Southwest, where Jennings became acquainted with A. V. Kidder, Edwin

Shook, Waldo Wedel, Emil Haury, Erik Reed, Charlie Steen, and others.

Amid this distinguished company Jennings gained early recognition as a major contributor to North American archaeology and in 1948 began a professorial career at the University of Utah, recommended independently to that institution by three nationally prominent scholars as the most promising young anthropologist of the day. From his base at Utah, Jennings went on to conduct major research in the Great Basin, Southwest, and Pacific, to train numerous professional archaeologists active today, and to build (from scratch) the award-winning Utah Museum of Natural History. After "retiring" as a Distinguished Professor at Utah, he moved to Oregon in 1980, continuing his teaching and research career as an adjunct professor at the University of Oregon. He is currently at work on a major synthesis of Great Basin prehistory, having just finished the autobiographical work that this note precedes.

Jennings's scholarly accomplishments are too many to discuss in this space, or even to list, but a convenient summary of the major honors earned over his long career is provided by the citation that accompanied the Distinguished Service Award of the Society for American Archaeology, which he received in 1982:

> The Distinguished Service Award of the Society for American Archaeology is given to a member of the society whose achievements have been clearly extraordinary in nature and have resulted in a genuine and lasting contribution to the archaeological profession. It was established as an annual award in 1980. It is with great pleasure that the Society presents the 1982 Award to Jesse D. Jennings, Distinguished Professor of Anthropology at the University of Utah.
>
> Dr. Jennings came to the University of Utah in 1948 from a background of Federal service, of which much was gained as an archaeologist with the National Park Service. He had received his doctorate from the University of Chicago in 1943. At Utah, he was the recipient of a number of academic distinctions, among them the Reynolds and Leigh Lectureships, the Distinguished Professorship he currently holds, and, in 1980, bestowal of the Doctor of Science degree. Furthermore, during his career there he established the Utah Museum of Natural History, developed the Utah Statewide Archaeological Survey, and directed the Glen Canyon Archaeological Salvage Project. Additional awards included the Viking Medal in Archaeol-

ogy (1958) and a Fulbright-Hayes Lectureship at the University of Auckland, New Zealand (1979). He was elected to the National Academy of Sciences in 1977.

Dr. Jennings's career is further distinguished by the extent of his service to the profession. He was a member of the Executive Board of the American Anthropological Association (1953–56), and Vice-President of the American Association for the Advancement of Science (1961). He served as Editor of *American Antiquity* (1950–54), and as President of the Society for American Archaeology (1959–60). He was one of the pioneers in the early development of salvage archaeology, and, more recently, a founding member of the Society of Professional Archaeologists. His record of fieldwork reflects well his diverse and untiring interest in archaeology, taking him from Guatemala, through much of North America, and ultimately to Polynesia. As an example of his many publications reporting this research, *Danger Cave* (1957) most certainly manifests his capabilities as both archaeologist and writer, as well as his interest and expertise in the Desert West.

However, it is perhaps for his syntheses and edited works in North American prehistory that Professor Jennings is best known. Among the major syntheses and co-edited volumes are *Prehistoric Man in the New World* (1964), *Readings in Anthropology* (1955), now in its third edition, and *The Native Americans* (1965) and *Prehistory of North America* (1968), now both in their second editions. His recent *Polynesian Prehistory* (1979) carries these talents to the Pacific. Most certainly these works constitute an extraordinary and enduring contribution to our profession by an extraordinarily productive scholar.

Jesse Jennings personifies the goals we strive for as archaeologists—a commitment to anthropological inquiry and scientific integrity, a diversity of geographical and temporal interests, an ability to synthesize and, most importantly, the determination to insure that the results of our efforts are published and presented to the profession with timeliness and clarity. Dr. Jennings is an exemplary archaeologist and a most deserving recipient of the 1982 Distinguished Service Award. The Award was presented to him at the Society's 47th Annual Meeting in Minneapolis, April 16, 1982 (*American Antiquity* Vol. 47, No. 3, pp. 483–484, 1982).

Thus, a brief sketch of Jennings's academic history, offered to contextualize professionally the remarkable career that is recounted in much more human terms in the memoir that follows. The remainder of this foreword offers a few impressions of the man himself. It has to be written in the first person, because what I have to report was learned at firsthand, as Jennings's student, his employee, and ultimately his colleague. Necessarily, considering the source, these impressions stem from a later phase of Jennings's career, after he became a professor of anthropology at the University of Utah and was well established as a major figure in American archaeology.

Jennings is most prominently defined, especially among his students, by his characteristically direct and demanding approach to both teaching and research situations. Never unclear about his expectations, he is dependably insistent and—if need be—forceful in seeing to it that they are met or their achievement at least vigorously attempted. Possessed of boundless energy himself, he expects to see it in others too. In the classroom or in the field—the latter one of Jennings's most important teaching venues—things are not left to chance, and things are not let go. Responsibility is demanded, of a seminar student scheduled to perform at a given time or of a field-crew chief coping with the many necessities of that position. Though good work is never left unremarked, neither is a failure to perform up to standard. Nor are too facile statements left unprobed, and a student who doesn't keep up the pace in a seminar presentation will be told to "kick it along." Helping to relieve the tension this regime can generate is Jennings's habit of lacing his interactions with wisecracks and asides ranging from groaners to the hilarious. Thus is engendered that certain blend of striving, nervous anticipation (for some verging on fear), and, ultimately, respectful affection for their mentor, that is known to all Jennings students.

The early chapters of Jennings's memoir seem to illuminate the origin of this *persona*. Clearly, his boyhood was dominated by the certainties of his strong-willed mother's deeply held Baptist religion. Although Jennings records that his own Baptist fervor evaporated during his college years, something manifestly remained of the fundamentalist sense of good and bad, right and wrong, and willingness to make and act on such judgments. Jennings was also schooled early in responsibility, by the obligations of helping to sustain house and home, which fell on him too heavily and too soon because of his father's frequent and prolonged absences and the extremely limited family income.

Jennings's students at Utah in the Glen Canyon Project days of the late 1950s and early 1960s expressed that certain feeling of respect, affection, and dread in the brief fad of rendering his given name, Jesse (via its obvious etymological connection to Jesus), as *Yahweh,* evoking the great and terrible desert god of the Old Testament. Similarly, he was referred to by a later generation of students as "The Dark Lord," after the powerful and implacable figure of J. R. R. Tolkien's *Lord of the Rings.* Jennings's often-uttered expectation that we would cope appropriately with whatever exigencies the wild canyonlands field situation might present was memorialized in a little ditty sung to the tune of "The Frozen Logger," accompanied by banjo and ukulele. The verses characterized our boss—not always flatteringly—in terms of various archaeological feats and incidents—some more or less real, some fabulous—and the song ended with the phrase, ". . . emblazoned on his forehead was the magic slogan, COPE!"

Those student exaggerations of Jennings's character and exploits seem to have reflected a sense of him as a kind of legendary figure, somehow larger than life. Manifestly, we at least occasionally thought of him as godlike, though not in any namby-pamby way. We knew about his previous work, of course, and certainly he was always a looming presence on the local scene. I know that in my own case I actually did think he was larger than life. I was greatly surprised to learn one day, in a conversation with his younger son Herb (Jennings regularly sent his sons Dave and Herb, then schoolboys, to the field on summer-dig crews for what they could learn about work and life in general), that Jennings was about five feet ten inches tall and weighed about 175 pounds. I was surprised because, fitting those dimensions almost exactly myself, I had always perceived Jennings as a good bit larger, maybe something over six feet and closer to 200 pounds!

After "cope," another favorite Jennings expression was "making mistakes." This applied to an archaeologist's role in directing an excavation. Jennings insisted on clear stratigraphic and associational control, but of course knew from much experience how hard it is to figure out the structure of an archaeological deposit while in the act of digging it away. A greeting to a neophyte crew chief, "so, Aikens, you're making the mistakes on this site," meant, "I see that you are in charge here," and was also a tip-off that this stern inspector could be understanding about an occasional error if it devolved from a reasoned attempt to get the thing right and so long as the error was clearly described and properly labeled in the field notes. Although he was not one to overtly "nurture" a student, I do recall being comforted by a Jennings statement that a man who never made mistakes was a man who never did anything.

On campus, a feature of Jennings's behavior that I only came to recognize as remarkable long after leaving Utah, completing graduate work, and becoming a professor myself was his total availability to students. Unlike the latter-day professor who typically schedules but a few office hours each week for student conversation and consultation, Jennings was always there and his door was always open. A student could depend on finding him interested and ready to act directly on the concern of the moment. A few snippets from a routine tenured faculty review, done shortly before Jennings's "retirement" at Utah, describes similar relations with students some twenty years later:

> Unlike many university faculty, he has faced the difficult task of providing direct and honest evaluation of his students so they all know where they and their work stand in relation to his judgment of quality.... Students, past and present, stress the great amount of learning that goes on in his classes as compared to other classes.... His involvement with students has been his outstanding characteristic. He is vitally concerned with their education, exceptionally active in finding them support during their studies and jobs when they get their degrees. His use of his many contacts for these ends has provided him with much vocal appreciation.

Subsequently, "retired" from Utah and offering occasional seminars at the University of Oregon, Jennings has continued this availability to students, who have in turn feted him repeatedly at term's end with luncheons and humorous reflections of the wit and wisdom shared in their classroom experience together.

As for Jennings's archaeological work in itself, the present book really does not say enough about that; this work is already well known to the professionals and students who will probably be the main readers of this memoir, but one not already acquainted with his research and writing could profit by looking up the latest edition of Jennings's *Prehistory of*

North America (Mayfield Press, 1989) or his *Prehistory of Utah and the Eastern Great Basin* (University of Utah Anthropological Papers 98, 1978). His most classic work, and a prominent milestone of North American archaeology, is *Danger Cave,* jointly published in 1957 as Memoir 14 of the Society for American Archaeology and University of Utah Anthropological Papers 27. The monograph on Danger Cave, a site west of the Great Salt Lake that was occupied over some 11,000 years, set a new standard for care in excavation and completeness in reporting and wove a tapestry of artifactual, biotic, and ethnographic threads vividly to portray an ancient and persistent Great Basin Desert Culture—a concept that has shaped all subsequent research in the desert west and will surely remain a point of reference for archaeological generations to come. In 1957, an archaeological report that discussed in detail excavation strategy, procedures, mistakes, and the excavator's evolving understanding of the deposits, that reported systematically and in detail not only the artifacts but also such unimpressive scraps as twigs, leaves, seeds, chaff, bones, and even human feces, and that integrated those data within a broad chronological/regional/ecological/ethnographic context was a marvelous novelty. *Danger Cave* did all that; and, as a result, the ideas that emerged from Jennings's laboring (inductively, be it noted) through his mountain of excavated and comparative data were taken very seriously by the archaeological profession. Happily, such monographs are quite commonplace today, and there is no doubt that the example of Jennings's Danger Cave work was enormously influential in stimulating this development.

Finally, it seems proper to note in closing, from the perspective of one who has known Jennings for some thirty-five years, that in this book the autobiographer presents himself in the same unembellished, matter-of-fact way that he might talk about colleagues in a graduate seminar or around a campfire (expletives and ribald humor deleted all around, of course). Jennings does not attempt a self-assessment of the value of his work and, in fact, does not even give an adequate sense of its remarkable scope; hence, the book is actually self-deprecating. But as an honest portrayal of character, the account is definitely "him." I recommend it to anyone who wants to know how an authentic archaeological legend got that way.

C. Melvin Aikens
Eugene, Oregon
January 1994

ACKNOWLEDGMENTS

As is already evident, I acknowledge my wife, Jane, first and foremost. I have been very fortunate in my marriage because Jane learned somewhere early in life that she had a mind and was expected to use it. Use of her mind extended to stating her opinions on events, affairs, incidents—the role of the stolid, docile female, always one step behind her man, had never occurred to her or, if it had, it did not appeal. In addition to supporting me endlessly in actions foolish or wise, she stated her opinion. Frequent disapproval of my perhaps hasty actions not only angered but also steadied and balanced me, I'm sure, a thousand-and-one times. Here I merely reiterate my awareness of my debt to my wife's forthrightness and independence of spirit, thought, and speech.

I need also to acknowledge the support and encouragement of university friends and many students. I have been encouraged to set down my memories by Warren d'Azevedo, Katherine and Don Fowler, Norma Mikkelsen, and Alice and Melvin Aikens. All have quite specifically urged me to do my memoirs. Dozens of other people in light conversations or at the close of an anecdote I had told would say, "You should write your memoirs." Of course, I appreciated their advice, but never intended to follow it. Then in recent years I was asked to do some retrospective lectures telling "How It Was in Olden Times." I want to acknowledge the several people who invited me to do that and let me learn for myself that raking over the adventures of the past was somehow fun: Raymond Wood, who asked me about my work in the Plains; Steve Williams, who elicited my views about the Lower Mississippi Valley; Shelley Smith of the Bureau of Land Management State Office in Utah to speak for Utah Archaeology week; Eldon Dorman of Price, Utah, who asked me to speak at the dedication of the new Price Museum; Melvin Aikens,

xvii

who asked me to offer a colloquium at the University of Oregon; and, finally, Samuel O. Brooke of the U.S. Forest Service stationed in Jackson, Mississippi, who asked me to address the Southeastern Archaeological Conference about my early years at the Natchez Trace. These people pushed me over the hump. Thinking about and preparing those talks made me realize that those people had done me a favor, and I acknowledge their role in whatever follows; no blame, however, should attach to them.

With great pleasure I acknowledge the cheerful assistance of Duncan Metcalfe, Department of Anthropology, University of Utah, Steve Williams of the Peabody Museum, Harvard University, and James Atkinson of the National Park Service, on assignment to the Natchez Trace Parkway, who promptly provided the many fine photographs I requested; each photograph is labeled in the volume as to source.

Especially I thank Melvin Aikens, a friend of many years, who, after reading the next-to-last draft, provided me with a careful, thoughtful critique and six pages of changes, additions, and comment that greatly improved this final version. I was equally annoyed by, but very grateful to, the anonymous reviewers solicited by the University of Utah Press. Meeting these criticisms greatly improved this volume.

Also I thank Mrs. Beth Johnston who transcribed my dictation through several versions and offered continuous encouragement.

Finally, I gratefully acknowledge William Woodcock with Princeton University Press, another friend (who also read the next-to-last draft), for his critique and encouragement—one might say his "quarterbacking"—in the final stages of manuscript preparation.

From the University of Utah Press I thankfully acknowledge Jeff Grathwohl, Norma Mikkelsen, and others who encouraged and guided me through intricacies of transforming a manuscript into a book.

INTRODUCTION

WHY DO PEOPLE WRITE? As I have pondered that question, it has seemed to me that novelists and mystery writers are probably bored with whatever life has given them and attempt an escape via the story or novel they create. To some degree, I also think, most novelists at one time or another draw on autobiographical material. Certainly I cannot fault the escape offered by reading creative writing when I have read so much of it. As for philosophers and religious writers, I presume they wish to instruct others either in their invaluable insights or in the details and rewards embedded in their creed. Some people write for money, although I gather that only a few writers are heavily rewarded financially. Scholars obviously and admittedly write to achieve the recognition of their peers; in fact, it is the written word through which scholarship is disseminated or preserved for succeeding generations. Statesmen and politicians are prone to save their letters and records so they or others, usually hired hacks, may write *their* version of their public accomplishments. In that way, I suppose, they hope finally to achieve the lasting recognition they feel their public spirit and good works deserve.

Why would one write about his own life? On the face of it, an autobiography is only an exercise in ego enhancement, although it can be more than that. In my case, I can rationalize that several people have urged me to do it, advice I appreciated as being perhaps a form of peer recognition. This account was dragged from memory because I never kept a diary and never—even today—keep letters or carbons of my responses to the letters. What I relate, then, will have been entirely from memory and will contain many gaps. The mistakes I have made cannot be ignored, but I have tended to gloss them over. Nor have I included any "kiss and tell" material. Neither have I included anything of family life:

the illnesses, the pleasures and frustrations and mistakes experienced as Jane and I tried to rear two boys to respectable manhood, nor our ever-present financial worries. I found that I could not blend the two—personal and professional—coherently, so I abandoned the effort. I have attempted to hold boasting to a minimum, trying always for matter-of-fact reporting of what I remember.

I should perhaps say that this task was far more difficult than I had expected. For example, one cannot be fully candid, although I have tried to be. Another interesting result of this effort has been to discover that by being more or less honest with myself I have learned far more about myself than I really needed to know.

In order to begin the story of one's life, something about an individual's childhood should be set out. This I fear could be tedious, largely because very little of apparent note occurs during anyone's early years. However, childhood, especially the first six or seven years, comprises the most important period in any life because it is then that the adult is formed, a truth that has long been established; the experience of living shapes one. The very fact of living teaches a great deal, as do precept, admonition, and the example set by those around a child. I am convinced that all those factors permanently mold everyone—thoughts, reactions, even motor habits. Thus, each person is unique to the extent that no one else has had the identical experiences; therefore, it seems necessary or desirable to inflict some of my early years on those who, for whatever reason, are reading this book.

This account, then, is principally about my life as I attempted to survive and perhaps to contribute something of value to the field of American archaeology. I have made no effort, except for the first twenty years, to keep the account chronological. The passage of time as such is a pretty monotonous thing at best, and to tell eighty-plus years of life experiences chronologically would be even more monotonous.

I think I have learned more writing this than I expected to, because as I looked back on my actions, some of which were clearly not to my advantage at the time, I came to know a little more about myself. I know that because of my early years I had a fear of poverty, a fear of failure, and there is no doubt that in high school I had developed a self-image as being a rugged, self-reliant "he-man," a concept implying physical strength and competence in any situation that arose. In distant retrospect, those three things, I now think, blended to motivate me. As I explain in the first chapter, I developed a series of behaviors for dealing with other people that now seem to me to be largely a defense mechanism against my uncertainties and an awareness of my inadequacies.

The Youthful Years

O N THE FACE OF IT, the first decades of Jesse David Jennings's life were ordinary, typical of most children of that period. I was born on July 7, 1909, in Oklahoma City, it is said on a kitchen table because my family probably could not have afforded lying-in facilities, even had they been available in Oklahoma City two years after Oklahoma became a state. Although the second of three children, I grew up as the oldest child since a brother born three or four years earlier had succumbed to diphtheria at the age of about one year; a sister, Alvina, was born in September 1914. As the oldest, I was expected to set the example of obedience, filial respect, and neatness for my young sister. Early on I had chores and other responsibilities which came to include tending my sister. My mother, Grace (Belle) Cruce Jennings, was a true believer in an omniscient, omnipotent, as well as a just and angry and vindictive God. Aside from the fact that my mother was fanatically religious, with a strong, unforgiving, fundamentalist Southern Baptist view of human frailty, my childhood was unremarkable. I was early—and thoroughly—convinced of my personal sinfulness in God's eyes and hence was fully aware of my unworthiness. The sense of unworthiness cropped up at inconvenient times in later life, but my belief in the disadvantages of sinning eventually evaporated as I observed that notable sinners prospered and seemed to suffer no supernatural sanctions.

I grew up in the normal conflict and harmony with half a dozen neighborhood children as do most boys and girls. Today the societal niche into which I was born would probably be called lower middle class. Although there was enough money to cover most things, frugality was seen as a prime virtue. Frivolous amusements were extravagances and rarely indulged in, and debt was abhorrent, to be avoided at all costs, for it was a sign of shiftlessness. From that childhood, I retain only scattered memories, but they do give some insights into later behavior. On one occasion a neighbor, evidently in great distress, asked me if I would take a package or message of some kind to her husband at his office in downtown Oklahoma City. I asked permission and my mother agreed that I could go, probably because it was the Christian thing to do. By then—at probably six or seven years of age—I had made several trips on the streetcar and knew the ropes. The neighbor gave me the object, whatever it was, and ten cents for round-trip streetcar fare. The trip accomplished, I reported to the neighbor. The matter must have been a true emergency, because she sobbed with relief and thanked me profusely, emptying her change purse into my probably dirty hands. Proudly I showed the coins—perhaps fifty cents in pennies, nickels, and dimes—to my mother, who promptly sent me back to return the money. The reasons given for return of the money were, first, that it was too much for a simple errand and, second, that the woman greatly needed help and the trip was no more than a freely given act of Christian charity. I pondered the matter for a long time, but without great understanding of the situational nuances.

Sometime later, another woman, also greatly upset, came over. She had a houseful of children, one of whom was so sick she couldn't leave home, and somehow she had failed to realize she was out of kerosene for her cookstove. It was late in the day, and what could she do? My mother volunteered me to go about four blocks to the neighborhood store and get her some oil. With a five-gallon can and twenty-five cents, I strolled to the store, gave the can and the money to the storekeeper who promptly filled it—kerosene, it seems, then being five cents a gallon. It turned out that the woman had told me to buy *two* gallons. The five gallons probably weighed more than half as much as I did, but I set out, struggling home with many, many rest stops. Dusk turned to dark; I was drenched from the waist down with oil because neither the can nor spout had caps, leaving me wondering how I got cast in the Good Samaritan role. Despite my protests, the woman, delighted to have the kerosene, forced five pennies into my hand. Reluctantly, I went home expecting to receive a reprimand for dallying and getting drenched in oil and then to be told to return the five pennies. There was no reprimand, and, moreover, I was allowed to keep the pennies because I had worked hard for them; evidently it was all right to receive pay for hard work honestly performed. That explanation made much more sense to me, and I never forgot that honest work deserves reward.

One summer, when the famous athletic evangelist, Billy Sunday, conducted a revival in Oklahoma City, I remember being sent every day to the morning services, having been given fifteen cents; ten cents was for the carfare and five cents for the contribution plate. The service was in a huge white tent which was breathlessly hot in the July or August weather; I there absorbed snippets of gospel and heard a great deal about wickedness, sin, and the devil as well as God's wrath. Sunday preached of heaven and hell and salvation; he climbed on the pulpit and challenged Satan to wrestle him; he exhorted the faithful to more piety and, wringing wet with perspiration, shed his coat and necktie toward the end of the sermon. He urged sinners to mend their ways and to embrace the opportunity to serve the Lord with him. At seven or eight, I believed the preacher's words and began to think that both God and Satan were individuals who had a personal interest in me, actually watching me and my behavior. Only when I was in high school did this conviction slowly diminish. In some mysterious way my regular attendance at sunday school and later, church services, while my less godly playmates roamed the vacant lots and nearby woods, led me to think I was probably, in God's eye at least, a cut above my playmates. To some extent that attitude persisted and later sometimes made easy relationships with others difficult.

Because my father (Daniel Wellman Jennings) traveled for a farm loan company owned by his older brother and was rarely at home, I was entirely a mama's boy, actually feeling that my father was a stranger in whose presence I was uneasy. One day, in fact, in tears I sought out my mother and sobbed, "That man who comes here Sundays just spanked me!" Later, when my father was home more, the strain between us was reduced, but never disappeared.

Despite severe respiratory afflictions, my mother worked tirelessly in the church, participated in the Women's Christian Temperance Union, and nursed sick neighbors occasionally. I recall learning at my mother's behest a temperance poem and reciting it to a group of women who were lavish in their praises as my mother beamed. Perhaps the most important element in my life other than religion was the presence of books and music in the home. The music came from a hand-cranked Victrola 78-speed phonograph on which I heard Caruso's best arias, the golden voice of John McCormick as he sang Irish love songs and ballads. To this day I thrill to the beautiful blended voices in the sextet from "Rigoletto." I have learned no operas, but my musical tastes still run to ballads and the classics, although I can name very few of the classic works. Eventually I developed a passable singing voice, first tenor and later baritone, and sang until I finished college.

But books came to dominate my leisure. In the house were complete sets of Mark Twain and Robert Louis Stevenson and other examples of good literature which I had devoured by the time I was nine, having learned to read before I went to school. That accomplishment—coupled with a good memory—made school and classes easy and exciting. Reading the *National Geographic Magazine*, which my mother subscribed to until the 1950s, always excited me. It also insensibly acquainted me with other times and places, animals, and peoples around the world, making so many of my adult travels more a renewal of past enjoyable experiences; I also feel that through the *National Geographic* I was preconditioned to an interest in anthropology. The classes in ethnology particularly were merely extensions of familiar and pleasant excursions of discovery into many things I had read about earlier. It should be noted that in those days the *National Geographic* was written more matter-of-factly and with far more accurate detail than is true today, probably because the explorers and researchers then did the writing themselves, whereas today the prose often sounds as if it were written by a photographer or tour guide, later to be polished by more flamboyant writers.

As I read more I ran less with the neighborhood children, while at the same time I came to be called a sissy because I enjoyed school and did well there, went to church regularly, and obeyed my mother. But worst of all, I didn't fight. Before the age of six I had fought anyone who wanted to, fought long and hard and often successfully, only when I reached home, proud, bloody and dirty, and with torn clothes, to be thoroughly thrashed and lectured about the peacefulness of Christ and the turning of the other cheek as Christ had advised. As I weighed the pleasures of combat against the more painful beating I was certain to receive at home and the guilt I was made to feel there, I slowly came to realize that fighting brought painful rewards, offsetting the occasional victorious, if awkward, scuffles. So, refusing to fight caused me to be slowly excluded from the boys' gang, and I even became ill at ease in the group, a condition which lingers in that I still find "small talk" social gatherings such as receptions or cocktail parties stressful, sometimes downright distasteful.

I remember pleasant annual visits by train to visit cousins at Wewoka, Oklahoma, sixty miles east of Oklahoma City, where my mother had grown up, Wewoka being the capital of the five Indian nations in the Indian Territory. Her father, my grandfather, named Jesse William Cruce, was induced by the tribe to come there from Texas in about 1895 to be the tribal blacksmith. He was evidently a great craftsmen who made custom matching bit-and-spur sets, engraved and inlaid with gold when there was time, or hammered out floral designs and other things that would today be called art. The floral pieces and the custom jobs were done in spare time, it seemed; most days were spent in wagon repair, shoeing horses, sharpening plows, and all the other things that a blacksmith did in those days.

After suffering a severe stroke, the old man came to live with our family. He could speak, however, and regaled me with humorous and frightening tales of his life in the Indian Territory and his childhood Civil War experiences. His family's "plantation" (likely a small farm) somewhere near Athens, Georgia, lay between Sherman and the sea on Sherman's famous march, so it was devastated—the crops and house were burned and livestock taken. Grandpa became angry again every time he described the booting a Union sergeant gave him when he tried to hide the milk cow in the bushes near the barn. Both grandpa and my mother told stories of Indian behavior. Particularly, she remembered a stick-and-ball game (the southern Indian version of lacrosse) between two towns that lasted all day, after which two men died from the beating they received during the fight that broke out in the late afternoon. I still have some pictures of that game. She also had a pair of the sticks, which my son David now has.

My grandpa was evidently a prankster and practical joker. One story he told was about a black in Wewoka who had a very painful bunion on one foot; grandpa and his helper, the helper being an enormous and powerful black, offered to cure the bunion if the man would come back later.

When he came the helper seized him, threw him to the ground with grandpa assisting, held him down, and applied an already prepared piece of red-hot iron to the painful bunion. It burned it off, of course, and actually cured the condition, but the poor man shunned the smithy thereafter. On another occasion, a troupe of traveling players came to town to present a few of the tragicomic plays so popular at the turn of the century. When the manager heard grandpa laugh, a deep, infectious belly laugh that made those around him spontaneously smile or laugh, he gave grandpa and a couple of ne'er-do-well cronies a dollar each to come to the play and laugh at the humorous parts. They came, collected their dollars, and remained mute during the comic passages, laughing uproariously at the tragic sections and especially at the death of the heroine. When accosted by the manager afterward, grandpa, of course, pled innocent, claiming to have misunderstood his instructions.

All such stories, combined with my father's stories, told on Sunday afternoons about his adventures in Alaska in 1898–1899 during the gold rush and stories of farm boy pranks and escapades in Iowa in the 1870s and 1880s, filled my head with romantic notions and fed my already lively imagination.

One strong memory I have concerns the terrible 1918–1919 flu epidemic which swept the nation. All of the family were sick; in sequence, my father, mother, and sister were confined to their beds, but I remained unaffected for about a week. I tended them and the fires as best I could, every four hours dissolving in a glass of water some white powder that came folded in a pink paper packet and administering it to each of them. I prepared food, mostly oatmeal, I think, because at nine I had only begun trying to learn to cook, and oatmeal was what I had first tried. However, I had already learned to wash dishes, peel vegetables, and otherwise help in the kitchen. After several days of this the flu hit me, but the others were recovering, possibly to escape the oatmeal. I recall being weak and feverish and unable to get out of bed, but have no idea which of the others tended me. I do recall getting out of bed eventually to find that my father had hired and installed in the kitchen a slattern who dipped snuff, spat everywhere, and cooked only fried potatoes. I also remember the sink stacked with dishes.

But flu evidently debilitated my mother enough that her frequent bouts with asthma and hay fever became longer, and she was much in bed. Her ailment had already been diagnosed as tuberculosis, and several remedies had been tried. One was goat's milk, which was thought to cure the disease, so my father acquired two milking nannies and taught me to tend them, which I did for about a year, finding the chore very distasteful at the beginning. For one thing, goats are rarely docile or good-natured and usually have their own ideas; they vigorously resist all attempts by humans to impose any other views. Since the goats outweighed me I was in constant physical conflict with the beasts. Being milked was particularly resisted by both animals. What with their kicking and lunging, milking time was a lively and angry exercise until I learned to tie their hind legs tightly together at the hocks once they were firmly fixed in the stanchion on the milking platform. Tensions eventually eased, although the goats never enjoyed being milked. I finally came to enjoy the goats' companionship. The milk did not improve my mother's condition, however.

Finally, after the doctors insisted that the family relocate in the high, thin air of the West there was, presumably, a period of search for the proper location and probably for employment. Other than farming, a little lumberjacking, and farm inspections as part of the farm loan business, my father had no work skills, so he intended, if possible, to open a branch loan office wherever the family ended unless something else turned up. Somehow the decision was reached. The family sold its equity in a very comfortable bungalow, most of the furniture, and headed west in June or July of 1919. The destination was Santa Fe, New Mexico, where my father was to meet an Alaskan comrade who had prospered and was negotiating for a huge tract of timber somewhere in northern New Mexico; the expectation was that my father would have some responsible job within the lumbering operation. During the trip, which took about twenty days, I turned ten.

The trip was a series of adventures for a ten-year-old. Even the camping at night, especially in the hot July weather, was a stimulating activity. Also, my mother felt better and was more lively than she had been in the previous months, so the whole trip was a pleasant, often exciting experience, not alone for me but no doubt for the entire family. I drank in the new sights: the occasional cowhands, the windmills, tiny towns, even the vastness of the prairies—all were strange and exciting, being outside my previous knowledge. The move was made in a Ford Model T touring car which had a grub box and a carrier for water and gasoline cans bolted to the left running board, with the result that the left doors on the car could not be opened. Wired on the left rear fender was a wooden crate containing a pet Buff Orpington hen that I insisted on taking. Oddly enough, even while bumping along the trail, the hen laid one egg every other day for the entire trip. A spare tire was wired between the hood and the right front fender, while a luggage rack attached to the back carried the bedding, dishes, camping gear, and a three-walled tent with a long flap that could be fastened to the left side of the car to create a covered open space between the car and the outer tent wall on the right side. The other gear was piled in the back, where my sister and I, a dog, and a cat rode. The life was comfortable: the family slept on the ground, bathed in streams, and bought groceries in the towns it passed through. Although there was a Coleman gas stove with two burners, cooking was sometimes done on an open fire when fuel was available. The entourage looked exactly like the first Okies waiting for the grapes of wrath.

Even driving the dusty roads was a continuous challenge. In 1919 transcontinental automobile touring was not commonplace. There were no marked highways, at least on the route, uphill all the way, from Oklahoma City to Amarillo, Texas, and thence to Las Vegas, New Mexico, along the Pecos River, through Glorietta Pass to Santa Fe. The travelers did not have to ask the way very often because of the unusual little maps available. Possibly the maps were the product of local entrepreneurs or even the nascent AAA, but I never knew nor wondered what the source of the maps was until recently. They were strips of green or orange paper, perhaps two inches wide by eight or ten inches long, usually with advertising for stores or the blacksmiths who repaired cars and sold gasoline and oil on one side. On the other side was a wiggly black line that took the same turns and bends that the next twenty or so miles of road would follow. Landmarks such as windmills, iron gates to be passed through, an occasional stream, and even prominent barns were all indicated when they were near turns or choices of road. Instructions were printed at the places where choices had to be made with mileage shown between the landmarks. The feeder roads were not marked, so sometimes wrong turns were made because most of the Oklahoma and Texas roads were merely two ruts (the right roads were no different from other roads that weren't directional). Of course, the speed averaged by the family was probably no more than ten or twelve miles per hour because of the time spent in making and breaking camp, the frequent flats that had to be repaired with cold patches and inflated with a hand pump, and early stops at likely spots to spend the night. Mother later estimated a daily run of fifty miles per day. There was no Sunday travel, of course, and if the camps were at a pretty spot the party would linger so that my mother could rest a day or two. It must have been a long, long trip, but it was continuous education for me.

The high point of the trip came one afternoon at Amarillo, Texas. It was raining, which was unusual in Amarillo, then as now. After the camp was established on a farm just outside of town, my dad and I walked back into town and saw a small crowd (which we joined) gathered in front of a mercantile store. A young, solidly built cowpuncher at the door of the store was bawling profanities and obscenities and inviting someone inside to "come out" and "take his whipping." A tall, rangy young city feller in white shirt, red tie, and wearing sleeve garters came out and followed the cowhand off the porch into the street, where they began an earnest exchange of punches. The cowhand was angry and impetuous and inexpert, whereas the clerk had a longer reach, was quite cool, and was, moreover, a skilled fistfighter. After several minutes of quite enthusiastic exchange, the poor puncher was groggy, bleeding from the mouth and nose, and had many cuts on his face, resulting perhaps from a ring the clerk had on one hand. When the cowhand had had enough he backed up, still impugning the clerk's ancestral antecedents, got on his horse, and thundered out of town, vowing to return soon with a gun. The sight of grown men fighting and the copious bleeding of one was traumatic for young peace-loving me. I was particularly upset and bewildered by the fact that a man, wearing a gun and a sheriff's star and watching the fight, not only didn't stop it but also exercised his authority keeping spectators back so the fighters had space to maneuver. I was stunned to have witnessed such a clear dereliction of duty by the Amarillo forces of law and order because I had been taught and firmly believed that the police were expected to stop, rather than abet, public brawls. Especially was this true when one understood that fighting was immoral and un-Christian. Perhaps it was here that my childish innocence began to erode.

But it is Santa Fe that I remember most vividly. It was still the provincial capital it had always been, and neither Fred Harvey nor his tourists had yet made any dent in the charm that the city fairly successfully perpetuates today, albeit in commercial, synthetic form. Close to the center of town, just east of the Santa Fe River, there was an entire vacant city block, covered with cinders, set aside for camping travelers. Today there is a fine motel on the spot; in the '30s there was a tourist camp called Orchard Camp. Apparently tourists have always stayed at that place in the city. Our camp was near the lone water hydrant, but at some distance from the public toilets that were not often cleaned. The river, so close to camp, was running very low in late July/early August and it so fascinated me (it was the first river I had ever waded in) that on the first day I undertook to dam it. For several hours, with sticks, stones, and sand, using the family shovel, I succeeded in creating a small pond about eighteen inches deep at the dam face. The project was rudely terminated by an irate Hispanic farmer who had been irrigating downstream and was investigating why his water had been shut off. He helped me out of the river and up the bank with a series of well-placed kicks, with the result that my interest in engineering forever languished. With dam building out of the question I began to roam the town. I went everywhere, gawking and soaking up the aura of romance and learning—never to be forgotten—that indefinable allure of the Southwest, a blend of climate, people, blue sky, architecture, the ever-present piñon and pineclad mountains, the spicy tang of sage and cedar, and the sweet perfume of burning piñon. Particularly, I remember the long trains of burros that filed through the streets bearing huge loads of piñon and cedar firewood for sale door-to-door.

But the brightest memory is the plaza. Although fewer than today, even then there were colorfully dressed women from the nearby pueblos selling jewelry, pottery, carved objects, baskets, and many other things they had made. There was a constant colorful movement in the plaza except at siesta time, when activity was almost entirely shut down.

During my exposure to the fascinating new Indian and Hispanic cultures, my father and his Alaskan partner were inspecting the forests and refining their plans. Ultimately the purchase of the timber tract fell through and there was no job, leaving the family literally adrift with no home, no job, and no prospects. After my father's fruitless search for work in Santa Fe, we packed up and headed south to the town of Estancia, center of a relatively successful pinto bean dry-farming effort in the Estancia Valley, some sixty miles south of Santa Fe. Estancia was near the farthest south of three large freshwater springs in the valley. Six miles to the north was Antelope Springs and farther north was Macintosh Spring. All three had been big ranch headquarters from about 1875 to 1910. The springs supported ponds, marshes, reeds, and abundant bird life and provided water for the cattle; especially beautiful were the flocks of redwinged blackbirds. Estancia and the other ranches were abandoned after a sheepman-cattleman war in which several sheepherders were killed as well as a few cowhands. The war is said to have been ended when late in the summer, at a predetermined hour, the sheepmen fired the grass along the entire western valley. The southwest wind swept the flames across, and in a matter of hours many cattle were killed and there was no grass for the survivors. The cattle outfits left the valley, leaving it to the sheep. The land was later thrown open to homesteaders, with the town of Estancia growing up just east of the old adobe ranch buildings and the big spring.

The west half of the valley was higher, more fertile and usually better watered, benefiting from the orographic rainfall as the clouds encountered the north-south trending Manzano Mountain range. East of the north-south line running through the town there was less rain, poorer soil, and very few farms. Cattle still ranged there, but few sheep.

It may be worthwhile to pause here and sketch the local physical and social environments, because they had both direct and oblique effects on my life. The Estancia Valley south from Santa Fe is an ancient Pleistocene lake with no outlet, one of the hundreds in the West. Like the bigger ones west of the Rockies—Bonneville, Lahonton, and Pyramid lakes—it had three terrace systems and a shallow salt lake in its southeast quadrant. The salt lake was called Lago de Perro, named, it was said, by Coronado during his early sixteenth-century march through New Mexico. The valley was thirty to thirty-five miles wide and about fifty miles long. On the east were the Pedernal Hills; to the west were the pine-forested Manzano Mountains, which merged to the north with the Sandias, which lie east of Albuquerque and the Rio Grande Valley. Albuquerque is probably less than fifty air miles from the town of Estancia. The Estancia Valley received all its moisture from the southeast, essentially monsoons from the Gulf of Mexico, in both winter and summer. The Manzanos stopped the moisture-laden gulf air so that their eastern flanks and the western half of the valley were well watered. Precipitation was lighter in the eastern part of the valley. The center was just about at the east edge of the dependable summer rain; in fact, local wisdom had it that "it never rains east of the railroad." The New Mexico Central Railroad ran south from Lamy, which is south of Santa Fe, through the center of the valley to Vaughn or Torrance, New Mexico, and perhaps farther. Since it came daily, the train was the valley's main link to the outside world. Roads, except for the main ones north to Santa Fe and northwest to Albuquerque and west to the mountains, were merely twin ruts in the prairie. Main roads were graveled but rough. Thus, the physical environment was set by the laws of physics. There was an arid east zone, where it was level and the soil tended to alkalinity, being the bottom of the old lake; the western half was where the well-developed terraces or benches lay, with rich and sandy soil.

The town of Estancia was typically western: one long street of four or five blocks running north and south and lined with false-fronted buildings. Shorter streets ran west, slightly uphill toward the mountains, which were about twelve or fifteen miles away. Most houses lay to the north and northwest of town. The railroad tracks were the east edge of town, about two blocks from and paralleling the main street. There were two general stores, one much larger with more goods and higher prices; both extended credit, hoping to collect after harvest or after the cattle were sold. It was again cow country, so no sheep were allowed in the valley when we lived there. There was a drugstore, a combined poolhall and barbershop which had once been a saloon where, it was rumored, an ample supply of moonshine whiskey was still available. There was also a meat market as well as a law office (I remember Mr. Ayers, the lawyer, very well as an awesome, dignified figure), a bank, and two doctors. One of the doctors was habitually intoxicated. He claimed he was better at his job than his competitor. Once when he was tending my mother he said, "I'm a better doctor drunk than he is sober." No one ever speculated (that I knew about) how good he would have been *sober;* probably it was so unlikely as to deserve little speculation.

Although there were only a few hundred people in town, there were at least four churches: Catholic, Methodist, Baptist, and a Baptist offshoot called Dunkard. The wealth was distributed by denomination. The Anglo-Catholics were the wealthiest, one of them being the banker. The Methodists were next, with the Baptists and Dunkards last, in that order. As already specified, we were Baptists and, with my family, I was there whenever the church was open. There may also have been a Catholic church in the nearby shantytown of a hundred or so Mexicans—whom we now call Hispanic-Americans. Then it was merely called Mexican Town. West of the last houses was the small consolidated school serving seventh through twelfth grades. Except for the few town kids, everyone came in on buses which were then one-ton Ford or Dodge trucks with dark, homemade wooden bodies, seats along each side made of one

twelve-inch plank, and a narrow door at the back and which were un-
heated and rough riding on the bumpy, often ungraded, roads. They
were quite uncomfortable. Usually the drivers were older school boys
who lived at the end of the route and who were safely in the cab, exercis-
ing no control or discipline over their usually unruly passengers. The
grade school was in the north part of town, much closer to the railroad
tracks.

Given the situation and time, it is not surprising that the social values
were entirely rural frontier ones—cattle, beans, and the weather dominated the conversation at any gathering. There were still bona fide cowhands dressed in the Levis, boots, and broad-brimmed hats that was then
the uniform and insignia of the working cowpuncher. Townsmen and
farmers, of course, wore shoes, not boots. The rare "drugstore" cowboy
was an object of derision. Once I saw one such robbed of his boots and
beaten up by a handful of real "cowhands" who had been lounging in the
pool hall. Manly virtues were clearly understood: self-reliance, physical
strength, hard work, a code of honor that required fighting if one was
called a son-of-a-bitch or a liar. Women were honored, desired, and held
somewhat in awe until, when finally wed, they were brutalized and sup-
pressed. The trait that is now called machismo was the image all males
strove to possess and display, so personal physical strength was, of
course, much admired.

I was excited about and a little fearful of the new home. The valley's
flatness, the scattered ranchhouses, the wooden windmills, and the
white-faced cattle were familiar from the trip across Texas and eastern
New Mexico, but the little town was new. None of the houses were
grand. Most were shabby and unpainted. They sat in treeless yards without lawns, although a few of the older houses and the little park around
the still-strong spring had huge, shading cottonwood trees. We camped
near the spring and began a search for a house to rent. The only one we
could afford was a four-room place on the northwest edge of town that
was built of rough lumber, the inside walls of plain boards unplastered
and unpapered. The privy was out back, and water came from a pump
over a shallow well.

All of this was more primitive than I knew in Oklahoma, but I was
unaware that my "quality of life" was now diminished because so many
other things were now on my mind. Nor was I aware that my childhood
had ended. I was hired to herd six or seven milk cows belonging to the

neighbor who furnished milk to the community. At about 8:00 A.M. I would collect the cows and take them—more accurately, follow them—perhaps two miles out to the rather extensive area of open range to the west. Here they grazed until about 4:00 P.M., when I headed them back for the evening milking. I did not stay all day with the cattle, but walked out part way a couple of times to check that they were all there. For this I received twenty-five cents a day. A second job came when a man with a two-acre truck garden next to our house decided it was too dry to farm because there was no irrigation water to the plot. He left to find work in California and arranged for me to tend the remaining garden. It did rain just after the man left, and I sold produce around town as things matured; I was to keep half of the proceeds, sending the other half to the man. The garden produced crookneck and pattypan squash, string beans, roasting ears, and pumpkins as well as a few cantaloupes and watermelons which I peddled from door-to-door. All told, I think I sold about $60 worth of vegetables. I also cut and shocked the corn after the roasting ears were gone and kept some of the pumpkins, from which mother made many quarts of pumpkin butter, thus providing sweets during the winter. I gave all the garden money to my mother since the family was without income; so, even with the strictest economies, the money from the sale of the equity in the Oklahoma house finally disappeared. I was, by then, becoming aware of the poverty to which the family had been reduced, and giving everything I earned to my mother seemed entirely reasonable. That pattern continued until I was out of college, and even then I sent small amounts home until about 1950. However, I was allowed to keep some of what I made herding the dairy cattle. With $15 of it I bought a skittish and thoroughly bad-mannered pony which I called Foxy, along with a broken-backed saddle. Neither proved to be a bargain. The saddle created saddle sores, but I didn't know the saddle was at fault; I credited my own ineptitude for them. However, I kept both the pony and the saddle throughout high school. The saddle and pony were merely the first of many bad purchases I have made throughout my life, but they were kept and used because I couldn't afford to replace them. But I never learned. My riding never became expert, nor did I ever learn that the animal could not be trusted. Frequently, while I daydreamed, Foxy would shy or stop suddenly or rear and send me flying over her head, sideways, or off her rump. Only once was I hurt, when she put me over her head and I landed on mine. Apparently I was out on my feet for about a day because, although I did my chores and behaved normally, the next day I remembered nothing but flying through the air. Yet another time the mare shied violently, dropping me in the cow path we were following, leaving me staring into the face of a coiled rattlesnake; I froze. When the snake eventually uncoiled and wandered into the brush, I trudged several miles home where Foxy had long since gone at an extended gallop.

When the first summer ended I started to school in the sixth grade, although I should have been in the fifth, having graduated from the fourth in Oklahoma. (I think it was the principal who looked at my fourth-grade report card, asked me some questions, had me read aloud, and then assigned me to the sixth grade. I had already skipped the first grade in Oklahoma because I could read when I started school, so was passed on to the second.) The first afternoon when I got home with my books, my mother established the routine that was to last for several years: read the assignments, do whatever homework was assigned (by sixth grade there was always daily homework in those days), then do whatever chores there were. Then, and only then, could I leave the premises. Being thus always prepared, I enjoyed school and did well, but being good in school was a handicap in the little cow town where book learning carried little prestige; instead, it invited suspicion because it was sissy, not manly. My being a good student, as well as a consistent if reluctant church- and Sunday school-goer, led to more opprobrium than approval among my peers. I have often said later in life that I did not understand what today's minorities complain about, pointing out that I had been a Christian in a godless community and a southerner—at least in accent—at a midwestern university; later, when my accent became less noticeable, I became a Yankee in the South, and, finally, for thirty-seven years, survived as a Gentile in Utah's Mormonland. I still believe that I have been a member of a minority most of my life, but am convinced that the minority status, real or fancied, along with the jeers and slights I experienced worked very much to my advantage. As a protective screen I deliberately developed an aggressive, even bellicose and at rare times a confrontational approach, to any new situation. At the same time, but without being aware of it, I also learned to avoid friction and hostility in relationships with people by joking and wisecracking, offering insults and sarcasm with a smile. Contradictory as the two stances were, the blend became my basic style from about age fifteen onward.

I have no particular memories of the sixth and seventh grades. Evidently I made good grades because I was promoted to the eighth grade, where I found myself in a homeroom with eight desks and nine students. After a few days on a chair in the corner, I was passed on to the ninth grade, becoming thereby a much-too-young high schooler at twelve, having already skipped two grades in elementary school. (There was then no junior high, or middle school, for the seventh, eighth, and ninth grades.) Thus, I faced competition from children mentally, emotionally, and physically far more mature than I, but, happily, I wasn't aware of the handicap my youth imposed until later, in college at sixteen, when I became painfully well aware of it.

I did almost nothing of an extracurricular nature in high school. I only came, went to class, and went home because the family usually lived in the country at a succession of small ranches or farms. I remember all told, between 1919 and 1925, eight places where the family lived. Most were only two miles from town, so I wasn't eligible for busing, leaving me and my sister, Alvina, to drive the buggy for about a year. Sometimes we rode the brainless pony carrying double. Thereafter we walked. Given my home chores—milking, woodcutting, tending chickens, getting me and my sister home—and the inflexible study routine, I had little time for such extracurricular things as the school plays, athletics, or glee club. Because of my meekness, I took some playground abuse from the older boys and was fairly low in the pecking order until my junior year.

There never seemed to be enough time. Wherever the family lived, on one farm or another, there was always livestock—two or three horses, from three to six milk cows, as well as a flock of scrawny chickens to tend—and in the frequent absences of my father, I tended the stock and milked the cows before and after school. For a while there was a milk route. Mother sewed a saddlebaglike canvas carrier with slots big enough for three quart milk bottles on each side. I would ride horseback to town, deliver the milk, collect empties, and return, often after dark. Then by kerosene lamplight I studied and did homework; then after morning chores and cutting the day's supply of firewood, it was off again to school. Probably four of the six years the family lived in Estancia were spent on farms. A total of eight moves were made, and I lived in three different houses in town for a few months each and then back to the next farm, always on a sharecropper basis, where the arrangement was the usual one. The owner was to receive one-half the proceeds of the crop. Rarely, in our case, did the owner or the farmer get any returns. The only good farm the family lived on lay west of town during the first two years of a four-year mini dust bowl that emptied the valley of all but the die-hards. When the crops failed and the grass was poor, farmers simply quit and left.

During all these years my father traveled, first selling butter and ice cream from the little creamery that had started in Estancia and, later, other things. He must have made some money, because the family was never completely destitute nor on charity. Also, my mother, a superb manager, kept us solvent with milk and eggs and her great skill as a seam-stress. For her needlework she had more customers than she could ac-commodate; in fact, she was actually still doing custom sewing at the age of eighty on the same ancient Singer she had acquired before her mar-riage. She consistently charged about half what her work was worth by going standards. But the family survived because she could handle money as expertly as any banker. I didn't realize that I was working hard; most farm boys worked the same way, as far as I knew, and by fourteen all of them did men's work, but for a boy's pay. For example, one summer I helped hoe beans which, of course, is weeding the long rows with a hoe. The work day was 7:00 A.M. to 7:00 P.M., with a lunch-nap period of two hours at noon, essentially a siesta. The work was hot and dusty as well as monotonous, but I remember that I kept up with the men all day al-though I worked for $1.25 a day, while the men earned $1.50; I never fully understood why, but to ask for equal pay never occurred to me.

Except for algebra (which I never understood, having been added to the freshman class two weeks late), I continued to enjoy school and to do well. My prestige among my peers remained low until my junior year, when I was fourteen. At that point I was six feet tall, wiry, thin, and strong, and one day decided I would no longer be the butt of the play-ground pranks. I had by then also become aware that even by local stan-dards my clothes were shabby and that my family was exceedingly poor in comparison to most others, none of whom were prosperous. So I be-came sensitive to every slight, fighting someone every few days. My mother's admonitions no longer disturbed me, particularly as I won more fights than I lost. Oddly, the fact of hurting someone made me sick at my stomach and I could feel hours of remorse remembering a stunned and bewildered look on a beaten opponent's face. Nonetheless, my senior year saw me still fighting (with the remorse still troubling me), leading the high school principal to tell me I was a troublemaker, a great trial to the faculty, a disgrace to my family, etc., etc., but I persisted. Except for one disastrous fight in college, I left physical combat in high school.

Because of farmwork I took no part in athletics except for a short season of baseball as a catcher in the spring of my junior year, which I played without a mask since the school didn't own one. I enjoyed it and did passably well until a foul tip hit me on the head, knocking me unconscious. I came to under a stream of water from the schoolyard pump and finished the game, albeit sluggishly. I tried a few more games, but a player who flinched every time a baseball came near his head was not very valuable to the team. I dropped out by mutual agreement. The following year as a senior, when I lived in town, I undertook two track and field events—the half mile and the high jump—at which I did well, winning both in two or three local meets. Later, at the Fourth of July rodeo, I beat all comers in the high jump which surprised and pleased me.

Another memory of high school that I think of occasionally is one which no one believes when I tells it. That year a friend and his sister stayed with us so they could go to school. Their family lived west of Tajique, a small Hispanic town in the Manzanos to the west, too far away to commute. The boy, Dave, was also a junior and helped with the chores. One evening in spring Dave and I had some obligatory school event (there's no telling what it was) to attend in Estancia, about two miles away. Walking back home in bright moonlight, we saw a skunk ambling up the road ahead of us. We stoned it until it took refuge under some scrap lumber that had been placed across a shallow dry well to keep animals from falling into it. Early the following morning we went back to the well and found that the skunk, as we surmised, had fallen and was still in the well, so we removed the lumber and killed the skunk by dropping boards on it. Then we went down into the well and retrieved and skinned the skunk, the skin being worth fifty cents. Throughout all this the animal sprayed his scent, none of which hit us directly, but it was dense in the well when we went down. We trudged happily home with our smelly trophy. Mother refused us entrance, handed us other clothing and breakfast, and told us to bathe at the horse trough and go to school. At school we went to classes, telling our story to no one, but within half an hour all the windows in the school were open with students and faculty alike complaining of the cold. By 10:00, a Mr. Brunnell, the superintendent/principal of the school (who also taught math) sought us out, inviting us to go home. I demurred, saying I had not missed a school day that year because I wanted a certificate of perfect attendance. Essentially I refused to leave, protesting that my perfect record would be spoiled and that to be sent home would be unfair. Evidently Mr. Brunnell saw it the same way, because he announced at a special assembly at 10:15 that school was dismissed for the day. Thus, Mr. Brunnell, a latter-day Solomon, saved the students from asphyxiation or freezing and my attendance record at one inspired stroke. Since neither of us had noticed the odor as being particularly strong, we were more than a little surprised at the action.

While in high school, I took any job offered; one I vividly remember was digging a trench silo for a friend of the family, where the digging involved operating his team of powerful mules pulling a Fresno scraper. Until the advent of power equipment the Fresno (probably in use nowhere today) was the most efficient earth mover in use. It consisted of a steel cylinder five or six feet long with ends blocked with steel plates. About one-third of the cylinder's side was missing in order to create an edge that constituted the cutting or scraping part of the tool. A long, curved iron handle extended behind the scraper with the team harnessed to a doubletree in front. The scraper was loaded by raising the handle just enough to allow the cutting edge to remove an inch or two of soil as the animals pulled it forward. When the cylinder was full, the handle was pulled down so no more dirt was removed, and the scraper slid forward on skids or runners fixed to each end. Dumping was achieved by raising the handle abruptly if the load was to be placed in one spot, gradually if it was to be spread. It sounds and seemed simple, but it proved to require precise coordination of team, driver, and the angle of attack established by the position of the handle. A bite too deep caused the scraper and handle to tip forward forcefully, sometimes carrying the operator with it unless he turned loose. A shallow cut could be jerked free by the team, causing the handle to fly sharply downward, effecting severe blows on the head or shoulders of the operator. In sheer self-defense, and to avoid the jeers of the neighbor who hired me, I more or less mastered the mules and the scraper during the first day. Sore and battered, I returned the next day and eventually succeeded in creating the twelve-feet-wide, eight-feet-deep trench of the required length of something like fifty or sixty feet. Later I assisted in filling the silo with silage which was, in this case, chopped green corn. While filling the silo the owner decided to pack the edges down by having someone ride up and down inside the trench along its edges. I volunteered to ride my tricky pony for the job. She didn't like it. As often before, I grew careless, and when the pony leaped violently sideways, unseating me, my foot caught in the stirrup as the pony careened across a large field at a gallop, occasionally kicking at me as I thumped along the ground alongside. Finally, I loosened my foot; the pony broke through a fence and started home while I limped back in the hope of finding less hazardous work at the silo.

One autumn, with some of the money I earned I bought a few small steel traps. Rabbit skins were worth ten cents a piece then, and the pastures I walked through to get to school supported many jackrabbits and cottontails. Setting the traps on the way to school, I planned to collect the animals on the way home, dreaming during the day of untold wealth. On that first day there was a cottontail in the first trap. As I loosened the trap, the rabbit struggled and escaped, leaving me holding the paper-thin skin as the rabbit's naked body sped away glistening in the afternoon sun. I was instantly violently ill, retching and vomiting for some time. When recovered, I slowly ran the trapline, springing and burying all the traps, and since then I have never hunted nor fished. The slaughter of domestic food animals or sick and aged pets, however, has never affected my sensibilities, possibly because in the case of the food animals they were destined to become food anyhow and putting down sick animals was more humane than leaving them alive to suffer.

On two occasions I went on stock-judging competitions. I had enrolled in the Smith-Hughes agriculture program established by federal law. At that time, through the extension departments of A & M colleges, high school teachers were provided for local high schools, where they offered classes in shop, blacksmithing, animal husbandry, and various other things. One of the rewards the students strove for was the opportunity to judge stock, for which the teacher arranged a lot of practice sessions during the year. In the spring in a Model T, four excited boys and the instructor, whose name was Jimmy Wayne, journeyed over rough roads to the New Mexico College of Agriculture and Mechanical Arts (or whatever it was called), now called New Mexico State University, to test their skills against other teams. The college was, as now, at Las Cruces, New Mexico. The first trip was a great success. We took first place, and some of us saw a big town for the first time. The second trip was less successful. The competition that year was close; the Estancia team was slightly ahead the afternoon of the last day, but it all hinged on the final event, sheep judging. I knew I was least familiar with sheep, probably because I detested their odor, but I pondered long and did my best. My team took second place thanks to me, because I had completely reversed the animals, giving first place to the poorest one, second to the next worse, and so on to the end. The second place was not too bad because there were several teams, but to have been the cause of it embarrassed and depressed me for some time.

Because of the agricultural classes, my work for other farmers, and an optimism that has never diminished, I undertook to farm during the summer between my junior and senior years. I prevailed upon my parents to buy two unbroken horses by means of a note to be paid when the bean crop was sold. My father selected them and brought them home; one was a shiny bright sorrel horse, a big strong four-year-old untouched by human hands except when he was branded and gelded. The other was worthless and was never used, while the sorrel held his head high on an arched neck. With the aid of a series of booklets by Professor Jesse Berry, a horse trainer of the day, I patiently gentled the horse to both harness and saddle without the animal ever learning to fight or buck. The horse, called Ginger because of his shiny sorrel coat, was intelligent, agile, strong, and eager to work, and fully obedient to command, and I planned to teach him high school tricks during the following winter. Farming proceeded until it was evident there would be no crop because of deficient moisture and the consequent dust bowl comparable to the devastating one to the east in the 1930s. The seller of the horses, naturally, came to get them when the note went unpaid, and he asked about their performance. I told him the truth—that one was worthless, but that Ginger was gentle, strong, and willing both in harness and under saddle. I failed to mention that Ginger was a one-man horse and that no one else had used or ridden or perhaps even touched him. I was much saddened to learn that Ginger had been sold to a cowhand who undertook to ride him. Probably, as was the custom, he treated him roughly so Ginger fought, kicking and biting, and finally was choked down to a snubbing post and saddled. The new owner then mounted. Ginger threw him and pawed him to death. The horse was so wild the other cowhands shot him in order to retrieve the saddle and probably, as well, because he had killed a man. I fear I felt less remorse about the man's death than for the loss of the magnificent animal that had also died.

That same year, 1924, the family moved to town. While most of my high school life was more or less standard for the place and time, my religious life was more intense than most boys experience. The little Baptist church usually had a full-time pastor, so there was Sunday school and two sermons each Sunday. I was there, as well as at the Wednesday night prayer meeting.

My churchgoing was less voluntary than merely a fact of life in my family. I sensed, rather than knew, that my father's enthusiasm for the church was as feeble as my own; nonetheless, mother prevailed. In that, our last year, I was hired as janitor of the church, making me responsible for sweeping, stoking two potbellied stoves, and struggling to keep four primitive Coleman lamps in working order. The wage was $4 per month. Annually, there was a revival meeting conducted by a visiting evangelist. I, of course, attended all sessions. The evangelists were all of a type, offering hell's fire and torment to those who sinned; they listed a wide variety of sins available to humankind, and repeatedly offered an alternative: one could avoid eternal damnation by accepting "Christ as a personal savior" and thus enter the kingdom of heaven. The same message is available today from TV evangelists. Routinely, many sinners always accepted the invitation, while my mother wept with joy. Equally routinely, the converts joined the congregation for three or four weeks after their conversion, then dropped out to continue their sinning, often to reappear and be saved again at the next revival meeting.

The Methodist church also held revival meetings with visiting preachers. One July they invited a woman; in consequence the church was full every night, including me in attendance to see the oddity—a female preacher. She was a handsome, blonde woman, with a Junoesque figure which she accented with soft, draping white robes, belted with a golden cord (à la Aimee Semple McPherson) that emphasized her ample charms. She spoke with a rich, strong contralto voice while she preached the standard gospel. The meeting was gaining momentum (usually these meetings lasted about two weeks), attendance was increasing, and the Methodists were preening over the power of their lady preacher. Even six or eight of the godless cowhands and the pool hall hangers-on began to come; on the sixth night, a Sunday, one of them went forward to signal his conversion, or at least to request a prayer and guidance session from the preacher when the services ended. However it was arranged, the preacher went off with him when the congregation dispersed. The sinner and his friends apparently took her out into the country a few miles, raped her repeatedly throughout the night, and released her bruised and nude on the outskirts of town well after sunup—or at least that was what I heard. At any rate, she left town on the noon train, so, not unreasonably, the revival was canceled; the scandal rocked the Methodist congregation, titillating the other sects. The event was forgotten only when the ten-day, well-attended Chautauqua program began in August.

Meanwhile, the drought continued. Some time in the spring of 1925 my mother decided to move to where a new Baptist college at Montezuma had opened in 1922 or 1923. There were two reasons for the move. There was decreasing opportunity for making any kind of living in Estancia, but more important, at Montezuma College, a boy could get a college education in a Christian, that is, Baptist, environment where the primary mission was to train preachers and teachers for their lifework. The curriculum was one that is now called liberal arts, with added required courses where the Bible and Baptist doctrine and dogma were taught. Further, and unknown to me, there was a third reason: at my birth mother had dedicated me to God's ministry, but I only found that out after the move.

My mother sold some furniture, any remaining livestock, including chickens, oversaw me while I created a cover for the rickety wagon, and the family started for Montezuma. The college lay six miles northwest of Las Vegas on the Gallinas River as it emerged from the foothills of the Sangre de Christo range, near a Hispanic village called Hot Springs (not the Hot Springs of central New Mexico that came to be called Truth or Consequences). She sent the few dollars in her savings to a bank in Las Vegas and shipped the remaining furniture by rail, her indomitable spirit or belief that the Lord would provide holding strong. The trip of about a hundred miles took six or seven uneventful days. It was another Okie trip, shabby and raggle-taggle, just a few years ahead of its time and, like the Okie trek, made in part because of drought and dust bowl.

 T W O

College

At Montezuma the family found a place to camp. Mother went next day to the college and, with a promissory note, bought the attractive lot where the family was camped. It cost $100, which I thought an astronomical figure.

The school was superbly situated in what had once been a magnificent resort hotel. It nestled on a bench of the south flank of a mountain overlooking the Gallinas River at a point where the river was looping eastward toward the water gap that opened to the plains of eastern New Mexico. Across the river lay a lower mountain, more foothill than mountain, that was covered with maples and oak brush and where the fall colors made a vast tapestry each autumn—reds, yellow, browns, pale greens—that gave an effect remindful of a Persian rug. But the chief attraction was the huge building, made of rich red sandstone quarried nearby; three stories high, its size was dwarfed by the huge round tower on the southeast corner. There were perhaps three hundred rooms, including a huge dining- and ballroom; there had once been a casino in the basement and a four-lane bowling alley, and there was still a large, richly paneled lobby dominated by a fireplace that would accept five-foot-long logs. The round tower contained four floors and an open balcony above, with a vaguely oriental dome atop. The four tower rooms had been used for bridal couples, important guests, and dignitaries, although one was

24

rumored to be haunted by the ghost of an inebriated guest who walked himself to death searching for a corner where he could put his suitcase.

Down on the valley floor, which was quite wide, lay a more spartan hotel for people who had come merely to take the waters, with a series of bathhouses scattered upstream over the several springs, exploiting the hot water and mud from them. The buildings had been built by the Santa Fe Railroad as a spa-resort in the early 1880s (the resort died quickly after the Santa Fe built a facility at the Grand Canyon in 1898 or 1899). One could come to the hotel to party and ride horses and gamble and bathe, or one could live in the much less expensive accommodations near the river and concentrate on the healing waters. The guests had included foreign royalty, Americans such as Theodore Roosevelt and famous prize fighters as well as hordes of wealthy easterners. The stories I heard about the fancy balls, the gambling, and the scandalous behavior of the guests both fascinated and shocked me, being things of which my rural background had left me ignorant, except in book accounts I had only half believed. My being where such things happened made them far more real and interesting.

The situation was ideal for a small college. Aside from having a spectacular setting and glorious climate, the donated building was entirely adaptable to educational use. The hotel that had served the less wealthy clients down near the bathhouses became the men's dormitory, while the guest rooms of the main building were used for the women. The kitchen and dining room uses, of course, remained the same as did the lobby. The lobby first-floor tower room and one or two adjacent rooms served as lounging and socializing areas. The meeting rooms, offices, and functional rooms became the classrooms. The tower, which sat high above everything except the mountains, overlooked the river, the winding brick paths, and the road wending its way west up the river and was a wonderful spot for a few moments of solitude. It was both soothing and stimulating. I often went there alone or with my friend Tom.

The day after we arrived, mother went to town to draw her money. Disaster!! During the seven-day trip the bank had failed, and we were literally penniless. But that same day I found a job as a laborer, helping dig an ill-starred well that was to have augmented the college water supply, but that later proved to be dry. Although we failed to reach water, I thought the money well spent since it had provided food for the family. Within two months there was enough saved for a load of rough lumber from which my father and I built a shed, about ten or twelve feet by six-teen feet. The shed housed three of the family—father, mother, and sister—leaving me to create a tent house which I made from the wagon box and the covering tarp, with a bed of pine boughs and branches at the back. Two years later, a small but proper house was built, incorporating the shed. Mother provided the plans and the drive, I willingly supplied the labor because the house enabled me to move out of the canvas-covered shelter where I had spent two years, including two frigid winters.

I remember and say little about my sister. We were never close; being born five years earlier, I had been nursemaid and sitter, but we rarely did things together. I was a student at Montezuma College while she was in grade and high school, so we rarely saw each other since I continued to work for the college at whatever was available. After short-term jobs on the college farm as a plumber's helper, electrician's helper, janitor, briefly a night watchman, and other miscellaneous short jobs, I was hired for a shift at the hand-fired boiler of the heating plant. I worked the shift from 1:00 to 6:00 P.M. Because the demand for heat was lowest at those hours I hauled in the coal for the next shift and manually cleaned the flues—a filthy, sooty job—but I also had two, sometimes three hours for unin-terrupted study with no distractions. As a result, I fully grasped the first-year course material and established a reputation for both prompt assign-ments and high grades, and—important later—I learned always to trust my first thoughts on examinations. Just after Christmas in my sopho-more year, and without any significant experience, I landed the second-cook and meat-cutting spot, which had suddenly become vacant in the college kitchen. The job entailed getting to the kitchen by 4:30 A.M., building fires in the huge iron range, preparing some parts of the break-fast, and especially preparing the beef or pork or whatever meat was des-tined for lunch and dinner. Then from 7:00 to 7:30 I served the breakfast; athletes always had the waiters' jobs. The kitchen served meals to 250 (more or less) people per meal with food much better than most institu-tional fare today. The cook, Mrs. Nettie Crowder, was a rotund, five-foot-tall woman and an excellent cook as well as a highly competent planner. Additionally, she was also a tyrannical martinet who allowed no deviation from her myriad of established rules. One dividend of the job was that from her I learned how to cook, even to enjoy it, although I never was successful in pleasing her completely. One constant source of friction was my appetite. Since I was not a boarder, but lived at home (although rarely there except for a few hours' sleep), I was not entitled to eat at the college, and she knew it, forbidding me to eat. I, however, was always hungry and there was always food at hand, so I ate breakfast, lunch, and dinner by means of a continuous snacking system. A soft and steaming buttered biscuit, a piece of fried ham, a crispy corner from a roast beef I was carving, or an unguarded piece of pie all helped sustain me. This and other failings led to an almost constant bickering with Mrs. Crowder. I was never fired because I was more punctual and long-suffering than any student helper had ever been before, so I kept the job until I finished school. And it was a good job for me because it paid my own and my sister's tuition and provided a steady, if small, income for my mother. She, as before, got continued work with sewing for faculty wives, including even Mrs. Crowder, the cook. Because I had to carve the meat and serve the other food at lunch and dinner, I put in an average of six and a half hours daily. The three-way split shift meant I had to arrange classes, study time, athletics, and limited social activity around the work hours. Although I resented it at times, the crowded schedule was of lasting value in that I learned to concentrate when I read assignments and to allot blocks of time for study as well as all the other activities. By always needing to hurry to the next thing I had to do, I also missed out on discussions with others of the facts or data or ideas that cropped up in class. This, as I later realized, was a handicap. Even so, classes were fun, the standards were not high, so my grades remained high. I ended the four years with enough credit hours in Greek, English, and History to claim a triple major. Having begun Greek as a freshman, I probably enjoyed those classes most of any, being particularly taken with Xenophon's *Anabasis,* which the class studied in the second year. English I took because it was easy, and I was enslaved by Miss Louisville Marshall, who handed out criticism and praise as deserved. All the other required freshman classes, which I had missed, not knowing they were required, I took in the senior year; and my complete indifference to Ed. 101, Introduction to Educational Psychology, is still strong in memory as total boredom. But I had learned to admire the Greek warriors and to revel in the power of good literature.

At the end of four years I was second in the class, again surpassed by a girl as had happened in high school. I was chagrined, but knew I was at fault because I had devoted less time to classes (because of subject matter) and more time to competitive activities, including four sports and debate during my senior year; as a consequence I had reduced my class preparation considerably. Moreover, I failed to win athletic letters in either track or tennis, although I had lettered in basketball and football. I also led a debate team that lost more meets than it won. Had I not attempted so much, things might have gone better.

Because the school was Baptist, run by Southern Baptists, religion and its values were a dominant force in all activities. Naturally, because of previous conditioning, fear of losing my job, and constant pressure from my mother, I was active in the church from Sunday school to the choir. My faith had evaporated during high school, but I played out the charade until the end of college. After that, I never entered a church except for weddings and funerals, nor do I listen to religious cant today.

Perhaps the most treasured experience from college was my friendship with Thomas M. Wiley. Tom was the son of a well-to-do orchardist and creamery manager in Albuquerque, and he, too, had grown up doing farmwork chores, but with evidently more leisure for play and mischievous pranks, as Tom told it.

Tom not only grew up doing farmwork and chores but also shared with me a strong Baptist upbringing. We met a few days before school started while working together on the college farm and hit it off immediately, establishing a friendship that lasted until Tom's death decades later. The relationship was, from the start, marked by an intensely competitive atmosphere, beginning even as we hoed the crops (probably cabbage) on the farm and where each tried to beat the other to the end of the row. Everything we did, from climbing a mountain to shining our shoes to cutting wood, was inevitably a contest; even after college, the rivalry, although still friendly, resurfaced whenever we met. But each of us appeared to derive genuine, if vicarious, pleasure from the other's successes. At least I was deeply proud of Tom's thirty-year progress from grade school teacher to superintendent of Bernalillo County schools, the most difficult and most prestigious education job in the state. I was particularly impressed (and I constantly told Tom so) that for him to have returned to an acre on the farm where he grew up and to have succeeded as a school teacher in the same system he attended, ultimately to go to important state jobs and finally to return to his hometown in the important superintendency was quite remarkable. I realized full well the truth of the Biblical statement: "A prophet is not without honor save in his own country." For Tom to have done so well where he had also been a prankish kid greatly impressed me.

Tom was the school electrician for the college. He had been appointed to that position because he had earned a certificate/diploma while still in high school from an eastern correspondence school, completing with high marks a course in electricity. Whether the course was theoretical or practical or both, I never thought to inquire, although I worked a few weeks with Tom as his helper until the steam-plant job opened up. Although we rarely took the same classes, we spent as much of our limited leisure time together as we could. We hiked, climbed, explored the hills, talked about many things, including fantasizing about girls and our ill-formed dreams for future careers. It is noteworthy that neither of us planned to be either a teacher or a preacher. My job at the boiler room, of course, greatly restricted my lounging and loafing time, but the few bull sessions I did have with Tom were, as a result, even more valuable. I had had few such sessions in my life, Tom being the first close friend I ever had—a new experience and I reveled in it.

We actually became closer in our sophomore year. Due largely to extreme peer pressure, we both tried out for the football team. Despite lack of experience—neither had ever played before—we both made the team because of our size and strength and, of course, our eagerness, but mainly because only about twenty-five of the college men even tried for the team. The coach had little choice, merely picking the bigger ones. As players we were pitifully inept, improving somewhat with each game, but both of us enjoyed it thoroughly. With Tom at right guard and me at right tackle, we were, of course, teamed on many plays and reveled in the sport. The team had a perfect season, losing every game to such outstanding schools as Plainview (Texas) College, Gunnison (Colorado) Teachers College, the University of New Mexico, the New Mexico A & M College, and others of equal fame. I played again in my senior year and being now older (nineteen) and much stronger played at center and spent the season with a Sunday headache because helmets were then far more flimsy than those of today; the headaches, of course, resulted from the pounding the opposing centers administered. I, of course, energetically pounded the other center's head when I was playing defense. I also played defense because there was no platooning in those days, so you played the entire game. The record the second season was like the first— eight games lost out of eight played.

But our intimacy almost disappeared toward the middle of the sophomore year. Tom completely lost his head over a wonderful girl from

Colorado. He exercised great ingenuity in seeing her anywhere at any time: in the tower at midnight, in the kitchen storeroom at noon with my connivance, even once or twice in the early morning hours in her dorm. They were finally observed by the president of the college (who often looked for just such things with stealth and flashlight), so both were expelled some time in the early spring. Tom got a milk-route job from his father, built a small house on an acre his father gave him at the farm, and sent for the girl. Her name was Beulah Turner. Tom eventually taught grade school near his house while he earned a B.A. at the University of New Mexico at night. He then became superintendent of the state reform school, was elected New Mexico's superintendent of schools for several terms, and ended his career as superintendent of Bernalillo County schools. He had long since earned a doctor's degree in education during his work career. He died at the hands of drug-crazed youths when he surprised them burglarizing his daughter's nearby home. I had always visited and stayed with them when I was within reach of Albuquerque, and we exchanged letters until Tom's death. Our wives were compatible and enjoyed each other equally.

Another friend, vastly different, was Pat Murphy, who entered the college as a junior or senior when I was a sophomore. Witty, friendly, and politically adept, he was elected editor of the yearbook. He asked me to do some odd jobs and named me associate editor, although I would today simply be called a "gofer." I was fascinated with the creation of the book and took on more chores, including learning how to copyedit and speak in the vocabulary used by printers. I spent as much time as possible at the print shop, and I still respond to the noise and odor of ink when the presses run. I actually saw the book finished, Murphy having left for a job some time in March. The next year I ran for, and was elected, editor.

The association with Murphy certainly enlightened me in many ways. He opened the world of writing and publishing to me, he taught me something of organization and administration at which he excelled, and I met many people the usual student never encounters. Pat Murphy and I were much at ease with each other and remained close for decades. Murphy, along with Tom Wiley, became powerful in New Mexico public school educational matters.

One of the major winter social activities at Montezuma was ice skating. On the Gallinas river upstream, west of the college, were nine wooden and earthen dams that created a series of long, deep lakes, which were filled each autumn and which froze deeply in the winter. When the ice was about eighteen inches or so thick, it was cut into large blocks with horse-drawn sawlike blades and stored in the icehouses, which were huge, wooden barnlike structures alongside the lake. It was cold enough that three crops of ice were cut each winter. When the ice got thick enough to support one's weight, many couples would skate away the short winter afternoons; there were often night parties as well. Once after the ice had been harvested and slick new ice had formed, a big group including Tom and me went up for a marshmallow roast and midnight skating on a gorgeous, frigid, cloudless, and windless night in December, with the full moon and clear air making it nearly as light as day. The skating was superb. The ice was thickest near both shores because the warmer current flowing down the center of the lake slowed the freezing and the ice was thinner there. Therefore, the skaters avoided crossing the lake except in one or two spots at the upper end where the ice was thicker. Tom and I, with a few others, were on the side across from the larger party near a huge fire when someone called to a couple of girls, who set out to join the smaller group by skating straight across the lake. They did not understand the warning shouts and so broke through the ice about twenty or thirty feet from the south shore where my group was. Immediately Tom started to help them; the ice cracked, but he flopped down to spread his weight so he would not go in and inched forward toward the freezing girls thrashing in the water. He soothed and coaxed them into resting their arms on the ice at the edges of the hole. Meanwhile, someone had secured a plank and a rope. I looped the rope around my waist, dug my skates into the rocks so I could anchor the rope when and if the girls grasped it, while Tom used the plank to support himself as he inched forward with the rope. The strategy worked. He got the rope around the girls and I hauled them in. They were terribly cold, but recovered within a day or two. Tom and I were heroes for a day, although I ruined my skates on the rocks.

Tom and I did other foolish things. In March of our freshman year when the snow was gone around the college and spring seemed to be close, we decided to climb "Baldy," or Hermit's Peak, a prominent peak about twenty miles upriver. We set out wearing high-topped shoes, with one blanket each, some bread, potatoes, bacon and onions, and one of my mother's famous raisin cakes, which Tom adored. We stayed the first night in one of the cabins at El Porvenir Lodge, a popular place which was not yet open for the season. Early the next morning, we set out up the switchback trail to the top, but halfway up encountered some snow, which grew deeper as we climbed. At the top the snow was three- to four-feet deep and heavily crusted, but not strong enough to support our weight, so we floundered around all afternoon. We struggled over to the east edge and looked out across New Mexico and Texas, and finally sought a campsite. In the lee of some trees the snow was shallower; here we built a huge fire from fallen trees and created a snow-free area. The plan worked well, but left a sea of mud, a development we had not anticipated. So we carpeted a small area with branches and prepared an evening meal, for it grew bitterly cold at that elevation, about 10,500 feet. Sleep was out of the question, but we created a flimsy shelter from our blankets and huddled there around a small fire, which we renewed by hunting farther and farther away for dry wood under the snow. I became violently ill, finally vomiting for some time, occasionally returning to the fire, trembling and cold. However, we stuck it out until there came a magnificent sunrise that signaled the retreat; the long hike home went faster than the ascent. That we could have died from the exposure or contracted pneumonia never occurred to either of us until years later.

Perhaps the most interesting summer I ever had was between the freshman and sophomore years. As soon as classes were over, an older fellow student and I went to Pecos, west of Las Vegas, New Mexico, to work at a mine that was being reopened after years of abandonment by the American Metals Company. Both of us were hired for the bull gang, a roving band of common laborers who did whatever hard, uninteresting work was to be done above ground. The above-ground facilities were being built while new shafts were sunk to open new lower levels of the lead, zinc, and silver ore to be exploited. The bunkhouses were roomy, the food at the mess hall was excellent and plentiful, and there were about six or eight college boys living in the dormitory to which we were assigned. The only miner in our bunkhouse was Louie, a powerful old hardrock miner who had been with the company here and there over the world for thirty or more years. He laid down bunkhouse rules of conduct, including no noise during the day because he worked the graveyard shift and slept all day. The rule made little difference. All the bull gang worked ten hours a day, seven days a week, so no one could have disturbed Louie's rest anyhow. I usually worked twelve hours because it was two hours more pay, but not at time-and-a-half, it being a nonunion operation. I was awed by Louie and all the other miners, who, after the superintendent and chief engineer, were the elite of the little society. They were also tough and probably dangerous, but I never saw or heard of any significant disturbances.

One way or another I was noticed. Late in the summer the superintendent offered me a four-year engineering course at company expense, with the understanding that I would work for the company at one of their worldwide holdings during the summers and then for a set period after graduation. Although the offer flattered and excited me, the certainty that math would be heavy in an engineering course led me to decline since I had barely squeaked through trigonometry and knew I could go no further with mathematics.

But the most remarkable part of the summer was the Sunday school. Some time in the spring of that year, 1926, I had gone with a student preacher to Glorietta to hold services at a mission there where I sang a couple of songs, led the hymns, and was as affable as possible. It turned out that the highly attractive wife of a carpenter at the Pecos mine was at that service. Soon after I got to the mine, she spotted me, told her husband to have me come to their tent and see her. I did, wondering. She and several other women asked me to direct a Sunday school for their children, teach them hymns, and teach Sunday school class for the women themselves. They already had lesson books and hymnals, so I agreed, seeing it more as a duty than an opportunity. So, for two or two-and-a-half months, I quit work at noon on Sunday, cleaned up, and went to a distant tent to meet with the women. They sang several hymns, I discussed the lesson with them, some woman taught the children, and after a couple more hymns the group disbanded. I wrote to some student preacher friends who came over, and thus, perhaps three times during the summer the women enjoyed a Sunday sermon. To my surprise, I enjoyed the whole experience—perhaps because I took a lot of lewd, ribald teasing from my roommates and even more from most of the miners and carpenters when they learned of my Sunday employment. Others thanked me for furthering the Christian upbringing of their children.

One of my greatest college pleasures was singing. My voice was strong and clear with nearly a three-octave range. I signed for half-time vocal lessons in my first quarter in school and continued throughout the four years. With training, of course, my control, flexibility, and tone improved. I sang at every opportunity: soloist in the choir, with the glee club, and at impromptu events. A friend and I, who had a high tenor voice, sang sacred, secular, and novelty duets. In the face of constant encouragement, I planned a singing career, and in my senior year, I consulted my voice teacher, who told me, "Jesse, you've got a good cornfield voice, but I don't know whether you can make it as a singer." Although I had just finished with a highly successful senior recital, I was crushed and completely abandoned the idea of singing for a living. The thought of consulting someone else never crossed my mind.

In my senior year, despite being busy with athletics, singing, and the occasional class, my frustration with the heavy denominational flavor of the college grew. What with the incredibly childish rules that were set forth and enforced by college administrators and the continued pressure from the college church's preacher for me to join the ministry, I became contentious and fractious, exhibiting spells of sullen anger or exuberant defiance without apparent reason. By deliberately breaking all the minor and a few major rules, I further alienated my mother, who was deeply disappointed at my apparent defection from the church and the gospel that she so adored. At the same time, I was aware of greater strength of body and perhaps mind and was less afraid of consequences, although I remained internally self-conscious and defensive about my failings. All the successful defiance added up presumably to confidence, or at least brashness or unfeelingness at some times; in fact, in retrospect I feel I was downright cocky through much of the senior year. This confidence in the face of the frustrating struggle against the local system, may sound paradoxical, but I think the two states of mind may really be two faces of the same phenomenon—a kind of belated or delayed adolescent rebellion which I had missed earlier. Certainly the flouting of the system without loss of job, without being expelled or losing face in front of my peers, engendered much of that confidence. In any case, I now feel that automatic resistance to vested authority and outmoded conventions became part of my personality during the last college year. There is no evidence that such an attitude is a social asset, but I never really overcame that tendency.

However, I never completely lost my head. Shortly before graduation the president, who was apparently also the chief fiscal officer, called me in and told me with a phony friendly smile that unless I paid some $90 owed for tuition, I could not graduate with the class. Although I reminded him that my account would soon have that much credit from the job, the president was adamant; no degree until the money was in hand.

Stunned, I left the office wondering what to do. I went into the registrar's office. The registrar was a strong, bright woman whom I much liked and respected. She, in turn, approved of me and particularly my singing. I blurted out the story and the crushing disappointment. She listened, turned away, and after a few minutes at the typewriter she gave me two certified copies of the transcript on which she indicated the awarding of the Bachelor of Arts degree. No charge. So, I had the degree, but the president didn't know it then or later, so far as I know. And as I had been instructed, I sat in the audience while my classmates were solemnly accepting their diplomas. I left the college the next morning at 5:30 and never saw the president or the registrar again.

At the close of this chapter dealing with my first and formative years, the reader may well wonder what relevance they have, if any, to a later career as an anthropologist/archaeologist. As I review the eighty-plus years I have enjoyed, I am certain that such success as I have attained can be credited to a few quite specific things I learned early that largely shaped my adult life. One I have already mentioned, that is, the cocky, direct, wisecracking, joking, often casual facade I usually wear in front of my inner thoughts. Another important residue from those early years is that, after a long period of reluctance and aversion to work as such, somewhere in the college years I learned to enjoy labor, whether easy or arduous, trivial or important, if I did it well, finished successfully, and if the job was aimed at a defined goal near or distant. I learned that any normal task, if done well and finished gracefully, was a source of a deeply satisfying feeling of personal pleasure, one of quiet satisfaction. Most important, however, was that during my college years I learned to ignore, or even appear to be unaware of or unaffected by, opinions other people held of me, whether good or bad. In fact, I am to this day embarrassed by and deal clumsily with compliments, tending to discount them or turn them into a joke with some wisecrack instead of the far simpler "thank you." Negative comments rarely influence my actions. I am not necessarily proud of my public attitude toward the opinion of others, nor do I fully understand it; however, I've had it a long time and will probably continue to behave in the same way.

 THREE

Chicago and Graduate Study

Eᴀʀʟʏ ᴛʜᴇ ᴍᴏʀɴɪɴɢ after I didn't graduate, I went with Professor Herbert Ball (my Greek teacher), at his invitation, to the University of Chicago, where he was working on a degree at the seminary there. Why he invited me I do not recall, but I suppose he had urged me to do graduate work there; he no doubt knew that the academic standards at Montezuma were not very high. I accepted his invitation, I suspect, because if nothing else it would take me fifteen hundred miles away from the suffocating constraints of the Baptist college. In any case, I joined him (with $30 in my pocket) and we left. The trip took longer than I expected because we went by way of Fort Worth, Texas, so he could visit his parents! But the trip was worth it. In Fort Worth I went to my first talking picture and heard Al Jolson singing to his "Mammy." Moreover, the theatre had for its vaudeville segment one of my singing heroes, Frankie Laine or Layne (correct spelling?), "The Yodeling Brakeman." I had a wonderful time, even though I shared my fifty-cents-a-night hotel room with a fine collection of bedbugs.

We arrived in Chicago on a Saturday after dark. The Balls knew of a rooming house for transients near the university, where we got rooms. Sunday morning I walked over to see the university, where I found the grey buildings, the quiet quadrangles, and the scattered trees, as well as the lush green grass, powerfully attractive. To my great surprise, I found construction work being done on campus that Sunday, so I immediately located the superintendent or assistant superintendent of the job and asked for work. He said he had work on the bull gang and told me to come to work at 7:00 A.M. the next day. He said, "You get paid on Thursday if you're still here." Evidently he had had problems keeping college boys and hard work together. Although I was fit, my hands were soft and my muscles were not used to the pace set by the profane little Irish straw boss whose tongue was like a rasp and who always carried a large Stillson wrench as his badge of authority, although I never saw him use it. The gang included two huge blacks, two compact little Swedes (newly arrived, with little English), three Italians, and me. By that night my hands were raw. I was dog tired and every muscle ached. The next day was worse, but by Thursday I felt I would survive and could eat as well since my money was gone. In fact, the Thursday payday came just as I spent my last dime on a hot dog for lunch at a cart that came each noon. That summer I dug ditches, wrecked concrete forms, dug ditches, hauled reinforcing rod, dug ditches, and many other nonglamorous things, including digging ditches. But the summer finally ended, as did the construction—actually it was the most physical summer I ever spent—before or since. It was a source of satisfaction to me to be left behind by the contractor after construction was completed to water the lawns we had planted. I was to water until the grass came up and set. Thus I had not only *stayed* on the job 'til Thursday, I had been the *last* one to leave—an ironic twist that pleased me.

One day I took time off from work to apply for admission to graduate study by meeting with a Dean Boucher, a very young-looking man, where I flashed my transcript from Montezuma. He was very kind, treating me with the civility and cordiality one might proffer a peer. In a couple of weeks he found me—I had told him I worked on the campus—and asked me to come to his office, where he told me they couldn't find anything about Montezuma College or even that it existed. He said that he doubted I could do graduate level work. I responded that so far I had never failed a course and reckoned I could keep up, so he put me on probation and said we'd evaluate my progress in six months.

Next I went to the head of the English department to be admitted to its program, where I confided that I was (and remain) an admirer of Mark Twain and wanted to do an M.A. thesis about him. The chairman allowed that such a thing would not be approved by his department. He then asked if I had ever read *The Bridge of San Luis Rey,* which, as it happened, I had read that summer. My opinion of the book: "I think it was thin and contrived—not much of a book." He turned somewhat cool, told me to forget any English career in that department, and dismissed me. Later I learned that he was *the* Thornton Wilder, the author of *The Bridge of San Luis Rey,* a best-selling book. It is interesting to me that Mark Twain's genius is today fully appreciated and widely recognized, while Wilder is not a household word, although he did later bring off *Our Town.*

I had also applied for a job as night orderly—11:00 P.M. to 7:00 A.M.—at Billings Hospital, with one day off every three weeks. I went to work about October 1, classes having started at about the same time. The hospital job paid, I think, $67.50 per month and offered all meals, but I lived about two miles away so only got breakfast and a 10:00 P.M. dinner of sorts.

But I entered the university a much different young man from the one who had arrived in early June. During the first months in Chicago, my rustic innocence was much eroded, largely because there was in my rooming house a young Irish reporter named John Fagan, from Indianapolis as I recall, who worked for the *Chicago Tribune.* Slender and pale, he was cynical, cocky, aggressive, and apparently worldly wise; at least he taught me how to use the elevated trains and streetcars, showed me Chicago's Loop and Michigan Boulevard, where I marveled at the tall buildings, and especially he took me to several burlesque shows. The sensuality of the writhing, prancing, dancing bump-and-grind strippers, the bawdy skits, the sweating audience, and the cries of "Take it off! Take it off!" were more than exciting to a green farm boy from Estancia Valley and Montezuma College. I was shocked, embarrassed, and fascinated, having never even seen a bare female breast before.

But I am forever indebted to Fagan for taking me to the Field Museum of Natural History. I had never been in any kind of museum before, and I was barely able to leave one exhibit to go on to the next; all of them were so strong and so exciting. I continued to go to the museum until I no longer lived in Chicago. All of the halls were gripping in their power, and I eventually began to return again and again to a few favorites. I realize now that the displays were not as wonderful as I thought, but I never got over the impact they made on me and my awareness of the world as it appeared in those cases. I resolved then that if it were possible I would be a museum person of some sort.

Educational as my trips to the Loop were, the six months I spent in Billings Hospital as a night orderly were even more so. I was usually on the surgical ward, where the helplessness, suffering, and frequent deaths, none of which I had observed before, kept me in an emotional turmoil for weeks. Eventually I learned to simulate a callousness that I learned from the nurses, who were hardened enough to avoid a deep identification with the patients. Many amusing things happened at the hospital. One scene that I remember vividly had to do with an elderly patient who had died at about 2:00 A.M. My job, it was explained, was to wash the corpse with alcohol, plug the bodily orifices with cotton, and wrap a sheet around it, after which I was to then load the body onto a cart to take it to the morgue in the basement. Needless to say, all the steps connected with the chore were upsetting to me. On this occasion the night supervisor, a large powerful woman whom I feared, came in and asked, "Jennings, did you remove the dentures?"

"His teeth are real. They won't come out," I explained.

"I'll get them out," she said. She tugged and tugged. No dentures. She muttered, "I know he has dentures," and climbed onto the bed astride the corpse and pulled again. Still no dentures. She stepped to the floor saying, "To the morgue," and stalked out. So I loaded the cart and left and went to the task. The scene while the nurse sat astride the old man and tugged has never faded from my mind.

The nurses were aware of my shyness and ignorance and treated me nicely, although they continually successfully shocked me with their stories and sometimes crude humor. Under their ministrations I lost much shyness.

What with working nights and trying to carry three classes—two in sociology and one in physical anthropology—I became nervous and jittery and could neither eat nor relax nor sleep and felt I had to quit the hospital, which I did as soon as I could after deciding. The chief nurse for the hospital was very upset. She was planning to make me an operating room orderly and took my quitting hard, but I was just as happy to be gone, because I was certain I could not have survived in the blood and what I thought of as brutality in the operating room. Thanks to the working hours and the monotony of the two sociology classes and the dull term-paper topics I had been assigned and seven days in the hospital in early December with a body covered with boils, I finished no class the first quarter, earning incompletes in all of them. The second quarter, except for an introductory class in anthropology from the famous Edward Sapir, was equally disastrous.

Therefore, Dean Boucher called me in, saying, "Aren't you the cocky kid who said he could do anything anyone else could do?"

"Yes, sir."

"How do you explain four incompletes and a B in your first two quarters?"

Thereupon I told him of my sleeplessness and offered other alibis and excuses, but showed no particular penitence so far as I recall. To my surprise and eternal gratitude, he laughed and chuckled and finally said, "Well, I just wanted to hear your story and to tell you your probation is lifted. Enjoy your graduate career." Why he did it I never knew, but I later often saw him on campus and a few times in what I called the Belgian Village (because of the ethnic ties of the patrons), a saloon near the university. He always remembered me, spoke cordially, evincing interest in my so-called career; his interest undoubtedly helped me as I slowly learned how to go to graduate school and enjoy it.

I was able to leave the hospital so abruptly because I had a chance at a job that paid more than twice what the hospital did. This being the winter and spring of 1930 in the beginning depths of the Great Depression, the students living on campus and moving around at night were being assaulted (it is called mugging today). A few girls cried rape or rape attempt, although I doubted then and now that rape was uppermost in the attacker's mind; it was sheer hunger and frustration, because they always took the victim's money. The burgeoning crime rate led the university to set up a campus police force. There were three of us: a chief, who had no experience, but had a couple of classes in police work from the famous August Vollmer; and the two patrolmen, a man named Anderson and I, who were equally ignorant. We endured all kinds of insults and jokes as we patrolled in our neat new uniforms. The students were amused at our presence, especially since we were unarmed except for nightsticks and shot-loaded blackjacks and our shiny badges identifying us as special deputy Cook County sheriffs. After a shooting on campus, we all began, without authority, to carry guns in holsters under the skirts of our tunics. I only used mine twice, both when I stumbled onto holdups on campus.

The man I shot died later of pneumonia; the other I must have missed. Except for the holdups and one or two occasions when football players attempted to beat me up for moving them and their dates out of the nooks and crannies where several holdups had occurred, there was no great excitement in the eighteen or more months I worked as an armed deputy. I walked a beat along 58th and 59th streets. It was about half a mile long, and I phoned in from buildings at each end. I also crossed the Midway every now and then to check in at the girls' dorm on 60th street. I made one trip an hour from 6:00 P.M. to 2:00 A.M., so I reckon I walked or sauntered at least ten, sometimes twelve, miles a night. Spring, summer, and early autumn were fine, but the bitter Chicago winter wasn't.

Interesting things happened. Once as I wandered past the girls' dormitory on the corner of 59th and University Avenue, there was a terrible crash right behind me. I wheeled around and saw the pieces of a large crockery pitcher on the sidewalk just behind me; as I looked up I saw two giggling girls retreat through a window that led off the fire escape on the fourth floor. Presumably they were the two girls whom, with their escorts the night before, I had urged to leave a favored mugging zone. The pitcher was full of water and would have driven me through the sidewalk had it connected with my head. Although I was in the university for several more years, I never went under that fire escape again without checking for hostiles.

Another time, just at dusk, I saw a man coming out of a small door nearly covered with ivy that led into the east end of Ryerson Library. It proved to be young President Maynard Hutchins, a man who remained controversial until his death. Together we walked eastward to his home, talking about many different things. That same stroll happened often, since my routine and his more or less coincided. I was expected to watch his house more closely when he was off campus, which he often was. One night in early June I met him, his wife, the famous Mortimer Adler, and a gaggle of distinguished-looking citizens all in evening dress walking down University Avenue toward the Commons to an important concert. Hutchins, very tall anyhow, was wearing a silk top hat, a scarlet rose in his lapel, and a crimson cummerbund; he was not merely handsome—he was beautiful. Strolling toward them, I smiled and saluted and said, "Prexy, you look very sharp tonight." He laughed, said, "Thank you, Jennings," and led his party past. I turned and watched while several members of the party turned to stare at me. Later he told me that the cheek of that young officer kept them talking for hours; he also thanked me for making his evening easier. Had I been smarter I would have no doubt asked him if there was a place in the university where one walked less and was paid as well. He would have perhaps found me one, but I never thought of asking. I just enjoyed his wit and optimism. Other people, both students and faculty, often strolled with me. They, too, educated me in many ways.

I stayed on the police job for another year or so, but nothing of particular interest happened that I recall. I enjoyed the higher salary, but since I had no plans for anything other than staying employed, I continued classes—social anthropology, ethnology, linguistics—because I enjoyed them. The police job, although it paid well, was more demanding than one would think. Since I went off duty at 2:00 A.M., it kept me from bed until about 3:00 A.M., so I only took late morning or early afternoon classes. I had little time for the library or the between-class interaction with classmates, leading me to be labeled a "loner." My relations with fellow students were a little uneasy anyhow, for they all seemed to know so much more than I did, dropping names I'd never heard of and arguing the fine points of the way in which kinship systems work, systems I have rarely worried about. I am aware now that as a student I was merely drifting, with no professional goals because my only strong personal goal was survival. I went to school largely because I enjoyed it and assumed that something good eventually would come of it, so I took all the required courses and let it go at that. After two courses in linguistics in which Edward Sapier had gotten me interested, I wanted to pursue that field; then, of course, he left for Yale, to be replaced by a Spaniard, Andrade, who encouraged me. An inflexible man, during my second or third class with him he assigned me a seminar paper that required me to listen to three specified radio programs for three hours every night for a month, after which I was to come up with a paper on the language and accent characteristics of American radio announcers. I protested, saying I worked at night. Andrade said, "Quit your job, then."

"I can't."

"Then drop the class," he said; I did, thus ending my linguistic career.

But by then I had met Robert Redfield and was much awed by him. For me, his quick intelligence, his brusque, incisive speech, and curt manner were intimidating, although I later learned that his mannerisms masked a gentle, sympathetic man I slowly came to know. More important, he, being precise in thought as well as speech, conveyed what little I know of intellectual or scientific rigor, leaving me greatly in his debt.

In those days the Department of Anthropology at Chicago was new, having been established, I think, around 1925; perhaps a little earlier. It was, of course, also small and one of six departments in the United States at the time. The head of the department was Fay-Cooper Cole, a physical anthropologist and ethnologist who collected most of the fabulous collection of Philippine materials presumably still at the Field Museum. Cole was a small, quick man, always in a hurry, being busy with committees, speaking engagements, departmental affairs, and one or two classes annually. I almost never talked to him except in class, being afraid as a mere student to take up his time. Robert Redfield, Wilton Krogman (then still a student), and Edward Sapir, and Harry Hoijer (also a student) were then (1930) the remaining regular faculty members. But Cole was able to lure the giants of the day to the department for full quarters or for brief ten-day stints. Among those I learned from in class or colloquia were Paul Radin, Leslie Spier, Bronislaw Malinowski, Alfred E. Kroeber, Ralph Linton, Robert Lowie, all of whom were then prominent scholars. Alfred R. Radcliffe-Brown, added to the staff a year or two later, attracted many students for reasons never clear to me, although I took all his classes (despite their dull repetitiveness) because he was so highly touted. The prominent visitors, of course, talked about their special interests. Radin dealt with the Winnebago, Spier taught an excellent class on the tribes of the Amazaon, Malinowski went on for hours about the Trobriand Islanders and their interest in sexual matters, Kroeber and Linton were more general in their coverage. I can't recall Lowie's emphasis, but it was probably the Plains area. As for Radcliffe-Brown, he endlessly discussed the Australian aboriginal Arunta in wearisome detail.

Cole was interested in archaeology, although he had done little or none. He had persuaded one of the Morton Salt family along with other lesser donors to underwrite the beginning of the study of Illinois archaeology. Work was done by students in the summer at what were called summer field schools. Cole himself, intermittently, some of the graduate students, and a convert from sociology named Thorne Deuel ran the schools at various times. Excavations had been carried out at various places in the state, but by 1929 or 1930 they were on or near a Morton company farm in Fulton County, where the Mortons also maintained a camp for duck-hunting guests who were invited down every autumn. I had heard vaguely about the field school, but gave it no thought because I couldn't go; I must have a job, and the field school offered only bed and board. There was no chance that I would attend.

But two things happened. In the spring of 1931 my father, then working in Oklahoma, became ill and my mother asked me to try and get a job in New Mexico and make some money in case my father worsened. I thereupon wrote my college friend, Pat Murphy, who was now superintendent of schools at Hope, New Mexico, for help, who proved to be delighted to have me fill an unexpected vacancy in his system; I was to report in late August. That took care of my family responsibility, and I gave notice to the campus police that I would be leaving in late August. But then the second problem arose when Dr. Cole sent for me and crisply announced that as a second-year student I was to go to field school. I had no interest in archaeology and told him so, explaining that I wanted to work with Redfield, preferably in Mexico, on his now-famous study of Mexican folk society. Cole said that was fine but irrelevant because field school was not optional since it was part of graduate education, at least at that time, at the University of Chicago. It was part of my education in anthropology and I should be ready on about June 10 for eight or ten weeks of manual labor. Although I was stunned, I simply said, "Yes, sir," and prepared to leave.

As it turned out I did well. I was strong and willing and unafraid of hard physical labor. Moreover, as I suppose any normal farm boy would have been, I was curious about things and I proved to be sensitive to soil, color, and texture, as well as fairly observant. In these attributes I was different from the city dwellers who made up the rest of the unwilling crew, which led, in a couple of weeks to Deuel appointing me a supervisor, and I began recording the rudimentary notes kept in those times during the excavation of the Goodall Mound, which lay somewhere to the northeast of Lewiston, Illinois, the county seat of Fulton County. I also dug, cleaned skeletons, and whatever else was needed.

The life was good. We were quartered in the duck-hunting lodge on the Morton estate, and had delicious food prepared by the lodge-keeper's staff. The varied, nutritious, and plentiful meals kept everyone happy. One or two nights a week Deuel let someone drive an old Buick touring car the department owned to Lewiston with a load of crew members. Our destination was a home-brew parlor in a basement operated by a farmer near town. Wild, bitter, and potent, the home brew, in quart bottles wasn't very good, but the trips to town broke the monotony of dormitory evenings when most of us read or played penny ante or engaged in bull sessions and talked of girls or all three in the course of an evening. I must have learned something that summer, but I didn't know, or worry about, why we were digging where we were. I know now that my main achievement was to develop a great impatience with ritual field procedures and with spurious meticulousness (I have elsewhere inveighed at great length against both of those). But I was asked by Deuel to return the next year as assistant to him, but this time there was a salary of $100 per month, from which I had to pay $50 each month to the lodge manager for my keep.

As earlier agreed, I left Illinois by bus in time to go to Montezuma, New Mexico, where I visited my mother, thence to Artesia, New Mexico, which lies twenty-one miles east of Hope. I spent the night in Artesia, phoning Murphy to come get me the next day. With some trepidation I approached a career as a high school teacher. My concerns heightened when I found that the new teacher inherited all the scut jobs; this meaning that I taught, among other things, freshman English, general science, shop, coached boys' basketball, and presided over the drama club, directing, of course, all the plays we put on. The drama club at a country high school probably requires explanation: Murphy had gone briefly to Stanford, and his experience as an undergrad with the Stanford Players had so inspired him that he built a drama program which, when I got there, carried more prestige in the Hope neighborhood than even basketball. As an afterthought, I was also appointed scoutmaster of the school-sponsored troop. Fortunately, I knew something about all of my assignments except drama and scouting.

Hope, New Mexico, was a very small rural community, the focal point for a few farmers whose fields were irrigated with the water from the Rio Peñasco. The stream was not strong, so there were but few farms. More people were struggling on the numerous cattle and sheep ranches to the west than on the farms. This being 1931, the area, along with much of the West, was terribly poor in the second year of the Great Depression. Perhaps not surprisingly, I felt quite at home in the little town; as in Estancia, money was scarce. There were again two general stores; the larger and more expensive one extended credit, while the smaller one charged less, had less stock, and gave no credit. There was also a combined drugstore and post office, a gas station, a barbershop (which also sold baths), a church with no regular pastor, the two schools (high school and grade), a hotel, and a small cafe. There was no electricity or running water, water being drawn or hand-pumped from the cisterns that were filled every few months when irrigation water was turned into a system of ditches. Sanitary facilities were outdoors. I stayed at the hotel and boarded at the cafe, augmenting the plain fare with fruit and Fig Newtons from the smaller store.

My first day at school found me downright terrified. Evidently the man I had replaced had been unable to control his students; fortunately, I had been warned. My homeroom contained all the freshmen, fifteen or sixteen in all. When the first class bell rang I invited them to be seated; only a few sat. I twice urged the others to do so, and eventually all sat down except one student at the back of the room. He was standing defiantly in front of the large bin which held the coal for use in the large base burner that heated the room in winter. The fellow was nineteen years old, only a freshman because he had grown up on a ranch near no school, so he had started school at about ten. He was also bigger than I was. When he refused to sit down I walked back prepared to wrestle him into a seat if I could. When I reached him, he stepped back and the front of the coal bin caught the back of his knees, causing him to fold backward down into the bin and be wedged helplessly with his feet in the air. I helped him out, said, "Sit down," turned my back, and went to the front of the room, keenly aware that a miracle had come to pass since I was unscathed and unruffled, with my authority intact. When I went to the cafe for lunch that noon, I learned that everyone in town was talking about how I had knocked the school bully into the coal bin. There were no discipline problems during the rest of the two years I taught there; only now have I denied even touching the man.

There are many incidents in the community that emphasize the cow-town nature of the place. On Saturdays the cowhands swaggered up and down the short sidewalks, one block long on each side of the street that comprised the main part of town. There were usually fistfights on Saturday nights after some bootleg liquor had been consumed, but with no saloon, no cinema, and no dance hall, the poor fellows had little else to do than fight. Although several were itching to try, no one ever invited me out into the street, possibly because I did not quite fit the "sissy-britches teacher" stereotype frontiersmen have long held. One or two evidently thought of challenging me. As I remember, one night while I was grading papers in my room two ranchhands whom I knew were spending the night in the hotel and, of course, had been drinking some moonshine, stopped in the hall outside my door. One said, "I'm gonna throw the teacher down the stairs." The other said, in essence, "That's a good idea. That would be fun, but have you looked at him? I think he could probably throw *you* down the stairs. That would be hard to explain."

Saved again. The man could probably have tossed me down the stairs, possibly over the hotel, but I had no yearning to fight him. I'd seen him in action on the streets, where he demonstrated that he was a strong, accomplished, rough-and-tumble fighter I had no desire to mix with; in any case, I was glad and relieved that I had no fights in the town. I had no fear of the fisticuffs; indeed, I would have welcomed and even enjoyed a brawl, but I was deathly afraid of being beaten. A physical beating could be survived, but losing the fight would leave a permanent scar on my public image. As I think back over my life, I think the odor of poverty and an obsessive fear of public failure have been the major driving forces of my life. Of course, I have often failed to achieve some goal, but only I knew of the failures, nor do I mention them herein.

In those days a teacher was expected to be a role model, possessing most, if not all, of the standard virtues, literally living in the public eye. Small wonder it was widely noticed and remarked that I didn't go to the occasional church service, nor did I call on the few available young women, I didn't drink bootleg whiskey with any of the cowhands, and was rarely invited to people's homes. Usually I went to Murphy's house every Saturday to wash my clothes in their hand-operated washer, where Murphy's wife, Jo, ironed my shirts for me and fed me.

Why I kept the community at a distance I am not sure. Perhaps my shyness was intensified by the fact that I was a stranger. Possibly I may have thought that I was cut from finer cloth and that country folk were not quite my social equals—after all I had lived in Chicago for two years!! Although I don't know why I was aloof, I *was* uncertain and insecure in the teacher's role. Whatever the reason, I placed myself outside the group and spent a lonesome two years; fortunately, I was very busy. For example, the drama club put on six plays in the two years I was there, with large casts. Murphy had told me to select plays with lots of characters. This meant a full house for each of two performances because all the relatives of any student in the play would attend. Four or five weeks of night rehearsals for three plays, with time out for night-long basketball trips for games with schools in nearby and no-so-near towns, took up most of my evening time. Our best plays were mysteries and comedies because the actors got into the spirit quickly and great acting skill was not required. For that matter, I brought no great skill as a coach-director, but the faults in the performances were either unnoticed or forgiven by the warm and enthusiastic audiences. Of all the things I did at Hope, I think I derived the most pleasure from the drama club chore. As for basketball, the less said the better. Although I had played enough college basketball to win letters, I didn't know the game well enough to coach it; I hadn't the vaguest conception of the way good coaches assess their players, create strategies around the players' strengths, or even how to shift strategy to exploit an opponent's weakness. Our basketball practice was held in the roofless shell of a burned-out building that had had a concrete floor. The pool of talent was not very deep. Only town boys reported regularly because we practiced after school and the school buses left as soon as school was dismissed; the ranch boys simply couldn't participate. To close this part of the Hope experience quietly and quickly, I only say we lost more games than we won the first year, but got to the district elimination meet at Roswell the second year, where we dropped out in the second round. I found little pleasure in our record or in the coaching itself. My performance in the classroom was probably more satisfactory and certainly was more satisfying personally. Although I was a novice, the progress the freshmen made pleased both the principal and the superintendent.

Scouting was a different matter, born as it was in the romantic British mind of Baden-Powell back at the turn of the century after he had read Cooper's *Leatherstocking*. It may have been what a few unfortunate British lads needed, but it seemed to me rule-ridden, stuffy, and bureaucratic in the extreme, if not downright silly. It stills seems so to me. Most, if not all, scoutmasters I met were as unfit as I to lead a group of unruly, ill-equipped teenagers into the dubious joys of camping out overnight. I was not a volunteer; I was commanded by Murphy to be a scoutmaster. So I met the troop every week, and attendance was very good, but progress with scoutcraft was slow. The attendance was good, I finally found out, because a girl scout troop also met that night, so the boys' real fun came after scouting was over. But I endured. Along about Christmas a stuffy Major Plummer, a regional scouting official (and a regular army officer who taught at the military school in Roswell), came to drum up attendance at the camporal to be held in the spring at Roswell 60 miles away.

Murphy suggested a mounted troop. The boys were enthusiastic, so I made the attempt. First, find the horses. One or two of the boys could borrow mounts, but I needed a total of seventeen—one for me and sixteen for the troop. Fifteen to go. I persuaded a man who raised pinto or "paint" ponies for sale to lend us what was needed; the animals were not ponies of Shetland size, but merely the well-known small western horses. He had a stallion, sire of most of his herd, and about twenty others, with all the young ones "painted" in the same pattern as the sire, but of different colors—black, brown, beige, sorrel, grey—depending on the color of the dam. Before we could have the horses there was one condition; it seems that only four or five of his animals were broken to saddle, so the boys had to ride and gentle about a dozen wild two- and three-year-old ponies. So we spent two Saturdays busting broncs with no one getting hurt, and the ponies soon responded to bit and rein. We needed a commander, so I chose a very small cocky boy with a loud resonant voice and borrowed a huge black animal seventeen hands high for him to ride, while I rode the mean-tempered stallion.

Subsequent Saturdays (all day) and part of each Sunday were spent learning some simple cavalry maneuvers out of a mounted cavalry drill manual I had found which gave us the diagrams of the maneuvers as well as the necessary commands. Eventually we could perform single file, column of two, column of four, column of eight, and troop abreast, and one or two more intricate moves. Each formation, as in close-order drill, required different maneuvers from one to another or back to an earlier one, with timing, of course, crucial. As always, practice, practice, practice leads to performance. When time came to go to the camporal we could perform all our maneuvers smoothly at a walk, trot, or gallop. It was very interesting to me that the half-wild ponies learned the commands and the maneuvers much faster than the boys; the animals actually seemed to relish the drills. Even my cross-grained patriarch showed spirit and life. I rode in the troop, with the commander on the strapping black a few feet outside the pack. I would quietly give him a command and he would crisply bellow it out with proper timing.

In the meantime, at noon at school I was coaching and training specialists in friction fire lighting, wall scaling, knot tying, and a lot of other useless skills for which competitions were scheduled. So as to involve everyone, I trained at least two teams or individuals for each event, and all

became adept because I trained them to higher standards or more strin-
gent rules than were actually required in the competition. By May I had
persuaded Major Plummer, who was in charge, to allow the troop to put
on a cavalry drill demonstration on the second day of the meeting. He
had also arranged an area for us to camp and keep our horses.

For the competitions I entered two entries in nearly every event. Not
one of us had a uniform. They cost cash money and none of my boys had
any way to earn money, nor could their parents spare any, so with the
money we made from selling fire drill kits (which we made in shop class) I
raised enough for official neckerchiefs for everyone. That constituted our
bow to the uniform requirements. On the school's truck we put hay and
corn, groceries, bedrolls, and clean clothes and rode overland to Roswell.
Two days later, on the outskirts of Roswell, beside an irrigation ditch, we
bathed and I shaved, put on clean Levis, blue shirts, and our new neckerchiefs and trotted up the main street of Roswell in a column of two, alter-
nating to fours, and back to two out to the camporal grounds somewhere
on the north side of town. Although the brightly colored ponies and the
flags were colorful, I'm afraid we were a ragtag lot.

Although the camporal ran its course I remember few details, but one
event was very funny. We had practiced wall climbing on a seven-and-a-
half-foot-high wall, whereas the one in the competition was six-and-a-
half feet high. I had worked out a scheme whereby the largest boy on the
team ran to the wall, put his back to it, cupped his hands just as the second boy ran to him and put his foot in the cupped hands, and was heaved
to the top. There on a small platform he grabbed all the other boys as the
tosser heaved them up. Two stayed on the wall, caught the tosser by both
hands, and hauled him up bodily. Although both teams were adept, I labeled the fastest one the first team, and sent them to the test; what with
the excitement and adrenaline and the lower wall, the tosser threw the
first boy entirely over the wall and the platform and he crashed behind it.
No one faltered. The next boy vaulted onto the platform and hauled up
the rest, including the one who went over the wall who had come back to
the start and went up again. The time was very fast, but the second team
did better because of the unscheduled free flight of the first team member.

In all the competitions we placed first or second, and we were all very
proud of the troop and each other. Imagine our dismay when none of our
wins were allowed. Why? We weren't in uniform and therefore had no
status. I was at first speechless, then too articulate when I lodged a protest

that was marked more by indignation and profanity than by reason. I thought we should have been barred from competition rather than later robbed of our honest wins on a technicality. I thought then and now that if we had not performed so well (the country clowns beating out troops from larger towns—unthinkable), we would have gotten our ribbons. It was a sad, dispirited bunch that started the long miles back. Leaving in the afternoon, we reached our predetermined stop at a windmill about sundown, eight or ten miles southwest of Roswell. When we were about half a mile away one of the boys challenged me to a race to the windmill. The patriarch I was riding had been a roping horse in his youth and, consequently, his shoulders were stiff. Of course he stumbled and fell, throwing me some distance ahead. I landed improperly, breaking my elbow, so after dinner, the truck driver and I went back to the hospital in Roswell. A young doctor set and splinted my elbow, gave me a sling, an aspirin, and a pat on the shoulder, and charged me $5.00—all the money I had. We rode hard the next day and reached Hope after dark to a hero's welcome when I told them of our wins. The boys spread the news of our technical losses at school next day. The mounted troop ended my career in scouting; I declined the chance to serve as scoutmaster the second year. The troop may have been disbanded—I can't recall. The rest of the school year finished without incident. I then hitchhiked to Chicago for the field season as planned.

While in Chicago I bought a 1929 Chevrolet coupe for $50 on credit because my father, then living with one of his brothers in Oklahoma City, was worsening and my mother asked me to bring him home to New Mexico when the summer's work was finished. She was an able nurse, unlicensed of course, but experienced, having raised her brothers and sisters, nursed her mother and father until their deaths, and got me and my sister through the then-common diseases of childhood. Additionally, she often nursed sick neighbors and understood the use of many home remedies and over-the-counter medicines, and was a remarkably astute diagnostician, I later came to understand. As always, she charged little or often nothing. Although I was unaware of it, she evidently anticipated my father's death and wanted him where she could nurse and comfort him. To this day I don't know what illness he had, but my mother apparently knew it would be fatal.

Upon arriving in Chicago I was told to gather all the equipment—from Band-Aids to wheelbarrows—that a field school, photo laboratory, and physical anthropological laboratory would require. The experience was invaluable for I learned what I came to call "anticipatory planning"; today it is called "worst case scenario" planning. Both terms mean simply, "be prepared for any contingency you can imagine or hear of."

For the second summer my assignment on the job was survey, then and now a slow way to spend the summer. During the season I had three successive companions for two or two-and-a-half weeks each. We spent the summer surveying every square mile of Fulton County, Illinois, a design imposed by Deuel. We walked endless miles, covering it section by section, while again I learned. By the time the summer was over I knew that the American Indian preferred to live where water was available, often on stream terraces with high ground behind; I also discovered what is now called "settlement patterning" and never again walked across endless, spreading plains when surveying. I looked first for water, then at the terrain. Also, I became aware of ecotonal positioning—locations between two different resource zones, although I didn't know what I was seeing.

Deuel, a West Point graduate and World War I veteran *cum* sociologist *cum* archaeologist was in charge of the entire school. He was a careful craftsman on the job, a slow thinker, and a martinet, but only on the job. He imposed many rules and faithfully applied them. While a stickler for detail and very careful with money and accounting, he was relaxed and pleasant socially. I think he decided on the countywide survey only because he knew I had acquired a car and because in previous seasons other survey parties that had searched the Illinois and Spoon River bottoms had located scores of large sites. I think he assumed the whole county was acrawl with them. I soon found out that compared to the rich valley and bluff zones, the rolling flat country back from the rivers was empty of settlement, although Deuel didn't believe there were so few; he thought we had simply missed them. We did find a few on minor watercourses.

For the survey, logistics were simple. Monday morning we would go to the designated area, find a farmer's wife who would feed us for five days, set up a tent somewhere near her house, and begin. We walked across pastures and fields looking for surface evidence, such as flint scrap, potsherds, and charcoal, and asked every farmer in every field whether he had any "Indian sign" on his place. We provided the farmers a great deal of harmless amusement that summer since they wouldn't believe that two able-bodied men were out looking for "dart" points, as they called them, presumably being paid to do it. Reactions ranged from laughter to clearly expressed contempt. However, most of the locations we recorded actually came from those sources. The summer rocked along—out on Monday, back to Morton's farm on Friday afternoon; seminars and discussions on Saturday; accounts with Deuel in the afternoon and loaf on Sunday; out again on Monday. One of the men assigned to me was Jean C. (Pink) Harrington. On the first day, we discovered that we had already met at the Pecos Mines where he had been an architect (that would have been in 1926), fresh from school, helping design the buildings then being built. I had seen him bustling about there, instructing carpenters, while he had probably seen me helping the plumber, remembering how young I looked. Our time together was pleasant. For one reason he was not lazy, as the first two had been, and the other reason was that he took an interest in what we were doing, volunteering to take over the note keeping and records. We ended the season at a rooming house in Canton, Illinois, where we began a report of the summer's work. I stayed on alone to finish it when Pink was called back to survey for one of the excavation crews, where, because he was experienced with transit and alidade plane-table mapping, he was needed to make maps of a dig that was going on near the Morton farm.

After squaring accounts with Deuel one day later than I had planned because he had a headache and promising to return next summer, I left for Oklahoma City to pick up my father. There I met several cousins I didn't know and went home. On the trip I came to know my father better than I had ever been able or willing to before. He seemed weak, but I had no idea he would be dead in a few months. My mother hadn't told me of her fears.

The second school year was very like the first except there was no scouting. I taught chemistry and general science that year, and my home-room group was sophomores, that is, last year's freshmen, who had asked the principal to be in my room. Most of my students were therefore familiar and many were fun to deal with, some being bright and eager. Unfortunately, however, I still had to teach freshman English, but to another group.

That year I devoted some of my weekends to searching for archaeological sites up and down the Peñasco River, where I found several, including a cave where I dug one trench, recovering considerable material comparable to the Archaic levels from Tularosa Cave. From someone, I heard of the Laboratory of Anthropology in Santa Fe and wrote them about what I was doing and asked that someone come by to examine and take the cave stuff. Stanley Stubbs came, looked at my sketchy notes, and took both the collection and the notes, where, presumably the material is still resting quietly on their shelves. I dug trenches in one or two others, but recovered little except at one location, which I named Peñasco Bend, where my trench went through two occupational strata. I continued there intermittently through the winter. Murphy went with me twice and was not excited by what he saw, although I was. We encountered a hard-packed caliche floor, one or two postholes, and gallons of potsherds in the fill and on the floor.

By Christmas of that year it was evident that Eddy County taxes would not be collected; the economy was essentially dead for the moment, meaning that ranchers and farmers could not sell their products and were therefore delinquent in their tax payments. The result was that it was decided to close the school in mid-March, not May, because the teachers could not be paid.

Thereupon I asked the lab at Santa Fe for $150 to excavate more at Peñasco Bend. Amazingly, they sent me the money. At about that time (March 1933), many banks closed, including the one at Artesia where I had about $50, but I had kept the Laboratory of Anthropology check so lost only those few dollars of my own. With the money, I hired two seniors, Rannell Jones and Philip Reed, who were glad of work for fifty cents a day and food. I spent half the money on four new tires, bought basic staple foods, borrowed a trailer and a few tools, and set up camp at Peñasco Bend late in March. As it happened, Reed was a very good camp cook; he took over that chore the first night, with the result that pinto beans with salt pork and baking power biscuits were our mainstays, although he made excellent raisin and dried apple pies among other things. The days were pleasant, the nights bitter cold. After a day in the trenches in the March and April winds, we were covered with dust, but the river was nearby, so bathing was simple although traumatic in the icy water. Getting out of the water was worst; as the water on our skins evaporated in the dry wind, hypothermia seemed inescapable. The dig drew many skeptical and amused spectators, as might have been expected since we were in full view, about three-quarters of a mile from the only road from Artesia to Alamagordo; many people stopped to see what the crazy school teacher was up to. The material we recovered was what would now be called Mogollon, but that term had not yet been coined. In any case, the site was, predictably, ineptly dug, with an equally poor report being written that winter. Unfortunately, it was published and remained my only research—flawed to be sure—in the Southwest proper, although later work in southeast Utah would also qualify as Southwestern research.

The day before I planned to quit and head for Chicago, where I was to receive better wages than before, a rancher from Hope brought word from the hotel keeper that my father would last only a few days. We broke camp and returned to Hope at once, where by midafternoon I had returned all borrowed gear, paid the boys, and started home. By driving all night I got to the my parents' house sometime midmorning the next day, exhausted. I talked a long time with my father, who seemed weak but alert, then took a nap. He died that night.

The next few days were spent in arranging the funeral. A small insurance policy covered the expenses and left a small surplus, enabling my mother to decide that for her and my sister Alvina to visit the Chicago World's Fair in 1933 was the best possible way to spend the rest. It was. She remembered the fair with pleasure for the rest of her life. They went up with me, and I arranged for them to stay with a friend's family. The friend was Carl Anderson with whom I had served on the campus police force and had kept in touch. While they went to the fair, I went to work on field school preparation as before. Because we were never close and I rarely thought of him, I was surprised to find I felt a strong sense of loss after my father's death, and for months I thought of him often, something I had never done before. Gradually, the feeling of loss and emptiness lessened.

During the summer Dr. Cole awarded me a service scholarship (although I hadn't applied for one) that paid tuition. Naturally I was surprised and delighted, and, my father's death having reduced the need to help my mother so much, I decided to accept and return to classes. The service scholarship involved grading papers, running errands for the secretary and Dr. Cole, and anything else any professor wanted. As a job it was neither arduous nor demanding—actually fun at times. For food I first washed dishes in the Commons, but was soon promoted to evening cashier. After much thought, I borrowed money for room, laundry, and other expenses, tuition being already paid and food paid for by the cashier's job. I had never borrowed before, and wasn't sure it was wise to go in debt with no idea how or even whether I would be able to pay it off.

An interesting thing happened in connection with the loan. I had already found and moved into a tiny room at a rooming house for very little money and thus knew my expenses could be kept low, but I still needed some money. When I talked to the loan officer in the bursar's office, he asked where I was living. When I told him he said, "Why not borrow from the landlady, then?" I understood the gambit and said, "I live there because I can't get into one of the residence halls. I heard they are full." He called across to the lady who handled housing who said she had a room in the Divinity Hall. Possibly a shortage of preachers? So I said I would take it, the loan officer opened an account for me, and I even borrowed later as well, but never very much.

I think that during my graduate years I was most influenced by Redfield, who took an interest in me as he did, but no more, of course, than he took in all his students. I took all his classes and hoped to work with him in the field. He offered me at least three field opportunities that I can remember; one was a year in Guatemala at Lago de Atitlan to study a village there—Panajachel, I think it was—where Sol Tax eventually worked; another was a year with him at a village in Yucatan or southern Mexico; a third was a four-month trip to northern Mexico with another student, Robert Zingg, about whom I was very uneasy. I was forced to decline all his opportunities because they carried no stipend. In those days students received only expenses, whereas I always needed some money because of my commitment to help support my mother. Redfield, however, continued to support me nonetheless.

By 1933 when I resumed graduate study on the teaching assistant grant, I had three full seasons of experience in the field school, and in everyone's eyes I *was* an archaeologist. It must be remembered that in the '30s, anthropology was regarded as the "mother" social science—at least it was labeled thus by the professors. The world would be saved as anthropological wisdom burgeoned and was applied to society's problems; hence, social (cultural) anthropologists were kings of the dung heap. Linguists, physical anthropologists, and archaeologists were ranked beneath them in that order; at least that was the students' view of the pecking order. At the bottom of the scale, the archaeologists with their low brows, dirty fingernails, and concern with dirt and mere things were seen as beings of limited intelligence and no social graces. This view seemed to have been all-pervasive in the discipline. For example, when Robert Wauchope, in 1956, wrote an introduction to a volume he had edited, he dwelt at length on the archaeologists' low estate, revealing in the process the depth of the psychic wounds he had received at Harvard. Other schools were, I fancy, about the same. Fortunately, at Chicago there was but one class in archaeology, Old World Prehistory, as it existed then, so all students took the social, ethnology, and physical classes and all seminars. Archaeology was learned in the field and library. I was never really convinced of my mental inferiority, but neither did I see any great future for the learning of kinship systems.

To return to Redfield: In December of 1933 he recommended me to the Smithsonian Institution as a supervisor for a WPA archaeological program at Murphy, North Carolina, where I was to excavate the Peachtree Mound, selected by John R. Swanton (of the Bureau of American Ethnology) as one of de Soto's stopping places (Guasili) as he explored the Southeast. Later, after I had finished my Ph.D. exams in 1936, he recommended me for a director's job at a series of WPA digs in the Chickamauga Basin north of Chattanooga, Tennessee. Finally, he got me a chance to work with A. V. Kidder in Guatemala at the famous Kaminaljuyú site, which proved to be important, serving eventually as my dissertation topic. In addition to all the overt support, Redfield was friendly, always offering encouragement and advice when asked.

According to the departmental secretary I even owe it to Redfield that I passed my Ph.D. exams. At that time we wrote four exams, spending one day on each of the four fields as then defined: physical, social, archaeology, and linguistics. I felt unprepared, but Redfield insisted I take them in May of 1936. I could only hope I passed. At the faculty meeting where the decision to pass or fail the candidate was reached, Radcliffe-Brown, with whom I had feuded and argued in class and out for years said, "Anyone who would write what Jennings wrote in response to my question should fail. In fact, he should *never* receive a degree." At this, Redfield reputedly replied, "I read your questions and Jennings's answers, and it is my opinion that the fact that Jennings could write anything coherent in response to such vague and ill-conceived questions shows he is little short of genius. I suggest we stop the discussion and pass him." At least this is what Dorothy Harrington, the secretary, who was present, reported. Small wonder that I respect his memory.

In the seven years spent in and out of the department from 1929 to 1936 I, of course, met and competed with many students. Several I had also met in field schools. Competition, of course, is what you make it. I felt, as I had told Dean Boucher, that I could hold my own. When I began to try to excel instead of merely hold my own, my participation in class and seminars probably became more aggressive than was called for. But I rationalized that I was up against a host of good minds; it was a case, as I saw it, of survival over the course of the training. I recall any number of bright people with whom I competed in class. Among them were Sol Tax, Fred Eggan, John Province, Kalervo Oberg, Corinne Brown, Charles Wisdom, Don Collier, Alex Spoehr, Joe Weckler, Florence Hawley, Edith Rosenfels (who later married Philleo Nash), John and Ella Embree, Philleo Nash, Robert Braidwood, Ned and Rosalyn Spicer, Millie Mott (later Millie Wedel), Horace Miner, Pink Harrington, Olive Eggan, John McGregor, Robert Zingg, James Griffin, Richard Morgan, Richard Snodgrass, and Georg Neumann. There were, of course, others whose names have faded. Some of them—Tax, Eggan, Kneberg, Griffin, Spicer, Hawley—achieved eminent positions in their respective fields. I felt, and still feel, that the quality of my training, whatever it was, flowed as much, if not more, from the competition than from the instructors. When people later asked me why it took seven years to do a three- or four-year stint, I always explained (only half in jest) that I had to wait until twenty or thirty people took their exams, that I didn't want to compete with the best there was at comprehensive exam time. I had become well acquainted with several; with some I socialized—Philleo Nash, John Province, Pink Harrington, and the Embrees especially. Among the faculty I sometimes had dinner or weekend invitations from only Hoijer and Redfield.

Student events were typical of student parties then and now, I presume. Classical music, poisonous liquor (each person contributed a pint or quart), conversation, one-upsmanship, and earnest efforts at seduction were standard features. It was a matter of honor that no liquor be left to deteriorate in the bottle. Usually the parties were on Saturday so that the hangovers could be treated on Sunday.

One party I recall was at Philleo Nash's apartment, which he shared with Edith Rosenfel's two brothers, who were premed students, enthusiastic partygoers and drinkers as befitted their premed status. Radcliffe-Brown was at the party and was surrounded as usual by a claque of admiring students who, as always, were enthralled by his British accent and sharp wit. After several hours of regaling his group with tales of his fieldwork in the Andaman Islands, and now deep in his cups, he decided to show us how the Andaman Islanders laid a cooking fire. Why, I don't know. People scurried around to get some scraps of wood and whatever else he needed and a metal wastebasket for the fire. He got it going, with flames leaping four- to five-feet high, and the wastebasket began to show a dull red glow. I went to the kitchen, got a saucepan of water, and threw it impartially on both Radcliffe-Brown and the fire, at which point the fire went out and Radcliffe-Brown went into an apoplectic rage. The party broke up soon after.

Another time Philleo and I, among others, went to some meeting at Madison, Wisconsin, where Philleo had earned his B.A. under Ralph Linton. Late one afternoon Philleo set out to show me the town; we went to all his undergraduate haunts and at three or four in the morning, somewhere out in the country, we were ejected from a tavern or speakeasy. After we debated who was best able to drive, I took the wheel. I soon discovered that the road was hard to follow, so we conferred and decided that since there was a white line in the center of the road I should merely straddle it, keep it in view, and follow it back to town; and I did. I recall meeting no cars nor do I have any idea how long it took, but I do recall eating very spicy chili and drinking milk at his favorite all-night hangout. We emerged as the sun came up, got back to the dormitory where we had been quartered, and I suppose tumbled into bed, leaving the meeting to go on without us. Nash went on to take a very good doctor's degree, but returned to his family's cranberry ranch or farm in Wisconsin, from where, shortly thereafter, he ran for and was elected lieutenant governor of the state of Wisconsin. I believe he did not run for a second term. Eventually he ended up as the commissioner of Indian Affairs under Stuart Udall, where he was, I gathered, a competent and responsible administrator.

One of the oldest of the students was John Province, a lawyer turned anthropologist (probably due to Redfield's suasions). He gave the most frequent parties. His wife was employed, so he was often able to provide liquor and well-prepared snack food for browsing. For some reason his parties were quieter and our conversation was better. In retrospect, I presume that was because John's status as elder statesman inhibited the noisier ones among us. I saw Pink and Dorothy Harrington much more frequently than anyone else. She had became the departmental secretary, a job at which she excelled, but she also took great interest in the welfare and social, academic, and financial status of many of the students. She seemed to feel that I particularly needed a lot of extra guidance. In any case, I was often at their apartment, profiting, I am sure, from her advice. Pink and I, when I was made a teaching assistant, were assigned to a basement office which we sometimes shared with other students, but were usually alone. We studied and discussed whatever topics were current. I remember that we studied French together to the disgust of Horace Miner, also using the office that year, who would leave when our French sessions began. He spoke French well and was horrified by our accents, mine being Spanish, while Pink had a flat Michigan one. Pink and I later shared the directorship of the field school for one year, a year that I learned enough about poker to learn never to play it again. Card sense I do not have, nor could I bluff successfully, while Pink made a few dollars a week in our five-cent limit, penny ante games. Pink didn't like camp life, being very uncomfortable without all the amenities. His employment at Jamestown National Monument or Park in 1936 or 1937 kept him out of the rigors of camp and led to a fine career in the National Park Service. Jane and I visited him often when we were in the east and during World War II when I was stationed at Norfolk. He and Dorothy separated, he to marry Virginia Sutton, a fellow student, while Dorothy married Fred Eggan, by then an assistant professor in the department.

I knew James Griffin fairly well. He had been a Chicago undergraduate and was an excellent athlete (I heard he had been a Big Ten diving champion for one or two years before continuing into graduate work). He was also a clever politician and manipulator. At one point he asked me to join "his" church basketball team in Oak Park, where he lived, which was at least an hour and a half away from campus. Although I had played college basketball and had been on a Roswell semipro team for one year when I was teaching at Hope, I saw no reason to travel so many hours just to get bruises and floor burns, so I declined. Later he asked me to join him and several others who disliked Thorne Deuel's style in an effort to get rid of Deuel. They contemplated visiting Dr. Cole to request that Deuel be removed and, I presume, replaced. Again I balked, saying that if Deuel got too troublesome for me I would have it out with him, not seek his dismissal. I suppose I simply didn't want to be on anyone else's team.

Jimmy went on to Michigan, and I've had continuous profitable contact with him throughout our careers. Years after our student time together he even offered me a job at Michigan, I believe to work with him in the ceramic repository he had built up, but again I declined. In 1955 I invited him to participate in a seminar I had been asked to conduct in Santa Fe in an effort to understand the infrequency with which North American cultures to the east had borrowed from or given traits, complexes, or artifacts to the Southwest. We didn't yet know that the eastern cultures were the oldest. It was called "The Southwest: A Study In Isolation." (Privately I called it "The Southwest: A Cultural Cul-de-Sac"). At our first session, as I laid out a series of steps for getting a coherent report out of six or eight scholars from outside the Southwest, Griffin objected to my agenda, as I had expected. I merely said, "I have outlined the way we will do it. All the rest have agreed to the format, and you are at complete liberty to leave." He withdrew his objections and contributed brilliantly to the seminar, which was later published as a Memoir of the Society for American Anthropology. That was our second cooperative effort. Earlier, at his invitation, I had written a chapter for his monumental *Archaeology of the Eastern United States,* a volume of enormous usefulness to young scholars for several decades. Despite my uneasiness with his personal style, I never changed my original impression that Griffin was bright, ambitious, and thoroughly competent. He proved to be an innovative scholar and a stout defender of his views. I have more than once been envious of the ideas and industry he displayed. He richly deserves the eminent position he holds today in American archaeology.

Robert Braidwood I knew for only one field season. After being with us one summer down in Fulton County he continued studying at Pennsylvania, where he switched from architecture to Near Eastern archaeology. When I knew him he had already worked with the University of Pennsylvania scholars on one of their digs as an architect. He was very bright, charming with everyone, and more than a trifle lazy, displaying even in the filth of the field the style of the country squire he eventually became. His scholarly achievements and charm lead to his appointment eventually as a professor at the University of Chicago, attached to the Oriental Institute. In describing the rise of Old World agriculture, he coined the phrase, "incipient agriculture," a term that puzzles me to this day. To me it has always seemed that the presence of agriculture is very like being pregnant: either you are or you aren't; either there is or there isn't agriculture. No matter. His phrase and his work at Jarmo together earned him his high place in the coterie of Near East scholars.

My relationship with Thorne Deuel has always mystified me. He wasn't a terribly bright man, although he had been an honor student at

West Point, which proves little. Having served as an officer in World War I, he was also a martinet—a stickler for detail; his handling of accounts was particularly maddening in that he would pay no expense account item that was not backed by a voucher or a receipt. I remember that I, along with Stuart Neitzel and my friend Carl Anderson, went down early to the Kincaid site to make it ready for our first season. The Kincaid site is in the Black Bottom across the Ohio River from Paducah, Kentucky, and we were to establish a camp in an old corncrib on a natural levee alongside the Ohio River. The crib was a relic of the days when farm products were moved largely by river barge. The building was perhaps a hundred feet long, with a wide center aisle—probably twelve feet wide—for loaded wagons to bring corn from the fields for storage until the barges picked it up. The cribs were about fifteen feet deep, so the barn was perhaps 100 by 40 feet in dimension. The cribs, of course, were alongside the aisle, walled with horizontal planks spaced four or five inches apart. We enclosed the central aisle sides and ceiling with screen wire and used tar paper as a "linoleum" to close and seal the cracks on the floor (a trick I have often used since), tar paper being a good floor covering, although that wasn't widely known. The object was to make the place mosquito-proof, which we succeeded in doing. I was very careful about that because the previous year, when we had begun our work at Kincaid, living in and under a school house on high piles, I had been infected with malaria so badly that I was having massive fever/chill spells daily and had spent eight days in the Metropolis Hospital getting sixty grams of quinine daily until the fever and chills abated. I took preventive doses of quinine for two years afterward because I wanted no reinfection or recurrence.

When the barn was ready and the crew had arrived, I brought my receipts and remaining funds for settlement. Naturally, I had bought several meals for all of us and a few other things I had noted, but for which I had taken no receipts. Deuel refused to pay them, leaving me in debt, but I had no money until payday. Deuel advanced the cash to balance his books, making me sign a note to be paid out of my first check. At other times and places he was, with his wife Nora, a gracious and considerate host. I later often borrowed small sums from him and he never pushed me for payment, nor did he ask again for a note. His social behavior was impeccable; in the work context he was insufferable. Soon after he got his degree he became the highly successful director of the Illinois State Museum in Springfield. Early in 1949 he offered me a job there when I was a first-year associate professor at the University of Utah, firmly convinced that on my record I had deserved a professorship. Deuel's offer placed me in a dilemma. I didn't want ever again to work closely with him, but thought an offer could perhaps be used locally to improve my rank. What to do? After days of vacillation I decided that for the much better salary I could endure the certain frustration of his nit-picking, so I accepted, duly notifying both him and the University of Utah of my action. I was quickly made full professor and received a significant, but not matching, salary increase; thus, I clearly owed Deuel my professorial rank.

I particularly enjoyed John and Ella Embree the one year they were at Chicago. Because she was a polyglot—English, Russian, Japanese, French, and German—she helped John and me study for and pass our German exams. While we studied, she worked at abstracting, or translating, Russian scientific journals into English for some agency or other. She could translate as fast as she could type. Embree and I, struggling with the German, would call out, "What does _____ mean?" Without stopping her typing she would give us the meaning. I am still amazed at her ability to work in three languages at once. In addition to studying there, I sometimes baby-sat while they went to concerts and similar events at night. John and their daughter were killed in a traffic accident after a stint of fieldwork in Hawaii. I met Ella many years later when I was a visiting professor at Hawaii, where she had become head of the French department at the Oahu campus and had remarried.

Probably I spent more time with Stu Neitzel and Donald Collier than with anyone else. Don, the son of the then-commissioner of Indian Affairs, John Collier, was attending the university on a Rierson Fellowship, the only fellowship the department had. Dr. Cole used it to bring new students to the department. Florence Hawley had earlier also held the fellowship for one year. When I inquired, I was told that people already in the program were ineligible to apply, but that was evidently not true, because Dorothy Harrington applied for it for me without my knowledge for my last year there, which was 1935–36. The department split it between me and Pink Harrington, who had also applied. That year it was worth $1,000, so we each got $500 for the year. But to receive it, one had to register for classes and pay tuition. That meant I got $67 per quarter, not a princely sum. I paid the tuition, but instead of going to classes I read for my comprehensive Ph.D. exams. I also wrote a report (later published) of the Peachtree Mound, North Carolina, excavation, which I describe later. But holding the fellowship was an unexpected honor. I was unaware that it was an honor, however, and have never cited it in my *curriculum vitae* or résumés. I don't know why I didn't realize that it was a kudo.

It was in North Carolina that I met Jane Noyes Chase, who was working at the John C. Campbell Folk School near Brasstown, North Carolina. Our courtship was relatively short, but our marriage was delayed until September 1935. Jane was immediately swept into my limited social circle. Our tiny apartment at University and 56th Streets was often invaded by Collier, Neitzel, the Wecklers, and others. We became particularly fond of Malcolm Carr, who later married Don Collier. As students, lacking either radio or gramophone, we only talked and drank beer, which was cheapest by the pitcher from the bar I called the Belgian Village, although I never knew its real name. The saloon was on University at 55th, only a block away from the apartment Jane and I had. I seem to remember that Collier was usually deputized to make the bar run, making many trips with our two pitchers. We often read books aloud, taking turns. I recall one whimsical author, Thorne Smith, whose far-fetched plots were screamingly funny, we thought, especially after a few pitchers of beer. We would read for a couple of hours, then put the book away until the next gathering when we would continue the reading. It was not riotous living, but was fun, and it was inexpensive compared to such things as movies or eating out. Jane and I never ate out except at a Chinese restaurant called Greater China somewhere off Cermac Road (or 22nd South) in Chicago. Eating there was something the department students did for several years; probably it was Dorothy Harrington who found the place and organized three or four jaunts a year, but Jane and I did it nearly every other week. She had found a job in the art department of Marshall Field, where she got paid every Friday. I would take the Illinois Central to town to meet her, and she would dutifully hand over her pay envelope. We would take a streetcar to Greater China, where we selected dishes that allowed us to eat for fifty cents each and be really out on the town. One of the waiters took a fancy to Jane and would filch one or two of the expensive shrimp, which she adored, from every shrimp order and quietly slip them onto our table. Thanks to him we often had a seventy-five cent meal. I remember my generosity very well; I never tipped less than fifteen cents.

I find it odd that the classes I took and the day-to-day events of the student years have faded so completely. I knew I was enjoying myself; I assumed that I would continue to survive and that I would eventually be employed. Long before I took the comprehensive exams I was classified in everyone's mind as an archaeologist, as I have said. I was willing to take archaeological offers of work because there was a salary attached; so, regardless of my expectations, I had only archaeological experience and thus became an archaeologist by default. And long since, I realized that I would have failed as an ethnologist because I would never have survived the fishbowl exposure ethnologists face in the field, while for linguistics I was equally unsuited. And my one class in physical anthropology had shown me that measuring bones and worrying about races of man was for me, at least, a blind alley. Perhaps archaeology appealed to me because it was physical, sometimes even arduous. Since it dealt with soils, I could utilize knowledge I already possessed from a childhood on the farm, and both my curiosity and skepticism were undoubtedly assets, as was my ability to observe. Like Yogi Berra I further learned to observe by watching. More important, I learned that the archaeologist on the job is in full charge, with the final say. Because a site is destroyed by the act of excavation, with records maintained by the archaeologist the only means of preserving the evidence, I very early realized that directing a dig was a challenging responsibility. One must see and save all there was, because there would be no chance to redo it. Obviously no one ever succeeded in recovering 100 percent of the evidence, but trying to recover it all sharpens eyes and skills. And the responsibility rests on one person. Evidently I have always preferred to be on my own, accepting credit if I got it right, reluctantly admitting the mistakes I made. Since I like to be free to do well or to blunder, it's clear that I do best if I am, or think I am, in charge. Obviously, for this reason if for no other, I am a very poor committee member.

Although in writing what I have I have by no means exhausted my student memories, I think what I have set down serves to illustrate the pleasant and haphazard route I took in becoming a professional archaeologist.

Parents' wedding picture.

Resisting a family Sunday gathering with (my uncle) Ivy Cruce's family. Daniel Wellman Jennings, my father, is on the extreme right; Uncle Will Cruce is center, 1916.

Ball game players, Wewoka, Oklahoma, 1902.

Mother Grace Belle Cruce Jennings, sometime before 1919.

The 1919 camp setup—Model T, awning and tent—at the campground in Santa Fe, New Mexico.

High School Senior Class, 1925. Jennings second from right, front row.

Off to college! (1925)

Montezuma Baptist College on the Gallinas River, northwest of Las Vegas, New Mexico. The bathhouse hotel is to the left of the photo.

With father shortly before his death in April 1933.

FOUR

The Early Professional Years

ALTHOUGH I MORE or less drifted into a professional status, I presume my professional life began in late 1933 when I took the CWA job for the Smithsonian Institution that Redfield had recommended me for. CWA was Franklin Roosevelt's first relief agency, the Civil Works Administration. Neil Judd and Frank Setzler took over when I reached Washington (after my first ride on a Pullman) by telling me that I was to go to Murphy, North Carolina, and organize the excavation of nearby Peachtree Mound. We were excavating the Peachtree site—an extensive village and a large earthen mound—because it had been identified as the Indian town of Guasili, one of the many visited by de Soto as he wandered the South from 1541 to 1543.

I was then twenty-three years old, cocky in my vast experience derived from three years in field school, and with absolutely no conception of what I faced on a major dig. Then I learned that I was second to an amateur collector named William B. Colburn, the brother of Burnham S. Colburn, a prominent Asheville, North Carolina, banker and mineral collector who had been influential in getting the project started. At that time my contempt for any collector was monumental, to be working under one was unthinkable. But I had already left the university, had no job to go back to, needed the salary, and my mother had asked for some additional money for some project she had in mind, so I stayed and went on down.

At Murphy I found that I had literally to organize everything every step of the way; everything from hand tools to typewriters had to be assembled. The CWA administrator had, until recently, been a regular county official of some sort and therefore was experienced in county matters, but was new to the CWA job, a job which required, among other things, familiarity with the dozens of CWA rules and regulations. He was horrified by my demands, but immediately began to help, being under terrific pressure to put men to work in an area that had been in extreme economic depression for over three years; things there were truly desperate. After about three days, Colburn, a tall, handsome man with a strong charismatic presence showed up and was able to take over the frustrating job of negotiating with and nagging the CWA staff. We were, I think, actually able to begin work just before Christmas.

I know that on that first day at the site I nearly fainted when 104 men showed up, none with any archaeological experience. My salvation was the young engineer I had requested; named Dale Lee, he was among the men assigned and proved to be not only very competent but also an intelligent, reliable—albeit religious—assistant whom I valued as a friend as well. I put him to work establishing map controls and a grid system as well as mapping the entire site and environs, a task that only absorbed six or seven men, three of whom were cutting stakes in the nearby woods. From the ninety-seven (more or less) remaining, I selected an unemployed warehouse clerk as timekeeper, picked two or three big men as foremen (alertness and size being the only criteria I used in the selection), and set all the others to digging three exploratory trenches, hoping for the best. All my choices for foremen proved to be good observers, interested, and willing; with their advice I later promoted three or four others to foreman status. They all worked out well and were my eyes as well as my great strength.

On the second day of digging when Colburn came out, he watched for a while and began issuing orders. I immediately asked him to go back to Murphy and straighten out something that had come up the day before about supplies. When he left, I canceled his orders, and work went on. That night (the hotel had us in connecting rooms with the bathroom between) I discussed our separate roles. We eventually agreed that I was the expert; I would run the dig, while he could visit but would keep his mouth shut. From then on he would handle the red tape and I would never darken the CWA office doors again, an arrangement that, as it turned out, worked perfectly for everyone. The CWA people soon ate from his hand, and for him no task was impossible.

It was easy to become good friends with Colburn, whom I only met at night since I left for the field at about 6:30 A.M., work starting perhaps by 7:00. By 4:00 or 4:30 I returned to the hotel, showered and changed after giving my notes to a woman who came at 4:30 to type up the day's record, a record that I sent each week to Setzler. I have heard recently the notes and many of the artifacts have since disappeared. (Since the typing was done in my room, the woman's husband came and sat on the bed, there being but one chair, the whole time). I went about my shower and change of clothes in the bathroom that Bill and I shared and then reported to his room, where by that time he had created a concoction of recently distilled, clear corn whiskey, orange or lemon juice, and grenadine. The whiskey we first got by the pint from Fred, the bellhop, but soon Bill developed his own source from a nearby moonshiner who supplied corn liquor in quart jars. Bill organized the whiskey run sometime during the day—at least we never ran out—but where he got the grenadine I never knew. I do recall that the bellhop was making a 100 percent profit by charging fifty cents a pint, whereas the moonshiner Bill found gave us a quart for the same price, but wanted his jar returned. After probably too many drinks and dinner, Bill played bridge with people in the hotel while I went to movies, a weekly square dance, or wrote my impressions or questions about the day's work, and to some extent planned tomorrow's work. One night I recall that the then-popular author, Sherwood Anderson, who was gathering material for a book, joined us after dinner. He was an interesting and charming man, and we drank our corn, sang, and argued until morning, leaving me going to work somewhat the worse for wear and with no plan except survival. Anderson, reporting the entire incident in the book he was then writing, nearly earned me a reprimand by referring to me at length in his book as "Dr. Jennings," a degree I had not yet earned and had not yet claimed. A university board of trustees member read the book and asked Dr. Cole just who was this famous Dr. Jennings; he asked me about it, and I reckon he believed my denial, although he did speak in generalizations about fraudulent claims.

Somewhere along the line, I was invited by Dale Lee (my engineer) to visit the John C. Campbell Folk School with him, his wife, and her sister on a Sunday afternoon. Of course I went, pleased to have a kind of date. There I met Jane Noyes Chase, later Jane Chase Jennings, and lost my head, later suggesting that she marry me, which she did a year or two later, actually on September 7, 1935. After more than fifty years, two boys of whom we are proud, and many years of scrabbling along on whatever my job paid, my affection and love for her and respect remain the same. She has shown great patience and forbearance, being always supportive, even when I made impulsive, perhaps wrong, moves.

At the Peachtree dig I had to learn a new vocabulary: "poke" for bag, "stob" for stake, "croker sack" for burlap bag, and other mountain words which presumably were Old English terms that had survived there in the hills. Among the other experiences I had at Murphy that I greatly enjoyed was meeting the owner of the Peachtree site, who invited me to visit while he trained his fighting cocks—good ones. Later he invited me to several mains (he called them "rooster fights"), where I always bet small sums on his birds because his were usually alive at the end of a fight. Probably I should have been shocked by the cock fights, but wasn't, although I did hate to see one or the other of the gallant birds die from a gaff to the heart or brain. The four-inch-long, needle-sharp "gaffs" the roosters wore on the stub of their cutoff spurs frightened me. Another local sport was fox hunting. There, and later in Tennessee, I was invited to go on one or two. Fox hunting required a pack of dogs, hills to run on, and wily old foxes, which appeared to be territorial. The men and the dogs would go to where a fox was known to den. There the dogs would pick up the scent, begin to bay, and follow the trail as the fox ran along the ridges for miles, while the hunters went to some place where the hounds could be heard. They would light a fire and stand or sit around, passing the jug and listening to the blending, bell-like tones of the hounds at work. As a pastime it sounds dull and foolish, but was, in fact, quite exciting, particularly when the baying changed as the scent grew warmer and then became frantic when the fox went to ground. When that happened everyone went home, the dogs straggling back over the next few hours, while the fox seemingly was unhurt and would run again another night. The foxes probably enjoyed the hunt as much as the dogs and men. Apparently the foxes ran about the same route every time, and the men could even identify "Old Rusty" or "Old Joe" by the location and length of the run.

I learned to square dance there as well. Although that activity is respectable today, at that time in Murphy the gentility frowned on square dancing as being a lower-class entertainment, so I perhaps lost a few numbers with the pillars of the community through my dancing. I was invited to the first one by a young woman I met at the hotel, and learned the rudiments from her; but at that first dance there was a short, plump girl who moved like thistledown, seeming to float through the measures. Moreover, she knew all the dances and conned me through them expertly. Thereafter, although I always took my sponsor, I sought her out when I got there and therefore thoroughly enjoyed every dance. The cost of admission for two was fifty cents (this was to pay the caller and fiddlers), to which the cost of a pint of moonshine had to be added, because at each break most of the men and a few of the women went outside and passed the bottle, which always came back empty—but no matter, at the next break another one was passed.

If one gets the impression that in Murphy and environs corn liquor was an integral part of all entertainment, one would be more or less correct. I learned early, however, that drinking unaged white whiskey requires both caution and fortitude. Once when I went to spend the night with one of my foremen, Hobart Hughes, he wakened me just before daylight and left me a water glass half full of a clear liquid as an eye opener. I drank it; it worked, truly opening my eyes. Within a few minutes, moreover, I found I had a fine appetite for breakfast.

Hughes and I spent a lot of time together. On the days when CWA didn't work we took Colburn's car and drove every road in Cherokee County searching for sites. The crew workweek was twenty-four hours, so we surveyed two or three days a week, with the result that I became more fully aware of the grinding poverty of the area. The houses of plank or log construction usually had one or two rooms, perhaps with a lean-to. They were essentially empty inside, containing a fireplace, beds or pallets, a few cooking utensils on the hearth, and little else. Some of the houses we visited belonged to workmen on my crew; those families were gracious and open. When we went to houses of strangers, I was treated with hostile reserve even though Hughes was with me. Of one thing I am certain: the much-maligned CWA saved the lives of many people in Cherokee County that winter.

Digging Peachtree taught me a little about picking and training helpers and led me to like and appreciate the "hillbillies" of the South; and possibly I learned more archaeological techniques, but of this I am less

sure. The site evidently was not Guasili, but was one of the first fully excavated sites of what came to be called the Late Mississippian Tradition.
The upper layers were built upon an earlier Middle Mississippian Tradition location. The final occupants were probably a Cherokee group of
early historic times. The main thing I learned was that I must read whatever I could find about a region *before* I put a shovel into the ground. I
would have made fewer mistakes and recognized the cultural affiliation of
the artifacts while digging instead of *two years later* in the laboratory and
library. Eventually I learned to prepare myself via the literature before
starting any fieldwork in a new area.

Sometime in April the CWA funding was exhausted and we closed the
dig, shipped our potsherds and other data to the Smithsonian Institution,
and I prepared to return to Chicago where I was expected in time for the
field school. Then, unexpectedly, the Smithsonian wanted me to go to
Florida to excavate the Ormond Mound near Ormond Beach, Florida,
under Matthew Stirling's direction. After two weeks in Asheville, where I
lived with a "courtesy cousin" (one of my mother's childhood friends)
and wrote a preliminary report of the Peachtree dig, I went to Ormond
Beach to meet Stirling.

The final Peachtree dig report (written in 1936, as mentioned earlier)
was eventually published as Bureau of Ethnology Bulletin No. 131, with
me as junior author, since Frank Setzler had told me that no BAE report
could be signed by other than a Smithsonian employee. Believing him, I,
of course, agreed to second billing, once more showing my ignorance and
naïveté, for there was no such requirement; however, that junior authorship proved beneficial later. When Walter Taylor wrote his all-inclusive
denunciation of archaeological practice up to 1948, Setzler got full credit
for wrong-headedness about the report I had written but he had signed,
while I was unscathed in the critique; I suppose everything evens out.

In Florida I met Stirling and his wife. They had just been married,
and were more interested in their Florida honeymoon than Florida archaeology and left after a couple of days. I discovered that I needed to
have a car—I had long ago given the little Chevrolet I had first owned to a
friend in Chicago, so Stirling loaned me the $125 I needed for a 1929
Model A Ford roadster with the rag top most cars had then. It served me
well; probably it was the best car I've ever owned.

I'd been able to convince the local relief authorities, now called Federal Emergency Relief Administration (FERA), that I needed "Doc" Par-

sons and Hobart Hughes from the Peachtree dig as photographer and foreman, respectively, as assistants. Parsons was a long-time friend of Bill Colburn and his banker brother Burnham, so when he arrived he had the keys to Colburn's Ormond Beach winter house. There Hobart and I lived in the servants' quarters of five or six rooms, while Doc lived in the big house where the kitchen was. He was a good cook, and he volunteered to take over the commissary and cooking chores. Naturally, I was delighted with having a place to stay, because the hotel where I was living was expensive; I had already foreseen that my room and food would cost more than my salary would cover.

I was assigned to dig the Ormond Mound, located on a property owned by John D. Rockerfeller, whom I never saw. Why it was picked I never knew. It was a low mound, forty to fifty feet in diameter. It proved difficult to dig; eventually it was studied and understood.

While the FERA officials were equal to the Murphy administrators in their ignorance of what the support of archaeology required, they were by no means as cooperative, saying they thought that archaeology was a waste of manpower, resisting me and my demands all the way. Every possible excuse was raised for delay and postponement until finally, with the help of a staff engineer, we got a crew and some equipment assembled. Things never got better, forcing me to spend part of every day at the office dealing with one or another unnecessary hindrance, but Hobart saved my life. He was a keen observer, he kept the crew alert, he understood context and association, he understood the mapping controls; he made the project succeed although I did not delegate the notes or strategies to him (I probably only spent half or a little more of my time at the dig), and I had no qualms about leaving Hughes in charge. Again our workweek was only three days, so there was time to explore the country. We also spent time on the beach, Colburn's cottage being between the beach and the coastal highway that I believe is today U.S. Highway 1.

The site was difficult to dig, being a sand mound. Palmetto roots formed a mat about three feet deep all over it, and a dozen or more pothunter holes dimpled its sides and summit. Even before the vandalism the palmetto roots had mangled and moved the many burials the mound contained. The sand slumped and made it impossible to keep a clean working face. While I could do nothing about the roots, I did control the trenches by sloping the working face at about a 70 degree angle instead of the usual vertical 90 degrees. So the stratigraphy (it was a two-stage mound) could be discovered, then observed, controlled, and photographed. The notes reveal that I agonized for days over the amount of time that had elapsed between the two construction stages. Finally on the evidence in the site I decided that there had been a hiatus of many years—I guessed several hundred. At that time neither I nor anyone else knew the local culture sequence, so as to the age of the artifacts I had no clue. Years later when Gordon Willey and Marshall (Bud) Newman (both of them then at the Smithsonian) and I prepared a report, my field judgment was confirmed. The artifacts from the lowest level were identified by Willey as St. John's I at least 500 years earlier than the second stage, identified as St. John's II. Our joint report was published as BAE Bulletin No. 164.

The site provided other problems. It was alongside a fairly important road; from the first day we were plagued with visitors, and since it seems to have been the most important thing going on in the county, the reporters were always there. On the third day a cocky young reporter who hadn't been there before leaped into the trench, caved in the working face, and demanded to know what was going on. Hobart and I heaved him out of the trench, promising to cripple him if he entered again. I then went up to talk to him and gave him a long interview, answered all his questions, and asked him to let me check his story for accuracy. He did let me see it that afternoon. He had written accurately—without mention of his ejection from the trench—and it was published the next day. On that next day, too, I created a rope fence around our working area and assigned our most literate laborer to talk to visitors about what we were doing. Of course, there was damage to the site when we weren't there, but people no longer messed around while we were working. The reporter became a regular visitor, and I always gave him all the time he wanted; I even invited him into the trench to see things, but he now always waited to be invited. Quite by accident and luck, I there and then established my relationship to the press from thence onward. The press has always treated me fairly because I gave them straightforward answers at any length they wished. So, at Ormond Mound I not only learned a great deal about archaeological problems and how to deal with them but, as a bonus, I also established an apparently effective pattern of dealing with the media.

The Ormond Mound dig was finished just as the FERA funds ran out in early June of 1934, so I drove back to Chicago for the annual ritual of setting up the field school. That was the year the Kincaid program was launched. Excavations, at least at first, were done by the field school. Kincaid would today be called a Late Mississippian site, being also the largest late site on the Ohio River. It is now, I believe, an Illinois State Park. I've already described what I did to the old corn barn the following year, arrangements which, as I said, were highly successful. That first year, 1934, I went down early and secured permission for us to camp in the small schoolhouse near the site. It stood on high pilings; the bottom-lands, being along the Ohio, flooded annually. I enclosed the bottom (i.e., the space under the building) with screen wire for a kitchen, dining area, work space, and lounge. Upstairs I unscrewed the desks, piled them in one corner, thus turning the schoolroom into the barracks. The situation was roomy and suitable, but stiflingly hot during the long Illinois summer. Since we were surrounded by cornfields and a few trees, there was never any breeze, and only Fats saved the day. Fats, whose name I cannot recall, actually was the glue that held the crew together that year. With the help of the banker in town I found him, unemployed, in Metropolis, Illinois, our outfitting town. Fats had been a riverboat cook in the waning days of that romantic era in American transportation; there he had learned to prepare beef, pork, lamb, fish, and fowl in ways none of us had ever seen before. In addition, his bread and pastries were superb. He and his swamper, Percy (who also waited table), working with a small coal-burning range, served up meals my taste buds can still remember. Fats took me at my word when I told him, "Order what you need to give us abundant meals of finest quality," and I bought everything on his list without demur, including 200 pounds of ice, on my semiweekly grocery runs into Metropolis. I felt, and still feel with Napoleon, that armies and working men travel on their stomachs and that good meals lead to good morale and fewer gripes about other things. Fats cooked for us again the next few years when we lived in the converted corncrib.

It was during these years of establishing camp facilities that I realized a very important thing. Nothing one does—no experience—is ever wasted. Even if something fails, one has learned not to try it again; that may be a negative value, but it is still a value. But my meaning is more positive in that I've learned that one calls again and again on past, seemingly unrelated experiences. A case in point with the camp setups is the logistics of camping: had I not once been a cook I would not have been able to list and purchase what one needs to outfit a kitchen and mess hall. And, had I not learned how to use hand tools in high school and on the farm, the enclosing of living space, creation of shelves and tables, and building of other features would have been beyond me. And I also learned very early that being congenitally lazy (and I fully qualified) is an asset in planning, meaning that if one can devise ways of getting the desired results with less effort, more is accomplished with no increased time or labor cost. It is nothing more than the age-old mini-max economic theory—minimum effort for maximum gain—which applies equally well to human effort.

At Kincaid, as before in Fulton County field schools, I directed an excavation crew for one year. In 1934 I had Horace Miner under instruction as a helper as we worked on a mound that was fairly complex. He kept notes when I was gone on camp-support chores. Beneath the mound was a building—a dwelling, as I recall. The second year (I can't recall who was with me as a trainee that year) I excavated in the village, finding two house patterns, one above the other. Excavating the houses posed two or three problems I had not yet encountered in fieldwork, so I undoubtedly learned a little more there. We also sampled the largest mound. I remember being awed by the size and extent of the Kincaid site. There was a tall pyramid facing south toward Avery Lake (an old channel of the Ohio River), a long, low platform to the north, and six or eight lower mounds to the east. I only spent two seasons there, but work continued at the site until 1941. The final report was done by Dr. Cole after World War II.

After the 1935 season ended I drove to Washington, D.C.; Deuel had given me expense money to analyze the Peachtree Mound material so I could write a formal report, which he would add to the long-running Mississippi Valley Pictorial Survey that he established and directed. The Southeast was then essentially unknown archaeologically, and Deuel's survey was aimed at collecting photographs and other data from existing private collections. The hope was that with the scattered data all in one set of files it would be possible to build a more coherent account of Southeastern prehistory. The photos from the University of Chicago field school researches from 1930 through 1941 were eventually included in the survey files. Nothing, so far as I know, was ever done with the survey data, probably because the CWA, FERA, and WPA programs generated so much new data, often under good control, that by 1941 the full sequence of early cultures and considerable detail about them had been established. Interestingly, in 1985 rehabilitation of the old Pictorial Survey photographs and negatives was undertaken. They now constitute a rich lode of historical data at the Illinois State Museum.

At the Smithsonian Institution Frank Setzler, head of the Anthropology Department of the National Museum, made the Peachtree collections and records available to me. He even arranged evening and weekend passes to the museum so that I could use all available time on the analysis. Except for the Peñasco material from Hope, this was the first effort I had ever made at analyzing and reporting a collection, and I was very unsure of myself, leading me to put in twelve- to fourteen-hour days.

However, I took one week off to go to Boston to meet Jane's folks and bring her to Washington, where we planned to marry. Susan Setzler arranged our wedding for Saturday afternoon, where she and Frank stood up with us and, except for one elderly woman who wandered in, were the only witnesses to the simple chapel wedding. After a drink at the Mayflower, Jane and I had dinner and drove around the Lincoln Monument before going to the room I had found in a private home. Sunday morning we went to work at the museum as usual. Probably the shortest but nicest honeymoon of record. By early October the Deuel funds were used up and we returned to Chicago. I've already touched on that final year and will leave it at that except to reiterate that in the spring of 1936 I took the written Ph.D. exams.

FIVE

The Southeast

THE DAY AFTER I took the Ph.D. exams, I went to Chattanooga, Tennessee, to take over (again with no idea what I would be likely to encounter), under T. M. N. Lewis, the direction of a dig in the Chickamauga Basin, a program sponsored by the TVA using WPA laborers. The Tennessee Valley Authority (TVA) goes back to the efforts of Senator George W. Norris of Nebraska, who in the 1920s conceived the grand scheme. The idea was to dam the almost endless Tennessee River to create a series of huge lakes for flood control, hydroelectric power, and recreation and, it was hoped, to ameliorate the poverty of those who lived on the edges of Appalachia in Tennessee and Alabama. Implemented by Congress, under Roosevelt in 1933, this unique government agency has continued and flourished beyond Senator Norris's wildest expectations. The Works Progress Administration (WPA) was the third and final form taken by the Federal Relief program from 1933 onward, finally to be dismantled in 1941. I had not realized it, but I evidently was "on relief" three times, with each of the New Deal agencies—CWA, FERA, and WPA. Sounds almost like I was a professional relief client.

That the TVA was interested in and sponsored emergency archaeological work is referable entirely to Maj. William S. Webb, a physics professor at the University of Kentucky at Lexington and an enthusiastic, indefatigable amateur archaeologist. When he became aware that the TVA was operative and that the Tennessee River Valley would eventually be inundated, he convinced A. E. Morgan, chairman of the TVA, that the hundreds of prehistoric sites must be explored before the flooding began. Webb was made director of the TVA archaeology rescue operation. He may also have designed and "sold" the wedding of the TVA and the WPA, a mating of resources and needs that apparently pleased both parties. By that I mean, the WPA sought useful tasks for large groups of men, tasks that required labor and little if any raw materials or equipment; the TVA was acquiring hundreds of square miles of river valley studded with large archaeological locations that were (according to Major Webb) crying for attention, particularly that which the TVA could and would provide. The program was strategically located in that there was, at the time, no extensive, systematic archaeological knowledge of any part of the South. Therefore, any new, well dug, and (one hoped) promptly reported archaeological finds would contribute heavily to the record of America's prehistoric heritage.

Aside from the value to the world of science we might recover from the project, I wanted to get to know Major Webb better for personal reasons. I had met him in one of the years I was hired to outfit the Chicago summer field school. At about 7:30 one morning I had gone to the office on campus to collect something, and I found a stocky individual who radiated physical power and some annoyance, trying to enter the building and muttering about slugabed academics. He identified himself, stating his desire to meet Dr. F.-C. Cole, the department head, at once. He also said he was in a hurry, was from Lexington and the University of Kentucky. I let him into the building, asked the secretary when she arrived about Dr. Cole's plans, and sat down to talk. For openers, I asked if he knew my uncle John Webb Willmott, who lived in Lexington. My uncle proved to be a first cousin of the major. We sat in silence a minute and he said, "What's your name, again?" I told him and we were again silent. Then he asked, "Was your mother's name Grace Cruce?" I said yes. He looked at me intently, then said, shaking his head, "Your mother was the most sought-after woman in the Indian Territory. I'd have been your father if it hadn't been for John Willmott and Wellman Jennings, because I had the inside track with Grace for a while." Thus, I gathered that my father got Grace, John settled for her sister, Irene (my aunt), and Webb left the Indian Territory to study physics in Kentucky. Webb later, on the Tennessee Hixon site dig, when he visited the job, talked about how he got his rank as major. Evidently he was a captain in the Kentucky National Guard when America was thrust into World War I. The governor of Kentucky offered full and unconditional pardons to any prisoners carrying a life sentence who would volunteer for army service. Major Webb either volunteered or was assigned as the commanding officer of the four hundred or so who volunteered. One Friday morning he reported to wherever the men were being held and assessed the situation. The volunteers were a tough-looking and unruly lot. Webb had also been given eight or ten tough, regular army noncoms, all sergeants, I believe. He called the noncoms together for a brief meeting, telling them he would be leaving for three days and that he wanted the convicts to be under control, disciplined, and learning how to be soldiers when he returned Monday. With that, he left.

The noncoms had already been learning, by observation and questioning, the convict power structure and who was at the top of the pecking order. As soon as Webb left, they called the leader in, beat him almost to a pulp (never hitting him in the face), and asked for his cooperation in establishing control over the mob outside. To that request he, unsurprisingly, agreed. The noncoms then called in his designated supporters, one by one, roughed them up somewhat, and gave them status by appointing them corporals, with the head man a sergeant. The newly created noncoms divided the rank and file into squads. Monday, Webb returned to find the entire troop marching, doing close-order drill, and smartly obeying any and all orders the sergeants issued. Major Webb then took over and began to build an artillery troop, which eventually served with bravery and distinction somewhere in France. The major was very positive in his views and language—his world was black and white; he was tireless; he understood the scientist's obligation to report the results of research and always did it. Eventually, either by himself or with a junior author he reported all the TVA work done under his direct supervision. I admire him and his memory very much.

I was surprised and delighted to find both Paul S. Cooper and Stuart Neitzel, alumni of the 1935 field school, already there and eager to let me take over. I soon found out why. The WPA crew, about ninety-five men from Soddy, Tennessee, a community in great distress, were all strong union men and very proud of it. Years before, the Soddy labor force had struck the coal mine there; the mines had remained closed, leaving them without work. In the '20s a textile mill was built and everyone got jobs and prospered; they again struck, and the owners promptly closed the mill. The Soddyites were proud of having closed the two businesses and were eager to strike and close me down as well, as it turned out. The grievance committee began making demands the very first day, asking for shorter hours, a rating or ranking of jobs, and differential pay, along with scores of other lesser demands I could not meet because the pay scale was already set by WPA regulation. A number of the men were hard cases, but aside from the three-man grievance committee and three or four of the committee's satellites who were always malingering and whining, most of the crew seemed willing to learn and work and did it well. But thanks to the grievance committee, which never let up, there was always an undertone of discontent and hostility. There was demand upon demand, which I could only refuse; that went on until the day I left. Even one time when I was incapacitated by a series of wasp stings that left my eyes swollen completely shut, the grievance committee came anyway. On the crew were several who had served penitentiary terms—one for murder—as well as many who were skilled, rough-and-tumble fighters of renown, and I was always in fear of some kind of trouble on the job—trouble involving me, that is. Nothing every happened, however, and for that I remain forever thankful.

As for the archaeology, it was again new and challenging. We first excavated the Hixon mound, a five- or six-stage Mississippian pyramidal structure, where we did a fair job of unraveling the sequence, finding several graves filled with exquisite burial objects in the process. The Hixon place was across the Tennessee River from our camp, so we ferried across twice a day. Ferrying was an added hazard because Lewis had leased a leaky and unwieldy, homemade, bargelike boat powered by a temperamental old Dodge motor converted to marine use; the boat was unsafe but usable. When we finished at the Hixon site, we began excavating at the Yarnell and Davis sites where I don't now recall anything except a large mound partially leveled by plowing and a large village site with an adjoining cemetery. But now the barge had to cross the river and ferry all of the ninety-five crew members across twice a day, giving the committee a field day; and with that complaint, for once I agreed. We secured a better, more reliable craft, and I ceased to worry about drowning half the crew in the Tennessee River.

The season there had many ups and downs. By the time I arrived in early June Lewis had installed the camp in two houseboats—primitive, leaky affairs—the houses merely corrugated-tin—covered sheds on ancient wooden barges, with one serving as a mess shack while the other was office and supervisory crew dormitory space. I took one look and immediately purchased a tent, which I pitched high on the bank. The situation was perfect as far as comfort went, with the boats moored under two large sycamores and thus shaded at all times, but nothing else was thought out. The cook knew nothing of cookery, and I very soon replaced him with a man who was in some kind of trouble with the law and wanted to get lost for a few months; at any rate, he never left the camp once he reported. He was a godsend—not as good as Fats, perhaps, but skilled in the kitchen. Jane joined me at camp after about two weeks. Our tent was comfortable and pleasant, and she busied herself with cleaning artifacts. She also discovered the Davis site which lay south of our camp and rediscovered the Yarnell site a little further along the terrace.

In midsummer, the river rose about four feet and the barges rose only about one foot until they hit the limbs of the huge sycamores and were forced underwater. About 3:00 A.M. I heard shouts and laughter and rushed out to see Cooper and Nietzel, our half-trained engineer (whose name I can't remember), and the cook climbing the bank from the submerged houseboats. I had long before decided that the houseboats were a distinct liability, unsafe, and impracticable and had already priced some tents. I walked out to the road, got to a telephone at Harrison (where we received our mail), and ordered the tents, along with enough lumber and nails to make tent houses for the crew, mess, office, and records; I also notified the houseboat owner where he could pick up the boats. When we began work at the Davis and Yarnell sites, we moved the camp to higher ground near the site, where it was also reasonably comfortable, even after summer passed, when we installed old-fashioned, airtight tin stoves in each tent.

The archaeological side of things moved well despite the administrative situation. Neitzel and Cooper were both good observers and kept adequate records of their excavation units. I, constantly on the move, tried to observe the critical aspects of all phenomena as they were uncovered and kept a set of stratigraphic and horizontal relationship maps and notes as well as a general log of the work.

Those three sites—Hixon, Yarnell, and Davis—have never been reported in published form, although a rather complete rough manuscript does exist, written by several authors. I had tried twice to get a National

Geographic Society grant support to analyze the material and prepare a report, but was turned down both times. In 1988, after I learned of the existing manuscript, I arranged to get a copy from Jefferson Chapman at the McClung Museum at the University of Tennessee in Knoxville. From the manuscript I learned that we had discovered that the deep Yarnell and Davis sites were stratified, the early material being the Middle Woodland Tradition (perhaps 2,000 years old), followed by a well-developed Mississippian Tradition occupancy. (In November 1991 I learned that Ms. Lynn Sullivan, of the New York State Museum, has secured the old manuscript just mentioned and has reworked it from the original notes, checked all the maps and tables, and will soon have an accurate and massive report of the entire Chickamauga program. Some twenty sites were excavated in addition to our three. There were scores of beautiful Southern cult objects, tons of pottery, hundreds of burials, and other items recovered. All have been analyzed, and will, I gather, be included in what will be a multivolume monograph, providing a detailed account of the prehistoric use of the Chickamauga Basin from before the time of Christ until historic times.)

From the first, my relationship with Lewis was never good. To begin with, I felt his notion of camping on houseboats absurd and was, as well, a clue to his common sense. Moreover, he had no professional credentials, either academic or in experience, that qualified him to be employed by the state of Tennessee in such an operation; nor was our dig part of any comprehensive plan that he ever discussed. Of course, in all fairness, I need to say that so little was known about Tennessee's prehistoric resources that probably no one, let alone Lewis, could have architected a research plan at the time. Therefore, I rarely carried out his off-the-cuff instructions on the occasions he was present. Fortunately, he visited us infrequently and spent little time on the dig when he was there; neither did he give me any help at all with my problems with the crew nor with the WPA administration. His subsequent elevation to chair of the anthropology department at Tennessee has always mystified me. He did achieve some credibility with his publications, which I have actually always credited entirely to Madeline Kneberg, who was a quite capable classmate of mine and who came to run Tennessee's Knoxville archaeology lab sometime in 1936 or 1937. In any case, Lewis is shown as senior coauthor, with her, of two of the best monographs from the Southeast, *Hiwassee Island* and *The Eva Site*. When they retired sometime in the '70s or '80s to Florida from the University of Tennessee, they were married. (In 1991 I discussed the matter with Jimmy Griffin; he credits the quality of the Tennessee reports to Bud Whiteford of Beloit. Griffin thinks that Whiteford, who was the laboratory chief for Kneberg at Tennessee, probably wrote the reports. That view clears up the mystery. Whiteford was an intelligent, well-trained man, and Griffin's version is easy to accept.)

The Guatemalan Interlude

J UST BEFORE CHRISTMAS in 1936 I received a reprieve from my travails, some of which I obviously had created for myself. Thanks again to Redfield, I was invited by telegram to work with the Carnegie Institution of Washington at the Kaminaljuyú site in Guatemala where Oliver Ricketson, who was to have run the dig, had become seriously ill, leaving A. V. Kidder in need of an immediate replacement. My acceptance was instantaneous. We received instructions to sail from New Orleans on such-and-such a United Fruit boat, which left ahead of its published schedule, so we missed it, leaving us seven pleasant and exciting days in New Orleans waiting for the next banana boat. We were very low on money, so our hotel and food were on a very modest scale, and we walked everywhere, soaking up the special quality of New Orleans in the 1930s. The steamship people knew I was with Carnegie because Carnegie had arranged for our passage; that connection made me an instant Maya expert. They asked if I could be persuaded to lecture to the tourists and guide them through picturesque Quirigua when we got to Guatemala as payment for my passage. I indeed would and hastened out to Tulane University to get the Morley guidebook to the site of Quirigua and try to memorize it. With half our fare saved, I breathed easier, given the state of our finances.

Even though the ship was a banana freighter belonging to the United

Fruit Company, it seemed to me to have commodious and near-elegant tourist accommodations. Of course, I'd never been on such a boat (or any other kind) nor been treated with such deference (even after I had given my lectures on Maya prehistory as I understood it). In the meantime, Jane came down with the flu and had a terrible trip, while I was healthy, reveling in all the food and other attractions of shipboard life, living, in fact, the life of Riley. At Quirigua the train dropped me and the tourists off at the ruins, then took a spur line up to the hospital, where Jane received further intensive treatment. After the ruins, the train backed down, picked everyone else up, and we went on to Guatemala City. There we were taken to the Pensión Geroúlt, and Jane went under the care of a second physician alerted from Vera Cruz by the ship's doctor.

Early the next day I left Jane, who knew no Spanish, in the care of the *pensión* and the doctor and went to the Highlands with the Carnegie Institution stationwagon and driver. I did, however, leave Jane with an American-Spanish phrase book. I don't remember why Dr. Kidder was so insistent that I go, but it was a wonderful trip, scenic and colorful. I also visited Sol and Gertrude Tax at Panajachel on Lago de Atitlán, where they were now fully acclimated, having rented a house and garden, bought two tiny Guatemalan horses, and were doing ethnology sixteen hours a day.

At Chichicastenango I was dumbfounded by the busy market, where every vendor was dressed in the distinctive costume of his or her own district, while the variety of items for sale or barter was unbelievable, totally distracting. Pottery from near the capital of Guatemala City; dried shrimp from Vera Cruz; copal and chicle from the Petén; corn, beans, eggs, onions, cordage, mats, blankets, string bags and hammocks, exotic fruits, and large round avocados from nearby—the list of items was seemingly endless. On the trip I learned that no one except tourists pays the asking price; part of the fun for the merchants, apparently, is in the dickering, finally to agree on an amount.

On a later visit to another market near Guatemala City with some friends, I spotted a fancy, colored string hammock that I coveted; the asking price was about $1.25. The merchant and I chaffered endlessly, until I finally got it for seventy-nine or eighty cents, or possibly less. Someone in the party later saw it and wanted one like it, so I returned to the merchant (who, I had noticed, had another one). Since we were leaving shortly, I thought to cut the dickering short and simply offered him ninety cents. The seller refused, saying, "No, no, señor. The *asking* price is only ninety cents. This hammock is of inferior quality." So I began over, offering forty cents, finally striking the bargain at sixty-five cents. He then shook my hand warmly, saying, "I've enjoyed our trading very, very much." One could only bargain in Spanish, however. All the vendors simply refused to haggle with English speakers, especially if he or she carried a camera (the universal worldwide badge of the tourist); tourists simply paid the asking price or didn't get the item. The market, full of handcrafted products, was remarkable enough in its variety alone, but when one also realized that every ounce came to market on men's backs or balanced in baskets on women's heads, the labor cost of the market institution is seen as staggeringly high, and one's appreciation of the products is somehow intensified.

The market and the traders and their goods moved from town to town, so one might see some of the same merchants at Huehuetenango two days after purchasing something from them at Chichicastenango. Naturally, the stock the merchants carried from market to market changed from town to town because they sell some things wherever they are and buy some local products that they know are desired further along on their route. (The incredible Guatemalan market merchant system is fully and sympathetically described by Sol Tax in *Penny Capitalism*, published by the Smithsonian Institution). Although what I remember best is the variety and movement in the market, my next strongest memory is the color—the color of the land and the color of the costumes on the people. Since each district had a different and distinctive costume, often in strong colors, the clothing identified the person, his or her district of origin, and moreover created a pleasing, ever-changing mass of color where there were crowds, as in the market.

Back in Guatemala City, where the work was scheduled to start immediately after my return, Dr. Kidder took me out to see the site, having already arranged for a crew of about eight men and a foreman or *caporal*. The site was a pair of low mounds facing each other from east and west across a long plaza. The site had been discovered when the slopes of the mounds were being cut away to extend the plaza enough to create a soccer field. The clearing and leveling had, of course, obliterated portions of the ruins of the frontal stairways of each mound.

The two mounds and the plaza between were but one small group within the huge Kaminaljuyú site which contained (when I saw it) more than two hundred mounds with their associated plazas, related structures (e.g., ball courts), covering more than five square kilometers. It lay west of Guatemala City, and had already suffered some losses as mounds and plazas were destroyed to make room for the city's growth. The site had been occupied from the time of Christ or earlier, but had apparently flourished from about A.D. 400 to 900 during what was the Classic period, when the Teotihuacán culture spread from the Valley of Mexico into Guatemala and the Petén. The location was evidently abandoned only after A.D. 1200 or later. We recovered ample evidence of the Teotihuacán dominance in our site. Aside from many architectural details identical with those in the central location, north of Mexico City, the lavishly furnished tombs contained stuccoed ceramic vessels and a few orange ware items that were actual imports from Mexico. Thus the site, known since the eighteenth century, but never before carefully sampled until our work, changed our knowledge of the Central American high cultures. Those findings made my dissertation (when eventually written) easy to defend, because the final report of our work had not yet been published.

The initial excavations the previous winter had partially outlined the foundations or bases of three successive pyramid constructions, with extensive stairways extending into the plaza. Each rebuilding or enlargement had happened after a deep tomb had been dug and filled with gorgeous grave furniture (intricate ceramics, shell, jade, and obsidian objects) and then roofed with heavy timbers. When eventually the timbers decayed, the earth and sometimes stone fill above had, of course, collapsed into the tomb. The outer three increments were made of adobe mud and pumice fragments—which Dr. Kidder called "tufa pudding"—faced with lime plaster. Just before the first season ended, a central trench into the front of the mound had revealed an even earlier stairway and pyramid, both made entirely of adobe. When work ended, the exposed material—walls and steps—had been protected by heavy thatch and had survived the heavy rains of the winter season without damage. The season's work had been first directed by Ricketson, who that year also could not continue because of an illness, so Dr. Kidder himself took over, with Robert Wauchope later assisting him. As a result of the change in supervisors, the notes, somewhat sketchy at best, contained gaps. The maps did not fit what I could see; I could not key in anywhere, nor did the descriptive notes exactly agree with what was now visible. So I dismissed the crew for the day, promising they would be paid, and tried to orient my-self well enough to begin work next day. Although I reread notes, exam-ined exposed elements, and measured things all day, I still knew I could not hook up with last year's controls.

Kidder was surprised that I had sat there all day without starting, but said nothing, nor when I did the same thing for the next two days did he say anything. By Thursday, the fourth day, I had a plan of action and kept the laborers, beginning training sessions for the crew. It was clear that the training classes were not well received by the *caporal*, Gustavo Espinosa. I think he had assumed that I would lack any skill with Spanish and that he would be my channel to the crew and would provide what-ever instructing was required. Although I regretted having earned his en-mity, I'm not aware that it did any damage to the morale of the crew, because they proved to be superb, the best I have ever enjoyed in any ex-cavation program I have directed. I should have known they would be good because they were laborers and they all understood tools; earth, with all its variations and textures, color and density, was familiar to them; they were quick to learn and they were proud of their jobs because Carnegie Institution, as an employer, carried a great deal of local clout. I convinced the men that they were my eyes and hands; willingly I credit our success at the site to them.

After I felt I was in control of the site and beginning to understand it, I asked Jane to help me with the sketching and mapping of last year's work as well as our own efforts. Soon, however, Kidder decided to exca-vate a tomb known to be in front of Mound B to the east; I was working on Mound A on the west end of the plaza. He quickly discovered, as I already knew, that Jane had infinite patience, was a perfectionist, and had an artist's eyes and hands; naturally he decided to use her on *his* dig. She worked almost exclusively at the exacting task of cleaning tombs, where all her qualities were assets. I greatly appreciated his decision to help with our *pensión* cost as recompense for Jane's labor, since my salary wasn't quite enough for both of us, although I am sure Dr. Kidder probably never had an idea how thin our resources really were inasmuch as the Carnegie Institution paid only token wages. The reason, I presume, was that all the staff that I eventually came to know had private incomes; Harry Pollock and Robert and Ledyard Smith were the ones I came to know best. As near as I could tell, their reward was prestige rather than money.

After about a month of work Kidder commented to Jane that he'd never seen anyone who could read and interpret and follow elusive archaeological evidence as well as I did, and he added that he had planned to send me home at once if I had failed to begin digging on that Thursday. Jane only told me about it after we were back in the States. Actually, since I had experience only with earthen structures and felt perfectly at ease with the site, I would have expected that I would perceive and be concerned with subtle soil changes. Later, I did notice that Kidder called me over several times to his area and asked what I would do next. After I explained what I would do and why, he would say, "Tell the men to do it." He had already robbed me of the three best men, as well as Jane; they knew what to do and executed exactly whatever strategy I had outlined. One thing that I suggested made sense to me, but Kidder resisted strenuously at first, finally agreeing to try it. My notion was the simple idea of sinking a trench alongside but barely touching the deep tombs, which were two or two-and-a-half meters wide, two or two-and-a-half deep, and three or four long. Working from the side, it was possible to clean them more easily and with less trampling of contents than when work was done in the tomb itself with all the fill dirt being lifted up to the level above.

All of the work, from the first day, was demanding, exciting, and complex. There proved to be nine structures built in fairly rapid succession upon one another like the Chinese egg which opens to reveal smaller and smaller eggs within. When I began work the three successive outer pyramids, built of mud (adobe) and chunks of tufa (pumice) that had served as temple substructures, had been discovered, cleared, and identified. The next earliest structure, also a pyramid, with an intact stairway, was partially visible. This temple mound was built entirely of adobe. Eventually we uncovered a total of nine structural units, each larger and completely covering the earlier one beneath it. The first structure was a simple pen or enclosure (we called it a shrine) about six feet square, its walls built of stone and adobe. There followed two square platforms, three adobe pyramids, and the final three pyramids made of adobe and tufa, faced with lime plaster still strong and smooth. The sequence is clear in the cross sections in the illustration. There was a total of six rich tombs, three of which lay directly beneath the early structures. As the tomb roof beams collapsed, the later structures collapsed into the empty tomb, greatly distorting the remaining parts which we sought to under-

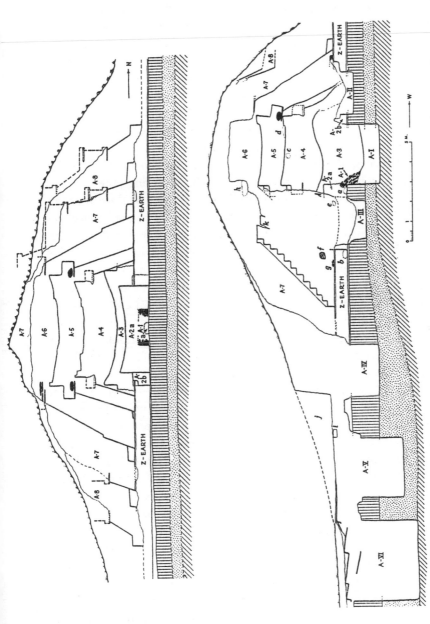

Cross sections of Mound A at Kaminaljuyú on the north-south and east-west axes of the mound. The slumpage of structures A-1 through A-6, after the timbers sealing tomb A-I collapsed, shows clearly on both sections. Because there was no evidence of "patching" or leveling of the top of the pyramids during use, it is assumed that the logs roofing tombs A-I and A-II did not give way until pyramid A-7 was under construction. (Peabody Museum, Harvard University)

stand as we exposed them. Small wonder the site was fun to dig and ultimately to unravel. (Readers who wish more detail should consult the full
report in *Kaminal Juyu* by A. V. Kidder, J. D. Jennings, and E. M.
Shook in Carnegie Institution of Washington Publication 561, 1946.)

Every day we spent in Guatemala was exciting in one way or another, with new experiences crowding in. Life in a good second-class
pensión, as run by Señor Lemus, was very interesting. A *pensión* is essentially a boardinghouse Latin American style, where guests have separate
rooms, but share a bathroom and eat along with the family in the large
dining room. There were two connecting patios filled with exciting (to
us) tropical plants, flowers, and trees, and there were perhaps half a
dozen servants who seemed especially to delight in serving Jane.

Perhaps the best known of the family was Frederico, a green parrot
said to be about seventy-five years old, whose apparent intelligence was
incredible. He immediately formed very strong, sometimes violent, opinions of guests; he approved of some (Jane was one), violently disliking
others. One of his enemies was a fanatic young man named Streipardt
who was a prominent member of the strong Nazi youth group in Guatemala, where the members included many of the German coffee growers
(who were later interned during World War II). Streipardt would stumble
home late from meetings, deep in his cups, and try to reach his room
quietly, but Frederico would lie in wait for him. When he came in Frederico would awaken everyone by stridently cursing him. "Streipardt—
drunken pig," "Streipardt—drunken fool," "Streipardt—baah" were the
calmest epithets I recall. When Frederico molted and couldn't fly, he was
pathetically skinny and small and seemed terribly vulnerable without his
gorgeous feathers. Once a buzzard swooped down into the patio at him,
but when he tried to run, he fell on his back, and screamed, "Help! Help!
Zopilote! Help Frederico! Help! Help! Zopilote!" Another time
Frederico saw a guest hastening to the bathroom. Just as the guest put his
hand on the doorknob, he heard a muffled "occupado," so returned to
his room. Again he tried, and again, "occupado"; frantic by now, the
guest went back the third time, ignored the "occupado," and went in. Of
course, the door was unlocked because no one was using the room,
whereupon Frederico called, "You fool," and burst into a gale of mock-
ing laughter. He also took part in the phone conversations he overheard
by making loud and entirely reasonable responses to the half of the conversation he could hear. I know, of course, very well that parrots only

mimic sound and don't know what they are saying—but I can't agree entirely. Maybe your parrot doesn't, but Frederico did! At least we thought so, especially when he came and crooned Spanish love songs to Jane one week when she was ill and lay in the sun near the tree he favored for observing and commenting on life in the patio.

The workday was long, from 7:00 A.M. to 5:00 P.M. because of the two-hour siesta. When Kidder and Jane were there, we talked through lunch; rather, we listened while Kidder spun yarns about his past and about people he knew.

One story that I vividly recall had to do with Edith Ricketson. It seems that Oliver had met her while she was a secretary to the historical division of the Carnegie Institution in Cambridge, Massachusetts. He had been working a crew at Uaxactún, establishing a headquarters facility there and clearing the jungle to create a landing strip so the projected long-term study of the site could be supported by air. When finished he departed, leaving a reliable Guatemalan employee to cut the grass and otherwise keep the strip open so the field could be used beginning at the end of the rainy season. (The dry, or digging, season begins about January 1 and ends on May 22 at 2:00 P.M.—at least it did in 1937, when torrential rain fell just as predicted by the locals.) Ricketson took his new bride with him to Uaxactún for a five-month honeymoon at the dig. The caretaker had done well. The strip was clear and the headquarters building intact, but he had also brought a bride, a mere slip of a girl very far along in pregnancy when the Ricketsons arrived. Shortly after they arrived the caretaker came to their cabin about midnight begging help for his wife, who was deep in labor, a call that clearly put Edith, a city girl, in charge. She was only just adapting to camp life in the jungle and was far from being an experienced midwife. Soon, however, at the lying-in bed, it became obvious the baby was huge; it was in a breech position, and the mother was weakening rapidly. To save the woman's life, Edith managed to get one of the baby's legs out, amputated it with a machete, did the other, pulled the dismembered body out, then nursed the mother back to life. To this story Jane and I reacted with expectable horror and shock, although Kidder went on to say that Edith, somewhat shaken by the experience, went back to work on the dig with no apparent emotional residue. By then Edith, still employed by the institution, was in Guatemala working on ceramics from Kaminaljuyú, where we met her at one of the frequent cocktail parties. I told her with utmost sincerity that I admired her bravery, courage, and fortitude and that meeting her was an extreme honor. She looked at me as if I were insane and asked, "What are you getting at?" I replied, "I've recently heard about your traumatic experience on your first trip to Uaxactún, and I think you are a marvelous woman." She was completely bewildered and asked again what I was talking about, so I told her the story just as Kidder had told it to us. Amazed and amused, she chuckled, then laughed, and confided that Kidder was indeed a terrible kidder and when he found a trusting audience would tell the most preposterous lies. That the Edith and baby story was one of those he cheerfully admitted the next day, leaving me chagrined and I'm afraid suspicious of everything of an anecdotal nature he told me thereafter, taking his stories with more than a little salt.

Our experience in Guatemala included a trip to Antigua, the old capital, for the days before Easter Sunday, when the country shuts down. There's no work, no travel, no business—nothing happens from Thursday through Sunday. We went up with Doug Byers and his wife, Faith Kidder (Kidder's youngest daughter), and an artist friend of Kidder's. We stayed in the Popenoe House owned by the famous botanist-geneticist who, while working for the United Fruit Company, had developed the delicious bananas we still eat today. We wandered the town, famous for its standing and ruined churches and gorged on large, round, hardskinned avocados, the like of which we had never seen before. Mostly, however, we stayed indoors so as not to offend by being on the street during the long processions where the saints and the Christ were given their annual outing. Being cooped up with friends in the gracious house attended by the skilled Guatemalan resident staff and spending hours at the windows watching processions was an idyllic interlude. We visited Sol and Gertrude Tax in Panajachel on a later trip, when we went as well to see Redfield and his family; Redfield had come down to work in a village across the lake from Panajachel.

Perhaps the high point was a flight to Copán in a TACA trimotor which landed on and departed from a strip that looked about as long and wide as a bowling alley. We were met by a squad of men with rifles and machetes who were to guard the plane. Evidently there was a revolution going on in next-door Honduras, although neither we nor the pilot knew about it. We did hear sporadic firing in the nearby town all the time we were at the ruin. The ruins, of course, were awesome. We were led around by the young architect making maps and architectural drawings of one of the structures. No other site except, perhaps, Nan Modal in Ponape in Micronesia ever impressed me so strongly. We took off to the sound of musket fire, having survived our first revolution.

When the dig was finally over due to the rains, we reluctantly said goodbye to the Kidders and the Lemus family and took an unforgettable eight-day train trip from Guatemala City through Mexico to El Paso, Texas, and finally to my mother's place in the shadow of Montezuma College, arriving there by bus. Our money was gone and there was no work available, so we settled down to sponge off my mother and see what would happen.

Wholly unexpectedly, but probably through Pat Murphy, I received almost immediately an offer to teach anthropology at a tiny Baptist college in Portales, New Mexico (the school now is Eastern New Mexico University). The pay was $1,800 (good for that time and place) for a nine-month year, but I felt that a Baptist school in 1937 was no place to profess anthropology when I knew the Baptist constraints would be in force and enforced. However, within a few days I had decided to accept since I had no better prospects and even had written an acceptance letter. But another letter came. This one was from the National Park Service Southwestern Monuments offering me a ranger job at either Wupatki or Montezuma Castle National Monument as of August 1. Moreover, the pay was $1,860 per year, with $5 a month going toward retirement. I had been picked off a list from an application I had made while in Tennessee for a National Park Service Museum specialist position. I still wanted a museum connection despite having twice been rejected by Paul Martin of the Field Museum on grounds that I was fully unqualified, as he put it. Nonetheless, I accepted the Montezuma Castle job because it would at least get me into the National Park Service and perhaps I could eventually end up with the museum branch.

Although we had no car, my mother's credit was good, and with her cosigning we acquired a badly abused Plymouth four-door sedan with ragged tires, but which ran well. What with the heat, two blowouts, the gravel roads, and other distractions, it took us until midnight to get to Montezuma Castle near Camp Verde, Arizona, from Las Vegas, New Mexico. Expectably, we arrived dusty, tired, and hungry. The custodian, Earl Jackson, and his wife came out to meet us. He put a powerful flashlight into our eyes, played his light over the car then back to our faces, and opined, "That's a mighty shabby car for a big-shot Ph.D. to be driving. I expected a Cadillac at least." When I asked him to spare our eyes, he did, asking, "What's the matter? You got bad eyes?" This gracious greeting, after hours of driving strange roads for perhaps eighteen hours, set the tone for our personal relations from then on. We were shown to our quarters, a fourteen- by eighteen-foot tent house containing a bed, a wood-fired cookstove, a folding table, a two- by four-foot closet behind a curtain, and two chairs. It being August and pleasantly warm, we fell on the bed and slept as if dead, with neither sheets nor blankets.

The next morning I reported for duty and was "indoctrinated"; among other things the briefing entailed explaining that he was custodian (the head man) while I did the scut work, which meant I pumped water to the gravity system (the one-cylinder gas engine worked nearly every time), washed cars, picked up, cleaned the public restrooms, emptied garbage cans periodically, and read the weather station instruments every morning at 8:00 A.M. Also, I guided tourists through the Castle (in those days tourists were allowed to climb 118 feet of ladders up to the then well-preserved rooms and wander through them). I soon learned enough about the ruins and regional archaeology (as it was then understood) to offer a short orientation lecture to the few tourists who found their way to the monument. So, to some degree, I found the job tolerable, even sometimes pleasant, because many of the people I met were interesting in their own right. Jane and I actually fell in love with the location, including our tent house. It was well arranged and we had few possessions to clutter it up, so it was almost roomy. It sat on the banks of Beaver Creek, where an intermittent stream attracted birds amid giant sycamores and hackberry, cat claw, mesquite, and one thousand crickets at night; the white glistening trunks and branches of the sycamores gleamed in the brilliant moonlight, always reminding me of ballet dancers. Small mammals abounded, as did birds. We first met Gambel's quail, canyon wrens, ruby-crowned kinglets, chaparral, and other desert birds there. Never had we enjoyed a home site so much.

We had been at Montezuma Castle only a few weeks when my mother hinted rather strongly that she was lonesome and could she come and live with us? Thereupon, I purchased a twelve- by fourteen-foot tent, got permission to use some good scrap lumber at the monument, and built her a snug tent house, just like ours but smaller, fifty or sixty feet upstream from us. With a little airtight tin stove, so common in the West in those days, installed and a scrap of carpeting by the cot, over the tar-paper floor, she was warm and comfortable. She ate with us, although she spent much time alone enjoying the leisure and the sunlight, reveling also in the Gambel quail, kangaroo rats, doves, ducks, and other wildlife. She had a few interesting habits, one of which was the cold bath when she arose. Once, during the only cold snap we had that winter, I took some coffee to her and found ice on the stoop by her door; in the ice were her footprints! Truly a cold bath, taken out-of-doors. Having her there in a separate location proved to be more enjoyable than I had expected. When we were later transferred, we dropped her off at her Montezuma house.

We had two days off each month, which we took together; twenty-eight days on, two off. On the off days we sometimes went to Clarksville for a maxi shopping spree, whereas on some we merely drove to enjoy the country. Flagstaff, Black Canyon, Mogollon Rim, Jerome, Sedona were some of our destinations. All in all, the time passed quickly and more or less quietly, except that Jackson and I continued to grate on each other's nerves. Nothing major—just scores of little nit-picking criticisms to which I usually responded in a bellicose way.

He must, however, have given good reports of me, because in March of 1938 I was summarily transferred, to be acting superintendent at Ocmulgee National Monument in Macon, Georgia. The superintendent of the Southwestern Monuments was "Boss" Pinkley, who refused to let me go. In fact, I didn't know of the transfer for some time until the Washington office told Pinkley to ask me whether I wanted the transfer or not. Thereupon he invited me and Jane down to headquarters at Casa Grande National Monument to "discuss" it, a discussion which opened with his statement that for an "easterner from Illinois" I had adjusted nicely to the Southwest and its quite different people. He had never read anything in my résumé and was totally unaware that I had grown up in the Southwest, arriving there long before he had; he knew only I'd gone to the University of Chicago and must therefore be a product of the asphalt jungle. He then offered me the custodian's job at Aztec Ruins near Farmington, New Mexico, further explaining that the Southwest was grandaddy to all other prehistoric cultures of North America and that I didn't want to go to the muggy South. This went on for two or three hours and I said very little. Finally he said, "Well, what about it?" "What about what?" I asked. He said, "About staying with us where your future is assured." I merely said, "I've listened patiently. I came here wanting the transfer and I still do. Please make out the papers. Washington seems to be in a hurry." With ill grace he dismissed us, and in a few days the transfer notice came to Montezuma Castle.

Since our scanty gear was already packed, we immediately piled it into the Plymouth, and started to Georgia, with few farewells but with qualms about a new job for which I had no background and wondering why I had been chosen. Later, from Herbert E. Kahler, the coordinating superintendent of the Southeast Monuments—all of which were historical or military except for Ocmulgee—I learned that I was the only person in the entire National Park Service with any apparent knowledge of Southeastern archaeology. Ocmulgee being an archaeological preserve, I, of course, was the man for the job!! No questions asked about administrative experience or construction experience or how much I knew about the National Park Service, even though the program at Ocmulgee was one of development and construction. I was quite right to have been apprehensive about the job.

As I have indicated, I was at Ocmulgee because I was an archaeologist, but for the moment that was a secondary consideration.* My mission was not to establish an archaeological presence in the community—that had already been done—but to establish a National Park Service presence in the community of Macon, Georgia. I was, of course, fascinated by the archaeological record, but my role as I interpreted it was to protect, preserve, and interpret—the three principal National Park Service missions—not to extend or expand the archaeological research. I will dwell here on my highly personal story of creating a local Park Service image for the area, only touching on the archaeological effort I expended there.

As acting superintendent I was also the first bona fide National Park Service person assigned to the area. I came complete with civil service status and *vast* (eight months) experience! Arthur Kelly, who had been acting superintendent before me, met me the first day at the monument and

---

* What follows about the experience at Ocmulgee is a lecture I gave in 1986 at the fiftieth anniversary of the establishment of Ocmulgee National Monument. I use it here because it pretty well describes the thirteen months I spent on the job there. The original lecture, reproduced here as given, was modified and printed as "Macon Daze" in *Ocmulgee Archaeology, 1936–1986*, edited by David J. Hally, University of Georgia Press, 1994. (Reprinted by permission)

showed me around, leaving me with the impression that no one was in charge. I was actually totally bewildered. There proved to be a large work force: a 200-man CCC camp and a 200-man WPA crew. Except for Gordon Willey, none of the CCC staff was an archaeologist or historian or what you could even call academically oriented. Gordon I welcomed as a new colleague, we having never met before. For the WPA, there was only Kelly, who promptly left for Washington, D.C., to a new assignment. Within two days I fell into a profound depression which I can only describe as nearly complete paralysis of mind and body, but I was aware enough to remember that development of the physical side of things, as I understood it, was my task. It was clear that I had come into a chaotic mare's nest of misdirection, indirection, and indecision, and I was swamped. Jane, however, recalls that during those first traumatic weeks I slept like a baby; it turns out that what she meant was that I'd sleep for a couple of hours, wake up screaming, and sob for a while. (I apologize to Pepper Martin, who phrased the thought fifty years later.)

Of all the people I met that first week, I felt only one knew what he was doing, except, of course, for the ones I met in the restroom. That man was a CCC enrollee of about eighteen or nineteen who was the clerk for the monument—the office was then in the old Dunlap house, where the last owner had lived. That man—his name was Jacobs—knew his job; he knew the Park Service paper work, his files were in good order, and he seemed to me both stable and dependable. I came to trust his judgment very much about Park Service rules and procedures after I spent some time learning from him how to follow the paper trail. Out-of-doors things were still confused, and I was making no headway learning what was going on. When I'd been there about a week a big engineer barged into my office, announcing that his name was Woodward (actually he said he was Wood'ard), a CCC inspector from Atlanta. He proved soon to be unhappy (to put it mildly) about our CCC program. He talked a long time about its shortcomings, seeming to hold me accountable for all that was wrong around me.

I remain in Wood'ard's debt because he explained flatly that *I* was the *boss*. All that the monument needed, he said, was action—any kind of movement, a source of clear-cut simple instructions, any forward-looking thing, particularly if the source of authority was someone who could take responsibility and make decisions. There was the expectable great confusion about the role of the WPA and the CCC at the monument, although there wasn't much or any overlap in their assignments and not any cooperation that I could notice. Wood'ard simply told me to take charge, which, in my innocence and ignorance, I believed I could and which I set out to do, conferring with the few older members of the CCC supervisory force who had had work experience. Most of the politically appointed foremen were inexperienced youths, so I ignored them. Based on my evaluation of the advice I got, I did take action, and of course Wood'ard was right in that every one was delighted to be told unequivocally to do this or that or not to do this or that, and except for one or two individuals at the CCC foreman level, I enjoyed support from most of the supervisory level people in both the CCC and WPA groups.

The first two or three weeks, however, were long days of deepening frustration, but then there came the late Herbert E. Kahler, who was my immediate administrative superior. Kahler was the superintendent of the Fort Marion National Monument at St. Augustine, Florida, as well as coordinator for the rest of the area, who had come to offer advice, sympathy, or whatever else I wanted or needed. Without Kahler's encouragement and support, combined with his composure and calm, unflurried approach to any problem, I probably would not have survived that year at Ocmulgee. His stabilizing influence kept me sane; he merely made casual suggestions to which I listened carefully, and I don't recall that he was ever critical. My affection and respect for him continue to this day. Kahler did me a second great favor when he talked to me about the past problems of administering the monument, which was regarded as an eyesore and a source of both annoyance and embarrassment throughout the entire Region I, which encompassed most of the East. When he left after two days he said to me, "Just don't bother me. Don't call me every time you have a little problem. Do something about it." He further gave me instructions not to embarrass the National Park Service and not to antagonize the three local backers of the project, men I had already met: C. C. Harold, Walter Harris, and Linton Solomon. They were politically powerful men, all natives of Macon, who had gotten archaeological work started at Ocmulgee; they were, in fact, the driving force behind the establishment of the monument. They had strong opinions as well as strong political affiliations, and their views on everything related to Ocmulgee were strong and positive.

When I arrived, the physical development as planned and approved by the regional office was under way, but the resources offered at the monument for public enjoyment were limited, although it was open for daily visitation. There was an approved road, not always in the best condition, then being constructed as well as an approved museum plan which I thought then, and believe today, was the least appropriate museum structure I had ever seen. It has since been modified and vastly improved. The famous council chamber had been reconstructed within its concrete dome, however, and was a most impressive display, as it still is.

As for my behavior as superintendent, I systematized things as best I could in both construction and archaeological work, conferring often with three people: Tom Winchester, an accomplished engineer who was the superintendent of the CCC camp; Frank Lester, another engineer and the senior CCC foreman; and, finally, Reaville Brown, a tough engineer with largely South American railroad experience, who was superintendent of the PWA (Public Works Administration) force continuing the construction of the unfinished museum building. All three were supportive and generous with their experience. Practices I initiated because of wasteful procedures (of both time and money) I had perceived permitted me, with the help of those men, to have things operating more smoothly and toward a series of unified goals within perhaps four or five weeks.

As far as archaeology is concerned, when I got there the laboratory was operating because the materials from the Macon Plateau, which had been dug over a period of years, were still being processed in the basement of the museum. By then, Kelly, who had directed all the archaeological work up to that point, had been absorbed into the National Park system, I think on a temporary basis, and called to Washington. But there was still some kind of undirected, piddling excavation program still going on on the Macon Plateau under a supervisor named Jackson, a local artist who had been trained by Kelly. Since the object of the excavation was never clear to me, I closed it. Under Gordon Willey there was a mobile CCC unit doing what he called "strati-tests" over half of south-central Georgia, but there was no other archaeology going on. The fact is that the area looked like neither an archaeological project, nor a national monument, nor a park, nor a very effective construction activity. There were construction scars and raw earth exposed nearly everywhere, but there was not even a decent trail to get from the temporary parking area over to the council chamber. Almost at once I gave a training course for a large WPA guide force in which I gave them some rudimentary archaeological concepts, (e.g., that stratification provided some knowledge of time and its passage) and tried to pass on the things I had learned about dealing with the public as an interpreter while I had been a ranger at Montezuma Castle.

For the guides I also outlined the sequence of the cultures as they were then known: the earliest, the Swift Creek, was a Woodland variant of some age; next was Macon Plateau, about 1,000 years old, now re-garded as the Early Mississippian Tradition; next came Lamar culture, which was observed by de Soto; and then came the brief historic Creek occupation. The guides were to explain that sequence as best they could.

What I accomplished at the monument can be quickly listed. Inci-dental to the construction of a levee (never finished) around the Lamar site, we sampled the site, which lay in the Ocmulgee River bottoms and was subject to regular flooding. The sampling consisted of a continuous trench just inside the boundary of the tract. That project provided and publicized (in a short report I wrote) the first stratified evidence that Ma-con Plateau ceramics were older than those of the Lamar culture. I was also able to discover that the Lamar site was built on an island in a swamp and that it had been completely palisaded. Jackson was the supervisor on the site, although I was there daily and set the strategy of the research.

The museum construction was resumed, roads were pretty much fin-ished with gravel surfacing, and the mound C shelter, which I tried mightily to prevent, was designed and built. Mound C had earlier been partially cut away when the railroad was built into Macon and points west. The mound had been enlarged several times, serving as a temple substructure that contained many important burials. The part that had been left after Kelly's crew had excavated a portion showed the several layers very plainly. The shelter was planned and built to display the last working face so that the contrasting strata could be displayed, but no ef-fort was made to stabilize the earth in it. It was simply an impractical idea; it was not in any sense a success and has long since been taken down.

With Jane's help and advice we built a nature trail. It was possible for her to make recommendations and suggestions about the trail because she knew the entire area, having volunteered shortly after our arrival to con-duct a one-year bird census and banding program on the monument itself. Her records of that census may very well be somewhere in the monument files even today. At my request she laid out a very effective round-trip nature trail, about half a mile in length, which came out about where it started. It proved popular and got a great deal of use through the years. (It is very gratifying for her to find that it is still maintained and much used today, being called the Opelofa Trail.) Mound A was eroding badly where people climbed to the top, so I had the CCC repair the erosion and erect a sturdy wooden stairway to facilitate access to the summit; the stairway, of course, was used. I'm sure we did many other lesser jobs, although I don't recall any right now.

But I do, however, recall situations I had never faced before that had to be dealt with. Probably the most unusual came when an earnest young man came to me, announcing that I was to close the monument for twenty-four hours on Saturday so his group (a local splinter group of a well-known cult) could have a great spiritual experience in that the members would camp on Mound A, which stood forty or fifty feet high, praying the night through, and then on Sunday greet the dawn with songs and rejoicings. "Why?" I asked. It transpired that American Indian beliefs were central to their beliefs and that Mound A was for them also a hallowed place and they wished to express their religious ecstasy there. I panicked. How important were the members? Crackpots or influential citizens? Did I dare refuse? Moreover, the problem was exacerbated by the regulations that I myself had already promulgated—closing the gates at 5:00 P.M. and opening them at 8:00 A.M. to reduce the monument's role as a local lovers' lane. Stalling while I frantically thought about what to do, I slowly negotiated a low-lying field near Mound A as the campsite, letting them use the mound for the rites as planned. I stipulated that the celebrants were to be gone by opening time, that is, 8:00 A.M. on Sunday, and that I would have the gates on the back entrance open from 6:00 to 8:00 P.M. on Saturday evening to allow the gathering of the faithful. On Friday it began to rain. It rained Friday night; it rained through Saturday; and the campground of red clay became a quagmire, while the rain steadily continued all night Saturday into Sunday. Not a soul showed up. Their fervor didn't include camping and praying in the rain. Not all the incidents that I dealt with were so amusing.

I must also mention some of my experiences with the three new friends who had initiated the Macon project. Dr. C. C. Harold was a cancer specialist; Gen. Walter Harris, an attorney and counsel for the railroad; and Linton Solomon, a farmer/dairyman. The three had grown up and gone to school together, but in addition to a lifelong companionship they shared an inordinate interest in Georgia history, Georgia natural history, and the Indian lore of the Southeast. Walter Harris was an authority on Georgia and the Creek tribes, while it was Harold who was more concerned with natural history, with Solomon the worst Indian-relic buff of the three. After we had a few rather tense sessions during which they gently but firmly explained to me how *they* wanted things to go at the monument and I, no doubt, somewhat less diplomatically established *my* position (based on my long association as *the authority* on Park Service matters). Sporadically and slowly they came to understand that I was consistent, that I would do nothing that fell below my interpretation of Park Service standards. When they finally came to realize that we wanted the same things, our relationships became more cordial.

After I had gained their confidence, they began inviting me on their monthly or semimonthly Thursday junkets. For years they had apparently been traveling over Georgia to look at things—almost anything—things as simple as a pictograph on a rock east of Atlanta, or an acre of rare wildflowers down near Savannah, or the site of the Creek Coosa village (wherever that was), and they invited me on many of these trips. Since I had never seen any of these features or points of interest, they took me to the places they liked best. The expeditions would begin about 8:30 in the morning when Dr. Harold, who had a proper doctor's car, a heavy Buick sedan, picked me up, but Lint Solomon, who drove fast, but with great skill, was the official chauffeur. Harold and I sat in the back, General Harris and Lint sat in the front, and all three of them took turns telling me what we were seeing and why I should appreciate it. But an equally important part of these expeditions was the shandy gaff. As near as I could learn, shandy gaff is half white port and half moonshine, rye or bourbon, with a dollop, I'm sure, of dynamite. These ingredients would be combined in a gallon Thermos jug which had a little ice in it, and as soon as we were well out of Macon—say by about 8:45—Lint would pull off the road, break out some Dixie cups, and we would all have a drink from the jug. They advised me, I recall, to brace myself on that first occasion. When I asked why, they said, "Well, if you've never had this, you'll need some support for that first drink." By midafternoon we had usually emptied the Thermos jug. They all had prodigious capacities for that vile stuff; I never equalled, to say nothing of surpassed, their intake.

What with the things we saw, the shandy gaff, and their incredible stories (all three men were accomplished raconteurs), the day, of course, went fast. Always on the second or fourth Thursday for several months we made our carefree return to Macon in the late afternoon. Mrs. Wilson, from whom Jane and I rented a small apartment, commented to Jane after a few trips that I most certainly enjoyed those three old men because I always came home so happy, relaxed, laughing, and enjoying life. Indeed I did on those days.

Other things I remember were the dubious pleasures of being a pioneer in a hostile land. I was the only archaeologist in the Park Service east of the Mississippi River at the time. That meant that anything having to do with archaeology was not only not understood but it was also neither appreciated nor taken seriously. That situation left me in constant, sometimes bitter, conflict with the stream of Region I office supervisory and technical personnel who came through saying we would now do this or that. Usually it was something that jeopardized the integrity of the archaeological reasons for the preserve, and an uneasy wrangle would ensue.

A word about the Region I office people at Richmond is perhaps appropriate. Almost none of them had previous National Park Service experience. The staff had been assembled by hiring state-park people because they had at least *state*-park experience in the East and knew the region, but the three National Park goals were unknown to them. Even the National Park Service presence east of the Mississippi River was then new. It only came about in 1934 when President Franklin D. Roosevelt transferred all the military parks (much against the army's wishes) to the National Park Service for administration. In fact, there hadn't even been a history branch in the service until then. So I was dealing with architects, clerks, engineers, landscape architects, and administrators who knew nothing of archaeology and but little about the National Park Service traditions of preservation, protection, and interpretation. However, Kahler, my coordinating superintendent, and Ronald Lee, assistant chief of Historic Sites in the Washington office, were both trained historians, and they at least understood my position and helped with the regional problems.

I learned at last not to argue all the time, but just to conceive and carry out necessary projects without bothering to tell the regional office. One was the nature trail mentioned earlier, while another was the palisade around the plateau which I built after reading Arthur Kelly's account of the "pit houses" on the Macon Plateau, described as houses hundreds of yards long. I couldn't accept those long trenches as houses, pit or otherwise, especially after I looked at the cross sections which Jackson, the artist, had created, and I read all of Kelly's notes. The sections were well drawn and well labeled, and it soon became very evident to me that the fill in those endless pit houses was nothing more than normal deposits to be expected from the disposal of trash and the erosion of a tall embankment on the west and north sides of a long trench. I reasoned, therefore, that they were not pit houses but trenches created when an earthen fortification, probably topped with a wooden palisade, was built. The Indians had dropped their garbage in the ditch; and upon site abandonment, slowly the embankment on which the palisade logs had been erected eroded into and filled the trench until the surface of the plateau was level. Without regional office knowledge, I rebuilt quite a long segment of the embankment, which had originally encircled the plateau, and sodded the embankment as well as a section of the trench itself with Bermuda grass. No palisade posts were put in—just the earthen wall. There was considerable consternation when some inspector noticed the completed but unauthorized project. By then the "damage" was done; the embankment and ditch remain as part of the interpretive scheme. I'm afraid that I may also have broken many fiscal rules, continuously ignoring the chain of command. But a great deal, I think, was accomplished.

There were many personal pleasures that we experienced. Gordon Willey would frequently visit us in the evening, as would Robert Wauchope, then at the University of Georgia, on occasional weekends for conversation and Scotch; Willey, when he dropped by, usually brought his own Scotch. Jane and I became briefly involved in a little-theater movement in Macon. There we met a lot of very fine young people, and I established a reputation as the least talented actor ever to grace the Macon stage.

About halfway through our period at Ocmulgee, Willey, over my protests and best advice, left Ocmulgee to work with James A. Ford as director of his New Orleans archaeology laboratory, which Ford had established as part of his ongoing WPA program there. My relationship with Willey was a strange one. Although I had, by the time we met, about two years' field experience—Peachtree, Chickamauga basin, and Kaminaljuyú—he seemed to feel, and even said, that he knew more archaeology than I did. I did not argue with him, knowing very well that "strati-tests" in Georgia didn't teach as much as a nested series of Central American pyramids did. After Willey left, Charles Fairbanks was acquired as his replacement, but rather than have him continue the "strati-tests," I simply put him in charge of the laboratory, where I needed someone with a modicum of archaeological background to be in charge. I told him to learn the material and read the notes; additionally, I assigned him—I think it was for ten hours a week while on duty—the reading of all Southeastern Indian history and ethnology and what archaeology there was. What he did with that period of self-improvement is well known. He became a respected and accomplished Southeastern archaeologist with particular interest in the protohistoric and historic periods.

I had hoped to help create the Ocmulgee museum, but I was suddenly transferred out of administration to a research position at the Natchez Trace Parkway. I had never heard of the parkway and had no idea why I was being sent there. Later, of course, I learned the reason: During the spring of 1939 I had had a great deal of difficulty with one of the CCC foremen who would be absent for periods of up to two weeks without explanation and who refused to sign sick-leave requests although he insisted he was seeing an Atlanta physician for an ailment he wouldn't specify. I felt, perhaps unreasonably, that his behavior was bad for morale among the supervisors, to say the least. He said he was sick but could not come up with a doctor's statement, and when he wouldn't sign sick- or even annual-leave slips, I suspended him without pay until he attended to these details. As it happened, he was a political appointee—the nephew of a famous Georgia senator, who was head of one of the most powerful Congressional committees.

It was unexpected and out of the blue one day in May that I received transfer orders to be complied with within *twenty-four hours;* the transfer involved my assignment to the Natchez Trace Parkway as associate archaeologist. Naturally I was more than bewildered by this summary order, but I, of course, packed up, managing to quarrel with my landlady in the process, and left, I believe, within the specified twenty-four hours, greatly agitated and upset by this unexplained chain of events. However, I reported for work at the Natchez Trace Parkway headquarters, then located in Jackson, Mississippi. There I was instructed to go up to Tupelo, Mississippi, and spend the summer excavating the putative site of Ackia, where in 1736 the Chickasaw had defeated French forces under Bienville. Armed with the historical information and other relevant detail, we went immediately to Tupelo in northeast Mississippi, where I began work as instructed, already knowing how to employ people, acquire tools, and so on, employing the correct NPS procedures and red tape.

One Sunday, perhaps in mid-July, a man came to our rooming house and introduced himself as a Department of Interior investigator. He told me that my suspension of the CCC foreman had angered the senator who, in turn, had demanded from Harold Ickes, then secretary of Interior, a satisfactory explanation or (preferably) my head on a platter; either one was acceptable, but should be soon. The man had a portable typewriter, was a skilled typist, and showed me the charges against me, after which he took my deposition. It being fresh in my mind I was able to give him almost a day-by-day and blow-by-blow account of my difficulty with the foreman; at the time it seemed to me this session went on all day. Toward the end of the afternoon, he and I began to talk about our pasts. It turned out that he was a New Mexico boy, as I was; he even knew one or two people I knew on the faculty at the University of New Mexico, and he went away after I signed the several pages of deposition. This was the first time I learned that the Park Service had given me a significant promotion—from $2,000 to $3,200 a year—and had saved my skin in order not to antagonize the congressman or Ickes. Nothing came of it: the investigator said I was blameless, that it was a conflict of personalities, and that the man and I must share equal blame; and so the matter blew over.

You can imagine my excitement much later when in 1950 I was invited to come to Washington and prepare—based on my previous experience and thoughts about it—a museum plan that was to be constructed under Fairbanks's supervision. I turned out a plan, which I submitted, complete with stick-figure illustrations and labels. It seems to have been followed rather closely in the creation of the first museum exhibits. However, today's new displays are a vast improvement, I'm sure, but I thought mine were good, too.

SEVEN

The Natchez Trace Parkway

T HE CONCEPT WAS to build a parkway with limited access to commemorate the Natchez Trace, the first federally funded road in our history. The parkway was to follow closely the old Natchez Trace from Nashville, Tennessee, to Natchez, Mississippi, which was created to speed communication between Nashville and Natchez, the latter recently acquired by the United States. (The dictionary definition of a trace is "a marked or blazed trail through woods or over open lands.") While the Trace was never heavily used, it served as a post road and as an overland route for various classes of travel, remaining in use from 1800 until about 1820. The invention of the steamboat led to less and less travel on the Trace and to its final abandonment in most places.

Because of the historical significance of the Natchez Trace, the National Park Service master plan for the area included interpretive centers and wayside exhibits that presented the history of the region. History, as defined in the master plan, included European, American, and Indian affairs as well as an account of the prehistoric cultures that the Trace traversed. My role was thus fairly well defined in that I was to provide ethnographic and archaeological data, but how I did it, as it turned out, was up to me. The first, however, and immediate reason for my presence was familiar—an excavation program. I was expected to excavate the site selected by the National Park Service historians as the location of the

Chickasaw village of Ackia, where a decisive defeat of a French commander, the sieur de Bienville, by the Chickasaw had occurred. The battle played an important role in confining the French to the Gulf Coast at a time when they and the Canadian French colonies were establishing dominion over the Mississippi Valley. I eventually decided that the village was not Ackia, but probably the Chickasaw village to which the Natchez had fled as a refuge after their 1729 rebellion against the French at Fatherland Plantation south of Natchez, Mississippi, the site of the tribe's Grand Village. In the 1980s the village of Ackia was actually discovered south of Tupelo, Mississippi, a few miles southeast from where we had excavated. After the materials from the summer dig near Tupelo were analyzed and I had again gone over all the maps of the seventeenth and eighteenth centuries of that area, particularly those of the Ackia incident, I wrote a report in which I outlined my reasons for rejecting the village as Ackia and listed the reasons why I thought it was instead an equally historic spot, the Natchez refuge village in the Chickasaw Nation. That report has never been published, possibly because the Park Service authorities at the time did not want to publish it; it made the history people, or at least the historian who had made the identification, look a little foolish. I did not keep a copy of the report nor did I know whether it still existed. (In 1991 the report was unearthed and is tentatively scheduled for publication in the *Mississippi Journal of History*.)

When the summer dig was over and the report written, Jane and I hied off to Cambridge, Massachusetts, because during the summer Dr. Kidder had offered me the opportunity to come and work on the Kaminaljuyú analysis and report. But to go, I needed and requested an educational leave from the National Park Service, which was granted as routine. The four months in Cambridge was in every way worthwhile. For one thing, Jane and I went each weekend to South Byfield, where her parents were living on her grandfather's farm. In that way I got better acquainted with her family, and ate many traditional New England baked-bean Saturday-night dinners.

I profited from the Carnegie Institution facilities and the Peabody Museum Library next door. For eight or nine hours each day I pored over my notes, the relevant literature, the excavation sections and maps, photos, the pottery analysis notes, and Manuel Tejeda's masterful watercolor copies of the tomb's ceramic pieces. I thus became familiar, but not expert, with most of the then-available Middle American literature in English and German (the latter in translation), and by Christmas I had written the excavator's report, a long comparative section, and some of the section on ceramics. As I worked it seemed more and more evident that J. Eric Thompson's hunch—that strong cultural impulses from Teotihuacán in the Valley of Mexico had reached deep into the Petén and Yucatán—was correct. I learned that Mounds A and B at Kaminaljuyú were almost pure expressions of the Teotihuacán culture, particularly in ceramics and architectural detail. At that time, this evidence, of course, comprised completely new data, more than sufficient to serve as a doctoral dissertation, which then as now was expected to be a "contribution to knowledge." Given the Teotihuacán data, mine qualified easily.

After Cambridge we returned to the Natchez Trace headquarters, still in Jackson, Mississippi, and began to work out how I would develop the anthropological aspects of the Trace story. Actually what I was working on is today called "research design." Then it was merely a "plan of work." There were several given conditions to be considered: (1) The study area was 450 miles long, from Nashville to Natchez, and averaged 400 or 500 yards wide (the usual parkway right-of-way), and traversed dozens of natural ecological zones. (2) All the literature on Southeast archaeology could have been carried in a small suitcase, so that the area except for Henry B. Collins's and James A. Ford's work in southwest Mississippi, the TVA work on the Tennessee River in Tennessee and northwest Alabama, and G. P. Thruston's work in Tennessee was a void on the archaeological map. Anything I learned would be new, although we now know that the Paleo-Indian, Archaic, Miller-Porter, and Mississippi traditions are well represented at various places along the route. (3) I would be working alone and walking long distances. (Sometime that winter we moved to a rental house in Tupelo, Mississippi, about halfway between Natchez and Nashville.)

What to do seemed fairly obvious. First, an intensive survey and site inventory of five miles, more or less, on each side of the right-of-way, collecting surface finds and noting details of site locations, was in order. Next, I planned to excavate a sample of sites near enough to the right-of-way that a regional cultural sequence could be derived and perhaps, at a few places, the right-of-way boundaries could be extended so as to weave some of the actual sites themselves into the interpretive fabric. Finally, I would attempt to design interpretive installations, incorporating historic and prehistoric Indian cultural data along with events of local, regional, and national American history.

Accordingly, I initiated the first phase of the survey, working one segment of the parkway after another. After ten or twelve days in the field finding the roads and looking for sites, I would return and see what I could learn from the potsherds and flint tools I had collected, and then go out to the field again. I established and kept an up-to-date comprehensive site file. After initial study, I sent the artifacts to Ocmulgee National Monument, where I had already deposited the records and collection from the Ackia work of 1938. Working that kind of schedule, I was able to keep at the survey winter and summer, and within perhaps fifteen months had located many sites. More important, I had arrived at some idea of the regional variations in the sites and their contents.

By August of 1940, after the survey findings had been analyzed as best I could, it became clear that the area in northern Mississippi where the Chickasaw central villages had been and which the Trace went through needed considerably more intensive study. I had already learned during survey that there was no literature regarding Chickasaw archaeology because it simply hadn't been systematically studied. I had as well become convinced that there was another older ceramic tradition to be found over most of northern Mississippi. I therefore proposed to Superintendent Malcolm Gardner that the NPS sponsor a WPA excavation program, a suggestion that I was told to pursue. When the program was authorized, I hired Albert C. Spaulding, fresh out of Columbia University, but with previous field experience, to help with it. He led the crew; I sometimes took out a smaller one.

Between us we excavated or extensively sampled eight locations which, as I had hoped, documented the existence of perhaps three cultural traditions in the area (Archaic, Hopewell-related, and the historic Chickasaw). When Spaulding left (the project was terminated in February 1941), I prepared a report after reading and corresponding with other Southeastern scholars so I could include a comparative section setting the Lee County work in something of a regional perspective. The report, which included a good excavator's report written by Spaulding before he left, was published in the *Mississippi Journal of History* in July of 1941. Any other reports of the survey and related studies that I prepared over the two-year period I had worked are presumably in National Park Service files, rarely, I presume, if ever, having been seen by anyone but me and the typist.

Spaulding was a pleasure to work with because he was a good observer, very bright, and critical; I'm sorry it was a short association. He was the only archaeologist other than Cooper and Neitzel I was ever closely associated with in my professional career, except, of course, during my student years. Together Spaulding and I devised the system of note-taking/recordation which I later simplified even more and have used ever since, as, I understand, do many of my students.

During the summer of 1939 the Trace had acquired, by transfer from some other agency, a cluster of twenty-five or thirty small, well-built houses sitting abandoned after a New Deal effort to establish a subsistence farm colony north of Tupelo had failed because the soil was exhausted. It was just west of Town Creek, one of the headwaters of the Tombigbee River. Being in the red clay hills and having been "farmed out" in previous decades, the small tracts now supported only scattered hardwood saplings, coarse grass, and nothing else, so, even though the project had failed, it was ideal for an administrative center. Four of the frame houses were put together to form a pleasant rambling office, with drafting rooms, file space, offices, and a research area where I shared an office with the historian, Dawson Phelps. A large maintenance area was created somewhere away from the housing area, while the staff, which continued to grow as construction and planning accelerated, lived in the other houses. Jane and I were in a string of eight or nine brick dwellings across the highway from the main area. Our house was typical: kitchen and breakfast space in one room; two adequate bedrooms; a small bath; and a fairly large living room with a nice fireplace which drew, rather than smoked. We enjoyed furnishing the place, and we also enjoyed the simple pleasures of country living without the need to do farm chores, such as tend animals, feed chickens, or cut wood. With the aid of much manure and effort, I even created a small vegetable garden, but the garden fully reflected my distaste for that art; far more, I enjoyed the flowers Jane teased from the red earth around the house and yard.

The years 1938–1946 at the Trace were pleasant, full of learning, and the satisfaction that follows the best effort one can make in an evolving task. More important were the friends and acquaintances of those eight years. The acting superintendent of the parkway was Malcolm Gardner, an Arkansan by birth and a historian by training. He alone of the staff tried to learn something of archaeological values, he being at least a scholar. In any case, he approved and encouraged my efforts, while he and his wife, Nancy, became our good friends. Almost as supportive was Dawson Phelps, a history professor recently escaped from a small college in southern Mississippi, with whom I frequently traveled. He and his wife, Molly, and daughter Lou Anne were often at our house and we at theirs. He liked alcohol in any guise, and we often had preprandial drinks together and we also played endless cribbage games. Our eight-year score was about 2,001 to 2,000. I don't recall who had the long end.

Other staff members we saw were the Gene DeSilets, Carl Gudat, Robert Smith, and Ed Zimmer families. All four men were landscape architects, Zimmer being the one in charge. Zimmer was able, prone to quarrel when drinking, but witty and charming otherwise. He particularly resented an anthropologist being around underfoot, because I could and did force him to deal with one other variable—archaeological values—in his planning of roads and facilities, especially their locations. In the beginning he simply refused because he believed he held more power than the superintendent. It was necessary twice to get the chief of Landscape Design, then Thomas Vint, down from Washington to settle arguments. Both times he flatly agreed with my position and instructed Zimmer to give equal weight to both scenic and archaeological values, including sign planning. Of all the staff, Reese Smith, assistant superintendent, seemed to me to be the most able. He was in charge of maintaining the parkway and the physical plant, and had a strong voice in land acquisition and land use matters. He, being a bachelor, worked bachelor's hours and ran a considerate but very tight ship, and, while he wasn't particularly social, he was great fun when he relaxed his habitual reserve and was universally liked and admired. Because I traveled the length of the Trace, I also came to know the rangers administering various completed sections of the parkway. Of the rangers, Bruce Wagner of the Natchez district and Jack McCormack at Ridgeland, north of Jackson, were more interested in the Indian history than anyone else I met, so we often talked; and they read material I recommended. Being able to discuss those things with visitors made their job more interesting, I presume.

I don't mean to imply that ten to twenty families all huddled together in the headquarters area, all working for the same outfit, all drawing different salaries, were one big joyous and loving family. There were petty jealousies, real and imagined discrimination, gossip flew like sparks, and a few deep enmities existed. Nonetheless, for us, the good greatly out-weighed the bad, and it is another period in our lives we remember with pleasure.

In the course of my work on the Trace I had many interesting experi-ences; a few I remember with a special clarity. On one occasion I was working some thirty miles north of Tupelo in an area where cotton fields alternated with strips of woodland. It was about midafternoon, I had been walking most of the day, I was soaked, it had been drizzling or mist-ing all day, and my feet were heavy with the mud on my boots. I saw on the edge of the woods a dog—a small collielike dog—whose dugs were long and heavy with milk. I had already realized that in my long ab-sences, Jane, out in the country with neighbors more than 100 yards away in any direction, would perhaps like a dog for both company and safety.

So, I threw a clod at the dog and said, "Go home," hoping that she would lead me to where the puppies were. She led me to a small clearing back of the woods where we were standing to a small, decrepit shack with a family of poverty-stricken occupants. The dog ran into a shed, I fol-lowed, and there found a litter of six or seven pups, after which I went on to the house to inquire whether they would sell one of the puppies. What would I pay? I said, "I can pay you a dollar," which the lady accepted with no hesitation and told me to take my pick. What I picked was the thin, emaciated runt of the litter with a rough coat, but he had a nice wide head and he proved to be nicely marked, although I could see no mark-ings at all on him then—he was just a dirty brown.

I wrapped him up in my windbreaker and took him home, where I put him in a box, carried him into the house, and invited Jane to see what I had brought her. She opened the box and I unwrapped him, whereupon she exclaimed, "It's a rat!" I explained that it wasn't a rat, but a little puppy for her, which we then took out; it was filthy. The first thing was to feed it, so we gave it some warmed milk, which it drank, so we gave it some more, which it lapped up, swelling visibly. Finally when it would drink no more, we decided to bathe it. There were several large ticks on it, and an unknown number of fleas. After its bath it was fluffy and, of course, being full, went to sleep. The next day we got the veterinarian's advice, administered worm medicine, got the food he recommended, and eventually we had a beautiful, small, but more-or-less classic, collie, which we called Mutt, that being the best way to describe what we believed his ancestry to be. He proved to be highly intelligent, badly spoiled, and an extraordinarily good watchdog, although we gave him no particular training; he just was a smart dog who, I guess, thought it was the better part of wisdom to obey the orders he received. He was indeed a delight.

We lost some faith in him only after our first son, David, was born following World War II, because apparently there wasn't room enough in the house for the two of them. At first Mutt guarded him; he slept by the doorway where David slept, and stood or lay between him and anything that was going on when he was outside in his playpen. But when the boy began to move on his own, trespassing on Mutt's favorite areas, he began to growl, and we realized we had to make a choice. From then on Mutt lived outside.

Some time during the spring or early summer of 1940, before we began the archaeological program I have just described, I was crashing around in thick canebrake north of Natchez on the banks of some creek searching for a site a farmer had told me about when I came upon a small clearing, perhaps thirty feet in diameter and absolutely clear on the edge of the creek. On the east was the butt of a huge tree that had been sawed and mostly hauled away except for one log. I presumed this one log was too big to haul away—it was about six or seven feet in diameter, taller than my head, and perhaps twenty feet long. It had been there so long that it was rotting away. Across the clearing, nearer the creek, was a crude shelter perhaps eight feet square, built of cane and thatched with cane and grass, open on one side. It was perfectly comfortable, with a little open fireplace maybe eighteen inches in diameter, and there were two or three blackened syrup or lard cans used for cooking. I assumed that it was someone's fishing camp and thought no more of it. I finally finished in the area a week or so later, and as I drove home I recalled the peaceful clearing and for my own amusement invented a story that fit the situation.

I envisioned a pre-Civil War plantation owner, developing his own lumber, who had cut the big tree and many others down there in the bottoms with his slaves. I remembered that as recently as 1939 I had seen a logging operation on the Pearl River north of Jackson being done with the aid of oxen. The system works this way: a large tree is cut down, two huge wagon wheels maybe ten or twelve feet in diameter, with a strong axle, are utilized—with the butt of the log suspended on a loop of chain from the axle—to drag the log out to where it could be milled. At the operation north of Jackson I had actually seen one log—I have no idea how long it was—being pulled that way by ten yoke of oxen.

Given that memory and a long road ahead of me, I worked out a story of encountering an aged black sitting in the shade by the hut who spoke to me most civilly and asked me if I'd seen Massa Robert.

"No. Why?"

"Long time ago we was down here cuttin' timber and someone from the big house come on a pony and called Massa Robert back. All the people left and took the oxen, but they left the tools. Massa Robert said, 'You, boy, stay here and guard them tools. We be back.' He never come back, but I'se still watching."

"But how do you get along?" I asked. "What are you doing down here?"

"I'se waiting for Massa Robert." He was dressed in clean, but very shabby, overalls and a ragged shirt, with no shoes.

I said, "How do you live?"

"Oh, the girls, they come see me. They's always some nice girls. They seems to get younger and younger. They's real nice to me. They brings me food and clothes and sometimes stays with me."

He went on telling me things—what he ate and such things—and I finally said, "How old do you think you are, uncle?"

He said, "Oh, I is pretty old. I reckon I'se about a hundred years old."

And I imagined that what had happened was that word of the Civil War had reached this young slave owner, who lived in the big house, and he had realized that things were going to change, so he stopped cutting timber and went back to the plantation on the bluffs, planning to check it out and return for his faithful slave and the tools, but never did. The tools which the old man showed me were still there, rusted, with the handles rotted out.

I thought that was a pretty good story, although I embellished it much more than I have here, of course, and I could then handle Southern dialect fairly well. One evening when we were entertaining guests—I don't remember now how many—I told this story, stringing it out for a long time. One of the ladies, who was emotional anyhow, became terribly agitated. Unfortunately, she knew the Natchez area and even knew the sheriff down in Adams County. To cut the story short, she went to the phone and began trying to reach the sheriff, so the county welfare people could go take care of my friend in the brakes. There was no way to stop her short of restraining her forcibly. Reluctantly, I told her the story was false, a total fabrication, and please, please to relax. I didn't know I had told the story so well, but I certainly got results, and I thereupon discarded the story. This is only the second time I have ever told it; I trust no one is upset by it, but I still think it could have been true. From the incident, I learned that stories told sincerely, with some animation and a straight face, tend to be believed and that I perhaps should curb my tendency to tell tall tales.

My service with the Trace was interrupted for exactly three years—to the day—in order to participate (willingly, but not eagerly) in World War II, where I started with a lieutenant, junior grade, appointment to the aviation branch of the U.S. Naval Reserve. About three weeks after Pearl Harbor I had volunteered after much soul-searching, although I had been until then, if anything, a pacifist and almost certainly an isolationist. But this was somewhat different, it seemed. Anyhow, in late September of 1942 I was told to report to Quonset, Rhode Island, for a ninety-day indoctrination course in how to behave like an officer and a gentleman. Although there was very little of practical value available during that course there, it helped me realize that the Navy runs on what the enlisted men know and do. Officers make the mistakes, and the enlisted men take the blame and clean up the mess.

I fear I was not a model officer; in fact, during the indoctrination period I was restricted to quarters for the full ninety days. It was a case of talking when I should have been listening. I was uncomfortable in the indoctrination program, which was diabolical and fully effective in that it was calculated more or less to brainwash us, essentially reducing us to "zombies." There were several hundred of us civilian volunteers—successful lawyers, bankers, businessmen of all kinds, a few teachers, all of whom were mostly in their thirties. All of us had egos and some measure of self-esteem when we arrived, and all of us were under threat of being sent home if we were uncooperative or otherwise unsuited to Navy life. We were a fine-looking lot, having all arrived in new uniforms glittering with gold braid.

Within an hour after arrival we were shocked and bewildered in a situation where all the rules were new. First we were stripped of all gold, with no remaining visible rank; next we were assigned bunks—upper or lower—in one of the several sixty-man barracks, then shown a small locker and told how to stow our clothing and gear, and finally told to make up our beds. Within another hour our beds had been ripped apart, our locker contents dumped on the floor, and we were told to do it again and do it right. My hospital corners and tight blankets passed muster after three tries, but some men, who had never made a bed, worked into the night. It took four tries on my locker, where everything had its place—a place not based on convenience, logic, common sense, or habit, but by Navy edict. We were eventually fed in the mess hall and instructed in our schedule for the next ninety days; we were also told about the demerit system: Demerits were awarded for lapses of memory, failure to carry out orders, talking in the ranks, etc. The magic number was ten; earn ten demerits and you were shipped home in disgrace and subject to the draft. What with the prospect of two hours of calisthenics and close-order drill, eight hours of classes, and the mandatory study hours, the days appeared to be full.

The loss of identity and of our accustomed personal and familiar social status we had at home, the hard living, the lack of familiar places left all of us confused and very unsure of ourselves. The indoctrination essentially robbed us of any personalities or any will of our own, leaving us, therefore, ideal candidates for instruction. In the mob, I found one friend, E. E. Overton, then dean of the Mercer Law School at Macon, Georgia, with whom I had played pool, particularly eight ball, when I was at the University of Chicago. We studied together, but only in the evening because we were in different platoons (platoons, based on alphabetical order, being the effective social group in that situation); his grades placed him second or third in the class, while I came in sixth or seventh. The classes I remember nothing of, except that Overton and I reduced the class on military courts and boards to a short table, which I consulted several times when I later served on courts martial. My main memory of that period is that my name always led the demerit list.

When we graduated I went to Chicago to meet Jane and have Christmas with her and, incidentally, to defend my doctoral dissertation, which I had written after volunteering in late 1941. I was terrified because I had no idea what a defense entailed. As I grew more and more nervous on the day I was to defend, I decided at least to enjoy myself and bought two bottles of wine, some Dixie cups, and reported to the examining room at the university. I sat in the examining room, stewing as the examiners (I only remember Cole and Redfield, but there were several more) drifted in. After three or four had come I said, "I'm new to all this, so I don't know what the proper procedure is. However, I have brought some wine to help the time go faster." With that I put the cups and wine on the table, offering everyone a cupful. All accepted, even Dr. Cole, although he was slightly upset and hesitant. Redfield was chuckling and soon took a second cup. In some vague way that action seemed to put me in charge of the session—at least people, and particularly Dr. Cole, sat and looked at me—so I asked, "What's next?" Cole said, "Please tell us what in this paper [the dissertation was a shorter version of what I had written for the Kaminaljuyú report] makes it important?" Thereafter I talked, answered some questions, parried others, and had a very good time for some two hours or longer. Then they finally decided to confer the degree, without even asking me to leave the room while they deliberated. When we came out, the secretary asked Redfield why the defense had taken so long, realizing that a long one usually means that a dissertation has been rejected. I heard him say, "Oh, we were just enjoying ourselves and the time slipped by."

In the navy my assignments were always the same. I served at the Newfoundland, Iceland, Bermuda, Buford (S.C.), and Norfolk air bases, with detachments of Headquarters Squadron No. 7. In Norfolk I was with the main Headquarters Squadron 7 first as personnel officer and later as executive officer; however, in detachments I was always the executive officer. Jane was able to join me in Buford and Norfolk. The commanding officers of detachments and the main squadrons were always naval aviators with the reserves (usually called "feather merchants" or "retreads" or "overaged destroyers") in all the other slots. I enjoyed being the exec where I habitually became the champion of the enlisted man, who needed one, given the navy's system at that time; possibly he still does today. After V-E Day I was instructed to disband the headquarters squadron, which involved absorbing and transferring all the detachments as well. Including officers, there were about 2,700 men. Of that number I was able to place over 2,300 in specialty schools.

I even found a school for myself where I would learn in twelve weeks how to command one of the 106-man detachments expected to be deployed all over the Pacific to support small bomber groups in the all-out war to finish Japan. Then came the atomic bombs and V-J Day. Under instruction at Milledgeville, Tennessee, in preparation for a role no longer relevant and therefore, I reasoned, surplus to the navy's needs, I requested a discharge and got it, getting home twelve days after V-J Day! I'm certain my request was facilitated by the base communications officer. Perhaps I was just lucky, but I was glad to be back at Tupelo in time to be present when our first son, David, was born.

I regret somewhat that, although I thought I had served conscientiously and well, I never got a 4.0 fitness report in any assignment during the three years. The record, of course, began at indoctrination school at Quonset. My continued willingness to fight for a principle or an enlisted man's rights, coupled with my willingness to question or ignore an order I thought stupid, kept my superiors a little edgy. They never knew whether I would be docile or difficult, an uncertainty that is reflected in my fitness grades.

Instead of shopping around for another National Park Service berth as many did, I resumed my work at the Trace by continuing to read ethnography and writing a long article, "The Prehistory of the Lower Mississippi Valley" at the invitation of James Griffin, which was later published in his *Archaeology of the Eastern United States*. That article, while already out of date when published in 1952, was my first attempt to describe the full culture sequence for that area.

At that time, too, I met the famed ecologist, Walter B. McDougall, who was assigned to the Trace to learn more about the succession of plant communities of the several ecological zones that the Trace traversed. The idea was that such a study would provide a data base for future "freezing" the natural vegetation types along the scenic, rural vistas of the parkway should this later be deemed desirable. Possibly the study is still being consulted, but to me the presence of an ecologist meant a new education; I learned from McDougall the systemic nature of all life. From him I came to realize that human presence and behavior had to be included as a factor in any ecosystem, an awareness that influenced all my future archaeological analyses or interpretations, although I never made a great point about having an ecological stance.

McDougall must have been well ahead of his time. He insisted that forest and brush fires were merely a part of the natural process and should be allowed to burn out unless they threatened homes and property; the National Park Service follows that policy today, sometimes to extremes, as witness Yellowstone. He told one story that carries within it the full beauty and complexity of the functioning of the natural ecosystem. Earlier he had once been sent as a naturalist to learn why the yucca on Yucca Flats in Grand Canyon National Park no longer annually beautified the area with its thin, tall stalks of creamy, waxy flowers. There he first identified the resident mammal and insect population and watched the interplay among the species. After watching the ecological round for one year, he merely recommended that three or four pairs of coyotes be released in the dense yucca areas. Why? The coyotes had been largely eradicated in the park for some reason, but coyotes eat mice, a plentiful and easy prey. With the coyotes gone, the mice multiplied and occupied their time in the spring eating the young yucca flower stalks as soon as they appeared; hence, no more flowers. After, I am sure, some qualms, the National Park Service acquired and released the coyotes; now the yucca blooms in Grand Canyon. For me, nothing so neatly exemplifies the complex relationships in a natural community as that one simple story.

Working with no supervision at the Trace I decided to devote some time to one of my overwhelming concerns: the interpretation of technical data—archaeology, natural history, regional and local history—into layman's terms for popular education and entertainment. For that, museum or field exhibits, alone or in combination, are the most effective; therefore, after consultation with the historians and reading many volumes on the regional history of the period 1775–1825, I planned three interpretive centers, each emphasizing the local scenes. One was to be at Nashville, one at the headquarters area near Tupelo, and one at Natchez. The plans were fairly detailed, including even a few labels for specific exhibits that I felt were appropriate for the location, and I felt that they were sound designs. They were submitted to the National Park Service powers in Washington and approved, I think, as preliminary plans, after which they were then consigned to the files, where they no doubt remain today, unseen. I understand, however, that a few of the interpretive ideas I suggested were followed.

In those days in the National Park Service, you were either an administrator, law enforcer, or technician (i.e., some kind of specialist). One of the tasks field technicians faced was promoting their own specialties or findings as being in some way useful to somebody. The parkway was the third roadway in the system, coming after the Washington and Blue Ridge Parkways were established. The eastern region of the National Park Service (Region I) included all three of them; developing the Blue Ridge had shaped thinking about how a rural parkway was to be developed and presented. The superb scenic values of Appalachia dominated the Blue Ridge planning, with a few spots along the road where pioneer mountain folkways were presented. The Trace did not fit the model too well, being commemorative of the creation of the Natchez Trace, and it was emphatically not scenically inspiring in nature; it was "merely" historic. The regional people, used to the Blue Ridge, couldn't understand how one could build a historical parkway. As a result, there was an endless stream of regional and Washington personnel who visited the area in order (1) to "see it on the ground" and (2) react (hopefully with informed intelligence) to the design, interpretation, and protection proposals that flowed from the field. The interpretive and other proposals, of course, had emphases different from those for the Blue Ridge, and therefore were deemed inappropriate. Visits, then, from the regional and Washington personnel, were frequent and not always adequately advertised in advance. There usually would be three or four or even five highly placed bureaucrats in each party, each representing a different specialty. It was necessary to organize a trip from one end of the parkway to the other, so the visiting decision makers could see or hear about all the historic spots, natural phenomena, and as many archaeological sites as I could slip into the itinerary.

I've already mentioned the fact that my familiarity with the entire Trace, resulting from my survey work, involved me in nearly all junkets. Although I was direct, honest, and as persuasive as possible in the field, I saved my most aggressive selling for after we had found our hotel, eaten dinner (Southeastern small-town cuisine in the 1930s and 1940s was not exciting), and settled in one of our rooms for a rehash of the day. I learned early, as have generations before me, that with a full belly and a glass of whiskey in hand there tends to be a relaxation of tensions and doubts so the bureaucratic mind, either broad or narrow, is then more receptive. I provided most of the bourbon on those junkets and did most of my huckstering after dinner. A result was that many of my proposals were approved. Some, if what I have heard is correct, seem to have been implemented. No doubt the success of my ideas can probably be credited as much to bureaucratic inertia as to the validity of my proposals. As best I can recall, I spent probably thirty days a year on such junkets. Rarely did my per diem allowance cover the bill.

Sometime in 1946 I drew up an archaeological research plan that would extensively sample several other important sites up and down the

Trace. It was approved and funded, so I expected to spend 1948, 1949, and 1950 in almost continuous fieldwork at six sites I pinpointed for extensive investigation. Among them were the Bynum and Pharr Mound groups in northeast Mississippi and the Emerald and Fatherland Mounds near Natchez.

As I recall the research plan it was fairly simple. I was certain from my study of the survey collection that work at Bynum and Pharr would extend or expand our knowledge of the Hopewell-related Miller site already dug during our short WPA program. With luck there might be even earlier Woodland remains and even earlier Late Archaic materials. The work in the Natchez area, of course, was to amplify both the historic Natchez record and the earlier Mississippian Tradition there. Some Woodland and Early Mississippian material might even occur below the later materials.

EIGHT

The Plains

I DIDN'T GET TO DO any of the fieldwork on the Trace because I was transferred on January 1, 1947, to Omaha in Region II of the Park Service, which had become part of the vast Missouri River Valley project to create a series of huge lakes behind earthen dams on the Missouri River and its tributaries. The agencies involved in the project were the Army Corps of Engineers, the Bureau of Reclamation, the Smithsonian Institution, and the Park Service, with the latter charged with the study of recreational uses of the lakes being formed and with safeguarding the recreational, archaeological, and historical values threatened by the construction. I was attached to a task force hastily assembled to deal with the recreational and other potentials of the scores of lakes to be created.

I welcomed the transfer for two reasons. First, it would expose me to a new series of archaeological data, thereby enriching and extending the limited experience I already had in the Midwest, Southeast, Southwest, and Central America. The second and, at the time, more important reason was that it would put me and my family in a better social environment. Our son David was already learning the degrading southern caste system of white over black, under which both Jane and I were increasingly restive and uncomfortable. For example, in 1939 we were appalled when the entire community condemned us because we raised the pay of the part-time girl who helped with the housework from fifty to seventy-

131

five cents a day for a six- to eight-hour day! Public pressure was so strong that we returned to the prevailing wage and began quietly adding several dollars' worth of groceries and/or clothing as equally appropriate compensation. In Omaha I was very lucky in finding a good house at a time when housing was very tight; the house was available through a forced sale and therefore reasonable. With the aid of a veteran's loan, I bought it at once. Jane and son David joined me in about three months, a lonesome three months in winter that I spent in a crowded rooming house which had no central heating and but one bathroom for eight roomers.

The recreational group to which I was attached included all the same classes of disinterested specialists and technicians I had dealt with at the Trace: landscape architects, architects, engineers, recreational planners, and one historian, along with the usual complement of fiscal officers, clerks, and stenographers. And, since it was at the regional headquarters, the regional director, assistant director, and all the regional level employees were also in the same office. Again I was the only archaeologist, sharing an office with the historian, Merrill Mattes, a careful, methodical scholar who controlled an immense fund of information about western frontier history. From the first it was a pleasure to sit with him and learn Plains and Missouri River history as he talked, although we had early problems because he, for some reason, assumed I was his assistant. We took only two trips together. On the first he essentially indoctrinated me in the historical material, showing me the cavalry forts, trading posts, and many other historic spots in three states. On the second trip he sent me to a courthouse in some Kansas town to check the chain of ownership of a historical location, while he went to interview a local county "shade tree" historian. Instead, I took my gear and went to the railroad station and caught the train back to Omaha, but before I left, of course, I explained the ways in which my conception of my role differed from his. He was not particularly upset, and our relationship remained easy and cordial. We shared a stenographer evenly, often had lunch together, exchanged visits between the families, and had a useful and pleasant relationship, but never traveled together again. His interest in prehistory was minimal, so I traveled alone thereafter, retaining my high opinion of his scholarship and abilities.

Actually, my job was vaguely defined as "liaison" between the National Park Service and the Smithsonian Institution as it carried out its commitment to survey, excavate, and study the archaeological resources threatened by the prospective reservoirs of the Missouri River Basin. In final analysis, as already mentioned, the archaeological values were the responsibility of the National Park Service, but it had, astonishingly, opted for having the Smithsonian direct the program, retaining no voice in the overall plans or strategies. This situation left me with no clearly defined assignment; moreover, in the entire regional office there was no one willing or able to be more specific. Therefore, I set my own agenda on the assumption that I was to interest myself in the research the Smithsonian was doing, assigning myself the following three tasks: (1) I must first get acquainted with the Smithsonian personnel at Lincoln; (2) then learn all I could about Plains prehistory as it was then understood; and (3) travel the length and breadth of the Missouri River Basin (MRB) itself to gain some sense of its terrain, rivers, and streams and, as it turned out, its vastness. I was more or less successful in blending these three self-supporting courses of action.

Within three or four months of travel and intensive reading, I felt I could participate to a limited degree, at least, in discussions of archaeological matters. Actually learning the outlines of the archaeology didn't take very long since there were only thirty or forty titles of any value in the literature at that time. Of these, Duncan Strong's 1935 synthesis was the most valuable and had the broadest perspective, while Waldo Wedel's Pawnee monograph and his numerous pioneering excursions into cultural ecology were the best reports of any research done up to that time. There were, of course, other authors: Earl Bell, George Will, Harry Weakly, Mildred Mott, A. T. Hill, Marvin Kivett, Alex Krieger, John Champe, and a few others.

Just what was the state of knowledge? Most of what was known lay in Kansas and Nebraska—the Central Plains, in short—where Duncan Strong and A. T. Hill had described the Upper Republic culture. Krieger had isolated and described the Antelope Creek fusion of the Upper Republican and Southwestern cultures in Oklahoma and Texas. Will and Thad Hecker had outlined three phases they could see in Mandan development. Wedel had identified the Lower Loop–Pawnee sequence. East of the river in Iowa was the Nebraska focus, and in Texas the Gibson-Caddo area had been described. All of these cultures were post-A.D. 1000. The earlier ones, Valley I, Sterns Creek, and other local affiliated Hopewell-Woodland manifestations had also been recognized and named. There was no hint of the Archaic and Paleo-Indian Traditions that we came to know during the river basin program. Although their work has been largely forgotten, both Will and Weakly had by then done what I thought were sound tree-ring analyses using cottonwood; that work was at least a step toward a real chronology. With that list, the data base in 1947 was pretty well established, with anything more that we know today coming since that time from the work being done then; actually, I would suppose that 95 percent of the new data resulted from the river basin work, first by the Smithsonian Institution, then by way of the continuing National Park Service contract system.

At Lincoln, at the Smithsonian Institution river basin headquarters, I was delighted to find Paul Cooper, an old friend from the Kincaid field school and Tennessee work, in charge. He was second to Wedel, who was the director of the Smithsonian Institution effort, but who was rarely in Lincoln except during the months of fieldwork because his real responsibility lay with the National Museum in Washington, D.C. Cooper's knowledge of the Plains was second only to Wedel's, and he generously instructed me continuously in its many details. The office itself was in an excellent space on the University of Nebraska campus, made available to the program by the late John Champe, then head of the anthropology department. In middle life, Champe became interested in archaeology, took a degree at Columbia University, and was added to the University of Nebraska staff. I don't recall meeting any other regular anthropology faculty there, although Fred Voget was there for a while on a temporary basis, working with a special grant on a segment of the Yale Human Relations Area files. Champe may well have been the only other staff member. A charming, witty fellow with whom I enjoyed many conversations, he was also very bright and much prone to give advice. He was deeply interested in the Smithsonian research and was always much in evidence around the lab. Other archaeologists I remember on my first visit were Wesley Bliss of Sandia Cave fame, Jack Hughes, a man named Cummings, and Marvin Kivett. It being winter, they were supposed to be doing analyses of the data they had recovered the previous summer and to be writing publishable reports, although in my view they all, except Kivett, were accomplishing very little. There was no apparent pressure to finish. I credit their failure to report to both Wedel and Frank H. H. Roberts (who directed the river basin studies), neither of whom had administrative experience on that scale. In addition to the individuals I met at the Smithsonian office on that first visit, I ultimately, during the course of my travels to all the digs during the summer, met a number of other people including Will, Wesley Hurt, Carlyle Smith, Gordon Hewes, Ray Wood, Alan Woolworth, and, of course, the late Carl Chapman.

In April of that first year—1947—I undertook to visit all the institutions of higher learning in the basin to try and persuade their archaeologists to divert their summer resources for research into reservoir areas where archaeological sites were in immediate jeopardy. I was sure I had thought up that idea by myself, but many years later I learned that such a strategy had been part of the design originally suggested by the Committee for the Recovery of Archaeological Remains for all the river basin surveys over the entire United States. Therefore, I suppose someone suggested it to me, but I had come to think of it as my own idea. Anyway, when I did put the plan into operation, I found the University of Missouri, through Carl Chapman and Professor Jesse Wrench, to be well ahead of me, having mobilized the entire Missouri Archaeological Society, which was busy surveying the Pomme de Terre Basin. The University of Kansas could not help in 1947, but did in 1948. Wyoming, through William B. Mulloy, declined; Gordon Hewes, then of the University of North Dakota, participated, as did the North Dakota Historical Society. And I think Elmer E. Meleen, at the University of South Dakota, also participated that year, but the director of the South Dakota Historical Society was monumentally disinterested and would do nothing. Wes Hurt, however, came the next year to South Dakota and participated fully. Champe, of course, at the University of Nebraska, was already contributing space and endless advice to the program. So that first year there were few participants, but by 1954 sixteen institutions were listed as collaborators. Their overall published production exceeded that of the Smithsonian Institution.

When fieldwork started I traveled almost constantly visiting digs, going to see famous sites, and thus began to get some grasp of such things as the Plains ceramic traditions. As well, I visited perfectly preserved prehistoric earth-lodge villages and abandoned cavalry forts—and as others had no doubt done before me, marveled at the rigidity, sterility, and unimaginativeness of the military mind as reflected in the layout of the forts. Particularly I pondered the futility of a cavalry operation against the mounted Plains tribes. In all my traveling I carried my sleeping bag, water, and canned foods so, if need be, I could make a dry camp whenever night overtook me and, after dark, watch the stars while the coyotes sang to me. One of my big thrills was a visit to the Spanish diggings in Wyoming, an aboriginal quarry where Plains Indians for millennia had secured a tough flint for their tools. But most of all, I came to appreciate the endless prairies, the interminable Platte River, the Missouri Valley itself, and the awesome power of that river. Although I have lived many places, I've had a love affair with only four: the Missouri River Basin, the Great Salt desert, the Glen Canyon of the Colorado, and Iceland, where I served in World War II. Those four are special to me, other places being just places. All dwarf man and his works, and all can be dangerous, even violent, at times, and each offers its own different beauty and challenge.

My association with the Plains ended in September of 1948 when, rather than accept a transfer to the National Park Service Washington office, I resigned and began the frustrating and equally rewarding life of a university professor at Utah. But before I left, in the summer of 1948, I made what I thought of as contributions to the study of Plains prehistory. The most visible contribution was in establishing the Plains Archaeological Conference newsletter, which I did after a conversation with John Champe about its possible usefulness. I remained its editor until the autumn of 1950, an opportunity I greatly enjoyed. Of course, the newsletter evolved within a very few years (after the conference was renamed the Plains Anthropological Conference) into *The Plains Anthropologist,* a very reputable journal. Also before leaving the Plains I organized the Sixth Plains Conference to be held in November of 1948. The conference, I thought, was highly successful, largely because I had asked Alex Krieger to develop and oversee the program. The other "contribution," also in 1948, entirely for my own education, was writing a self-illustrated mimeographed prehistory of the Plains (as I then understood it) that I called *Plainsmen of the Past* for distribution to the National Park Service's, Bureau of Reclamation's, and the Army Corps of Engineers' local offices; in short, it went only to all those involved in the Missouri River Basin Interagency Program. I also sent it to all the historical societies in the Plains, where it was widely read and well received. I doubt any modern reader has ever seen or heard of it, but it was the first entire Plains summary written since Strong's 1935 volume. I think it ran to about seventy-five or eighty pages.

My involvement with Plains archaeology extended even to technical matters. A disastrous flood on Medicine Creek destroyed a low-lying part of Cambridge, Nebraska, causing a few deaths by drowning. The citizenry demanded protection—which came at once since a large earthen dam and reservoir upstream from the town was already designed and approved, so construction could and did begin very soon after the flood. Moreover, the Corps of Engineers agreed to furnish a few men to investigate a village buried under two or more feet of loess on Medicine Creek that had been discovered when work began on the west abutment of the dam. Time was very short, and the small crew wouldn't have been able to accomplish any significant amount of recovery, so I began agitating for the use of power equipment. Wedel at first was adamant against it; he had many qualms, but he eventually agreed. Then we had to convince Kivett, who was to do the work, that he should use the power equipment. Although the idea repelled him, as I recall, he, too, finally agreed. He carried out the operation with good judgment and skill, and the use of such equipment since has become widespread. The amount of money saved in subsequent emergency archaeology all over the United States through intelligent use of power equipment is enormous.

Much later, in 1954, the National Park Service gave me a contract to review the status of Plains research, so I had a second chance to spend several weeks there. A report of that inspection was called *The Archaeology of the Plains: An Assessment*. In it I inventoried the resources: collections, facilities, personnel, and research plans from twenty institutions from all the states that were in or impinged upon the Missouri River Basin. Few have seen that report because it, too, had limited publication and citation was specifically forbidden. I think it was Merrill Mattes who prohibited its wide distribution, he having become regional historian after I had gone. Why it was restricted I never knew, but the restriction was a great disappointment, because chapter one was my second attempt at summarizing the culture history of the Plains (as was required by the contract). It was much better than my 1948 volume, at least. I've had many requests for it and have distributed many Xeroxed copies. In it I used Sellard's 1952 term "Llano" for the Clovis Horizon. I then proposed "Plano," which can mean either "plane" or "plain" for the varied but very similar materials that followed the Folsom culture. I had planned to use "Mano" for the Archaic culture; thus, Llano, Plano, and Mano would euphonically take care of the entire sequence through the farmers of the Christian era. The Mano suggestion never saw print because it seemed a little foolish upon second reading. I especially liked chapter three, an outline of a Plains research organization, in which I described the personnel, facilities, laboratory and field procedures, and the multi-discipline research design needed for systematic study of the Plains. The overall design came from the many people I interviewed during the 1954 visit, although the details were my contribution. I later drew on that chapter in establishing the mechanics of the Glen Canyon project, which operated reasonably well, but on a much lesser scale than I had used for the Plains proposal. The major benefit from the full report, however, was that it annoyed Waldo Wedel so much that he immediately set to work on *Prehistoric Man on the Great Plains,* which remains the definitive work on that area even now.

From those years I treasure some interesting memories. I recall visiting one dig where a well-known individual (now retired) was sampling a deep midden zone at a protohistoric village. I noticed that the workmen were blissfully ignoring a sharp change in soil color and texture about half-way down the one-foot zone they were removing in a vertical cut. I commented to the archaeologist that they appeared to me to be mixing material from two quite distinct depositions, suggesting that he should perhaps segregate the upper segment from the lighter lower one. He said, "Hell, I can't do that. I'm using one-foot cuts." So much for archaeology by rote.

For some reason I remember a visit to Lincoln by J. O. Brew and Fred Johnson, members of the Committee for the Recovery of Archaeological Remains, who were "inspecting" (there may have been two visits that have coalesced in my memory) the progress of research. During the conference they had called at the Smithsonian Institution's Lincoln offices, and one of them said that the CRAR wanted closer control over the research, that monthly reports must be provided, and so on and so on and so on. Although I had no status at all in the Smithsonian organization other than familiarity, I assured them that we (I was speaking without the *slightest* authority for the Smithsonian) "would do no such damn thing." I suggested the whole idea was presumptuous, that they weren't well enough informed to evaluate the reports, that they had no credibility or authority, and that they could stuff their instructions. Later when I provided an NPS car and took them and Wedel on a five- or six-day junket to a basinwide series of digs, the atmosphere on the trip was genial, courteous, and relaxed; no reports were made.

I've already mentioned the emotional effect the Plains had on me, but on a slightly more intellectual level, the biggest thrill I got there was realizing how shallow was the time depth that measured the actual American control of the Plains. The power of the hostile tribes had only been broken after about 1885, less than seventy years before my arrival there!! That realization explains one of the high spots of my experience, which was a call upon a Mrs. Thomas Riggs, whose large ranch lay on the river just north of the Oahe Dam in Oahe Bend, north of Pierre, South Dakota. The ranch was going under the waters soon to be backed up by the dam. She was then a perky little old lady over eighty, possibly ninety, years old (she may have told me her age, but I do not recall it). She was the daughter of the commandant at Fort Sully in the late 1870s. She told me of failed cavalry sorties against the Yanktonai Sioux on the west side of the Missouri, Sully being on the bleak bluff above the east bank. She told me about the young officers, all of whom courted her, took her on horseback rides, wrote her poetry, and (one of them) made for her beautiful sketches of the fort and the surrounding area, some of which she showed me. Of course, the young officers fought over her as well. But while the young second lieutenants fought behind the Bachelor Officer Quarters, a club-footed little Episcopalian missionary who worked with the Sioux would row across the river, take her on long, if slow, moonlit walks along the bluffs, and ultimately married her, whereupon the soldiers sulked. She later set up a school and taught the Sioux children whose families had taken allotments up and down the river near her house. The Reverend Riggs was no fool; he bought land from the Sioux as they gave up their allotments one by one and left, in the process building up a good acreage, which he began farming. By 1948 the ranch had long been famous for breeding high-quality Hereford bulls that fetched top prices at the annual sales. The entire ranch, of course, eventually drowned under the Oahe reservoir.

The half-day I spent talking with her passed in a flash, and I never forgot that I had listened for hours to a witness of the last stand of the Sioux in that area. I later called on the director of the South Dakota Historical Society, urging that he record her memories. He showed slight interest, so I doubt that he ever interviewed her, although he said he would one day.

My hoped-for field experience in the Plains, along with that I had already planned and discarded for the Trace, failed to materialize. Instead, I left the Park Service to join the faculty of the newly established Department of Anthropology at the University of Utah in Salt Lake City. That action was not an expected one, but resulted from events and developments within the Park Service over a period of months. One development was that my friends in the Branch of History in the director's office in Washington (Ronald Lee and Herbert Kahler) had both liked my work at Ocmulgee and had visited the Trace several times, supporting my recommendations. Both had also visited the Missouri River Basin activity and were familiar with my efforts there. Late in 1947 they proposed (and even issued orders) that I come to Washington to head a subbranch of archaeology in the Branch of History. I guess they assumed that my record of accepting transfers would lead to an automatic acceptance of this transfer and, I suppose, what would have been a promotion. But by then I had already had several short assignments and experience in Washington, meaning that I knew the frustrations and interruptions a Washington office person experienced, and I knew my own reaction to those frustrations. Too much talking and conferring and too few decisions leading to action were what I saw there; moreover, I also saw good men with strong research records reduced to clerks as they wrote letters for administrators to sign—anything from placating congressmen who did not have their "own" park or monument in their district to answering requests for instant information about Mt. Rushmore or the Everglades or whatever. I didn't like the housing situation, the traffic, nor the bureaucratic mentality, so I declined the offer.

Early in 1948, another transfer order came through. At that time an employee who rejected transfers three times was automatically resigning from the service, and even though I knew what it meant—I would be left with that either/or third time—I again declined the transfer.

The other development was at the Region II office, where by late 1947 my presence had been noted by the regional director who began to assign me tasks of an archaeological nature totally unrelated to the Missouri River Basin program; in short, he was using me as a regional archaeologist, an adviser to him. Of course, I did what he asked, at the same time requesting a change in status to regional archaeologist with a new job description and appropriate salary adjustment. It was carefully explained to me that Region II didn't really need a full-time archaeological specialist, and, moreover, had no such position available; hence he could not fund it. I listened and did not believe, but went on devoting more and more time to regional affairs. From him I also learned how hard it was to advise a timid man who was afraid of new things and immune to explanation, valuing his neck and his job more than a new idea or an appropriate course of action.

With William B. Colburn at Peachtree Mound as work was beginning.

The crew at Peachtree Mound, 1934.

Crew and gear being transported by barge from Paducah to the corn barn at the Kincaid site. Horace Miner and Jennings at the right front of the barge; Stuart Neitzel and Georg Neumann on the left front. Nearest the camera on the left is Charles Nash; second from the extreme right is Joffre Coe.

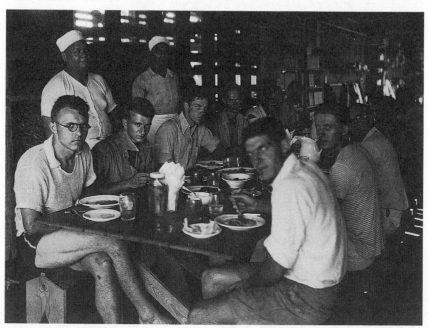

Lunch in the corncrib at the Kincaid site. Fats, one of the world's great cooks, along with his helper Percy, is behind Jennings on the extreme left. On Jennings's left is Ken Maynard, unknown, Georg Neumann, (?) Brown, unknown. Directly opposite is Stuart Neitzel, Horace Miner, Thorne Deuel, unknown.

Crew at Anderson Lake, Illinois, 1933 or 1934. Front row, left to right: Jennings; Jean C. (Pink) Harrington; Paul Cooper; Charles Wilder. Second row: Harriet Smith; unknown; unknown; Thorne Deuel(?). Third row: Kwong (?); Georg Neumann; Moreau Chambers. Fourth row: Jack Elliot; Marshall Newman. Top row: Robert Braidwood; Russell Hastings; unknown. At least six of this group went on to successful professional careers.

With Jane Jennings, 1937, Kaminaljuyú.

Alfred Vincent Kidder, gentleman and scholar. (Peabody Museum, Harvard University).

The last adobe pyramid (No. 6) and its stairway, and the "tufa pudding" fill and the lime-plastered sloping basalar wall of Pyramid No. 7. Work had stopped at this point at the end of 1936. The 1937 work began with the partial removal of the adobe stairway. (Peabody Museum, Harvard University).

Pyramid No. 4, almost completely exposed. The stub of the pyramid No. 6 stairway is visible at the extreme lower right. Estevo on the left and Gustavo Espinosa (caporal) on the cornice, with Pablo on the ladder. Estevo had the best excavation skills of the crew; he later became a full-time employee of the Museo Nacionál de Guatemala. (Peabody Museum, Harvard University)

Montezuma Castle. Note people on the ladders. Visitors are no longer allowed to climb into the ruins.

With Jane Jennings,
1937, while
Park Ranger at
Montezuma Castle
National Monument.

Mother's tent and
our tent on Beaver
Creek, with
Montezuma Castle
in background.

A section of the Old Natchez Trace north of Natchez, Mississippi, 1953. Here, and at many other places between Port Gibson and Natchez, the road traversed areas of *loess* (glacial flour) that erodes readily under traffic but never crumbles, although subject to columnar fracture when sufficiently weakened at the base. The loess is very deep along the east or left bank of the Mississippi River, thinning gradually inland from the river. The deep cuts result from decades of local use long after the Trace was abandoned as a national road. (Natchez Trace Parkway)

Emerald or Selsertown mound, north of Natchez. Dated to about A.D. 1300, it is a natural plateau shaped to serve as a base for several mounds (two of which are still visible, one at each end) arranged around a central plaza. Several smaller mounds around the edges have been leveled by cultivation. (Natchez Trace Parkway)

Mound 3, the main mound of the Anna group north of Natchez. Taken in June 1940 from the east, near the center of the plaza, the photo shows the ramp that supported a stairway leading to the tree in the center. The mound is about forty feet high. (Natchez Trace Parkway)

Mound A, the largest of the Lake George group near Holly Bluff, Mississippi. The photo, taken in February 1940, shows the erosion resulting from allowing cattle to use the mound as a refuge during the winter/spring floods that often occur in the "delta" country of western Mississippi. Jane Jennings (5' 9" tall), standing on the mound, emphasizes its height (about sixty feet). (Natchez Trace Parkway)

One of the burials—in this case lying on a cane mat—at site MLE 14. (Natchez Trace Parkway)

U.S. Navy, 1943 or 1944.

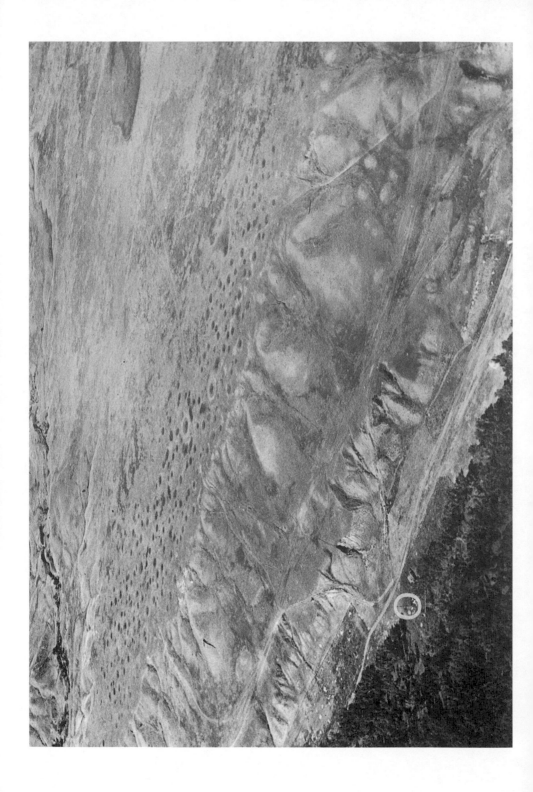

The Buffalo Pasture site, excavated and fully reported, was protected by a deep encircling ditch and palisade. It lies on the west (R) bank of the Missouri River, a few miles downstream from Fort Sully. (Smithsonian Institution).

Opposite: The Fort Sully site on the bluff or the east (L) bank of the Missouri River was one of, or perhaps the, largest site in the Plains. It lies a few miles north of Pierre, South Dakota. Sampled in 1960, it was occupied sometime between A.D. 1500 and 1700 and is regarded as being built by the protohistoric ancestors of the Arikara. Each of the "dimples" or depressions marks the location where a circular earth lodge once stood. The size of the huge town can be better grasped by comparing its extent with the church steeple circled in the lower left corner of the photograph. Normally the waters of the lake behind the Oahe Dam are twenty feet deep over the site. (Smithsonian Institution)

Occupied from about A.D. 1450 to 1550, the famous Huff Site is on the west (R)
bank of the Missouri River, which has eroded some of the site since this picture
was taken. The crowded rectangular houses, the encircling ditch and palisade, and
the evenly spaced bastions all show clearly. The site, located about twenty miles
south of Bismark, North Dakota, is now a state park. (State Historical Society of
North Dakota).

NINE

The University of Utah and University Life

WHAT WITH THE Washington transfer hanging over my head and the time I spent being regional archaeologist, I was getting nervous in the service. Out of the blue came an invitation to visit the campus of the University of Utah and consider an associate professorship appointment in the newly established anthropology department there. Despite the fact that I was now thirty-nine years old and had not been close to academia since 1936 and had never taught a college-level class and hadn't read any general anthropological material for fifteen years, the idea appealed to me as a challenge and as an escape from my twin predicaments. In late March of 1948 I went to Salt Lake City, leaving Omaha in a blizzard, with a foot of old snow on the ground. I arrived in Salt Lake City on a balmy early spring day to find a sheen of pale green over the valley, where the new bright leaves on the cottonwoods were about as big as a mouse's ear. The air was clear that day, the mountains were magnificent, and the feeling of spring was everywhere—sharp contrast with Omaha a few hours to the east.

I was met by Dean O. Meredith Wilson, recently from the University of Chicago, and was interviewed by him as well as by the new president, A. Ray Olpin, and by the dean of the faculty, Jacob Geerlings, who was a classics scholar. The then-faculty of the department included only Elmer R. Smith and Charles E. Dibble. Everyone made me feel welcome,

Dibble especially. He spent one day showing me the Salt Lake Valley and Brighton ski resort, intensifying my feeling of relaxation at being back among mountains and deserts and clean countryside. In none of the interviews was anything practical except salary and retirement plan discussed; I didn't know enough to ask about tenure or medical or health facilities available to me and the family, but I did note that retirement was an inadequate state system. I was offered the position and returned to Omaha.

Upon my return I found that the impossible had happened. In the three days I was gone I had been appointed regional archaeologist of Region II. Apparently there had been emergency action after I told my boss, the director of the recreational study group, that I was going to be interviewed for the teaching job. It was interesting that a few months earlier the position had not existed, but now with my possible resignation, it had proved instantly possible to create one and put me in it.

That night Jane and I weighed the matter carefully. We listed the advantages/disadvantages of the National Park Service vs. the University of Utah as we understood them. We listed everything we could think of: such things as housing (we had a very nice place in Omaha), salary (the promotion had brought me a nice raise so that I would be making 16 percent more than I had been offered at Utah), Omaha medical facilities, the hassle of moving, living in the Middle West vs. the West, familiarity with the National Park system vs. the unknown University of Utah, friends vs. strangers around us, as well as the Mormon constraints (little did we know). The list went on and on. No matter how we viewed the question of staying with the service or going to the university, all advantages clearly lay with staying put. Money, security, job familiarity, all argued against a move. However, there still loomed the specter of the uncertain transfer to Washington and consequent loss of professional and archaeological growth, both the latter clearly dependent on research and writing. The result was probably ordained. Waiving common sense, fiscal wisdom, and advice, we calmly decided to leave a comfortable future in the warm but restricting bureaucratic womb and try something new. Ever since, my advice to individuals uncertain about doing something or not has been to compare advantages and disadvantages and decide what action would be best for them. After doing that, they should next do what they *want* to do. Often these people, as did we, fly in the face of good judgment and follow their impulses; later they tell me they were glad they did so.

All this happened in March and April of 1948. I offered my NPS resignation as of September 1st of that year and went ahead with my summer plans. Those plans included writing the archaeological summary, *Plainsmen of the Past*, mentioned earlier, and to travel extensively to visit all the digs in the Missouri River Basin. In addition, I began to read extensively and develop lectures for the two classes I had agreed to give that first quarter at Utah. It was a busy and exciting summer, broken by a trip to Washington where Lee, Kahler, and Hillory Tolson, associate director of the Park Service, attempted to persuade me to withdraw my resignation. They were almost successful with their suasion, but were gracious with my refusal; we remained good friends.

I've already mentioned two or three special jobs I did for Lee and Kahler in later years, following up on things I had started while with the service. When they finally understood I would not stay with them, they asked for my suggestions for a National Park Service archaeologist for the new position being planned within the Branch of History. They gave me a list of perhaps six other men then in the service. I knew all of them, but none intimately, and, of course, I had opinions about them based on what I knew of their scholarly work.

The list included John Corbett, who, of the lot, seemed to have greater confidence, an almost patrician presence (he stood about six feet, five inches), a quick mind, and more diverse field experience. He, I thought, could find his way through the Washington jungle best of any, so I recommended him and he was given the job, soon proving to have been the right choice. He established single-handedly a National Park Service archaeological branch office that today employs scores of archaeologists and has great influence in Park Service and other federal archaeological decisions. Although he enjoyed participating in and manipulating the system, and thoroughly enjoyed being the successful bureaucrat without losing sight of his mission, which was to establish archaeology as a national resource, the pressures and tensions of the system contributed directly to his early death. His many accomplishments have been widely acknowledged by many North American archaeologists.

Leaving the Park Service was upsetting in many ways. Although Lee, Kahler, and Tolson had assured me I could return at any time if university life did not suit me, there was for us a feeling of finality, of severing strong ties—a sense of loss—that was quite saddening. We had friends throughout the service, we had spent eleven years embedding ourselves in the service structure, and we were, on the face of it, throwing all that away. With it were occasional moments of uneasiness, butterflies in the stomach, as we realized that while the university setting would be different, we didn't know exactly in what ways. There were times when I regretted the decision to go to Utah, and I'm sure Jane did also, but we never admitted our fears to each other. In any case, by September 1 we had sold our house, packed our then fewer belongings, and started west with the trauma of moving being intensified by Jane's discovering she was pregnant with our son Herbert and seeming, moreover, to be allergic to the fetus. The uneasy pregnancy added another measure of uncertainty to the move. On the trip to Salt Lake City, our aging and heavily loaded Chevrolet coupe, purchased ten years earlier in Macon, running uphill all the way, also ran hot, so we stopped often to let it cool. By the time we reached Vernal, Utah, Jane was too ill to travel. Jesse Lombard, superintendent of Dinosaur National Monument, had asked us to stay overnight at the monument with his family, but after one look at Jane, the Lombards insisted we stay until she felt better, thereby, I'm certain, saving the new baby. In three or four days we were able to continue, reaching Salt Lake City just at sunset by way of Parley's Canyon. Anyone who has come around that last turn to have Salt Lake City suddenly burst into view in the valley below knows how that dramatic panorama thrilled us, and we knew we were there at last.

From that moment of arrival, life was indeed different. We went to the motel that Dibble had reserved for us, where we found a small kitchen. I think we arrived on Saturday, early or mid-September. After we unloaded the car, Jane lay down to rest while I went in search of something to cook for dinner, beginning a period of about six weeks of which I have no clear memory, but a thousand blurred mental images. I do recall that the day after we arrived Dibble brought us some delicious peaches from his new orchard and said he would show me more of the university when I was ready. However, on Sunday, our second day there, I received a call from an Arthur Beeley, of whom I had never heard. He told me without the normal preamble of identifying himself as dean of the School of Social Work and head of the sociology department (where anthropology had been housed previously) that my wife and I were expected for dinner that night at 7:00 P.M. Jane, of course, was in no shape to go anywhere, so I refused. He then explained at length who he was, but I repeated my statement that we were not coming. Thus, I made my first enemy without having yet reported for work. He was a good enemy, complaining about me to the president, the dean, other faculty members—anyone who would listen. In so doing, I learned he had done me a great favor, for I met many faculty members during the next few months who mentioned hearing I had "had problems" with Beeley, smiling or chuckling as they said it. Almost always, too, they were cordial in welcoming me to the campus. I gathered that Beeley was widely regarded as a powerful and pompous bully, and anyone who stood up to him, even in ignorance as I had, instantly gained a certain stature and acceptability. Slowly it dawned on me, and I've never forgotten it, that one is judged as much or more by his enemies as by his friends. My knowing that Beeley had vowed to rid the campus of my presence helped me greatly in other ways in that I made sure that my every move was as carefully worked out as possible, that all contingencies and remedies I could think of were foreseen, and that the people who had to approve my proposals were aware of my ideas so that any Beeley charges against me would find me prepared to defend my moves. Probably I was overcautious; at least I was never aware of any later moves against me by him.

My first concern was Jane's health, so I immediately consulted the director of student health at the university, who recommended a general practitioner, E. Y. Hall, who in turn passed Jane on to an obstetrics-gynecologist specialist. That doctor, Laura Daines, fresh out of her internship, was deeply concerned about Jane's condition and feared an early miscarriage as highly likely and prescribed some drugs, as much bed rest as much as possible, and crossed fingers. She also insisted that we have a telephone because she wanted Jane to be able to get in touch with her day or night. Of course, phone installations were then running four to six months behind requests because World War II had caused shortages. Meanwhile, we lived in the tiny kitchenette apartment week after week while I went through the short list of meals I could cook six or eight times before we finally found a house. In Salt Lake City, like everywhere else, housing was tight in the wake of World War II, but we finally found a newly built house we could afford. It was tiny, ill-arranged, and on a raw, undeveloped lot on the southeast bench just south of Parley's Canyon some five miles from the university. The exact address was 2802 South 2750 East.

At the time there were no houses between our place and the Wasatch Range. Its only advantage was a full basement, which I eventually finished into four rooms and a bath. Dr. Daines was able, on the basis of Jane's precarious health, to get a phone installed in the house within three or four days. The phone was very comforting to us; at least Jane wasn't out of touch all day when I was gone. An even greater comfort was that despite a hard winter and all else that happened, Jane carried our second son, Herbert, to full term. Incidentally, phones remained hard to get for about two years, so ours was used by several families as houses were built nearby and the neighborhood grew. It was a terrible nuisance to have people underfoot day and night, but we realized that we were lucky to have the phone and it served everyone in emergencies. So we grinned (most of the time) and lived with it.

Our adventures with the house and the neighborhood were normal, I suppose, but we seemed often in a state of crisis over something. I will not dwell on domestic matters aside from saying that by doing all the work ourselves (except for a large living room we eventually added by contract) the house eventually became pleasant and livable. The first year was very crowded and very busy since I had several classes. First and obvious, I had to teach two classes each quarter. That meant in my case to learn or relearn and internalize enough anthropology to allow me to lecture on six different subjects. I went to great trouble to use examples and approaches different from the textbook, which meant I had to know what was in the text and find other relevant material to talk about. This being 1948, there were many older men going to school on the G.I. Bill in the classes, a fact that proved very advantageous for me because they often challenged me for proof or differed with me out of their own experience; therefore, the classes were often lively and stimulating and I tried always to find answers by next day for their questions. Undoubtedly I enjoyed and learned much that first year, probably more than my students; at least few later classes were as exciting as those first ones.

I had also been assigned custody of the anthropological collections that had accumulated since the 1900s, the collections having been initiated by the legendary Byron Cummings, then professor of classics, at the university. Excavation and collection of artifacts had gone on intermittently ever since his day, with artifacts from South America, Polynesia, and some from returning Mormon missionaries and local collectors also donated. Thus, a large but unsystematic body of fine exhibit-quality artifacts was on hand, including possibly the largest extant collections from Tsegi Canyon and Betatakin in Arizona. I discovered that the collection—the perishable parts of it—was slowly disappearing before the appetites of a massive infestation of carpet beetles that particularly liked animal products, such as woolen fiber, bone, horn, and antler. Before moving the collection from the top floor of the administration building to the new departmental quarters (we had been assigned the old World War II mess hall at Fort Douglas east of the main campus), I decided I should deal with the carpet beetles first. I hired a student full time for the fall quarter to spray or dunk every item except the record books in a DDT solution. Then he was to pack and move a few pieces at a time to the racks being built in the old kitchen of our building, where were also two large refrigerator rooms which I had caulked and sealed and used, with frequent fumigations, to store blankets, bone, and horn, and any new acquisitions. The move was finished by Christmas.

During that first quarter, of course, I got better acquainted with my new colleagues including E. A. Hoebel, the chairman, who had never been a chairman before. He was a tall, personable cultural anthropologist whose specialty was the law of primitive peoples, a field in which he had considerable stature; he also was interested in and had a smattering of psychology. Lacking administrative experience, he seemed unaware of the problems a new department, or even an old one, housed in a barren, echoing mess hall, faced. With no apparent problems, naturally there was no need on his part to solve any. What was worse, he worked at home and was rarely on campus except for classes. He, like Ronald Reagan thirty years later, seemed to be coated in Teflon—nothing touched or stuck to or affected him. Within a month I had begun signing requisitions and making the small but necessary almost daily decisions, actions which Hoebel either never noticed or more likely thought, "What the hell. If he does it, I don't have to." In short, I became departmental manager without portfolio or appointment, which meant that my projects at least moved more or less as planned.

There were four professors in the department: Hoebel, me, and the two local men who had been alone in the sociology department. As mentioned, one was Elmer Smith, with an M.A. in anthropology from Beeley's department; Smith also had been a student of Julian Steward for the two years Steward had been at Utah, but had taken mostly sociology classes. He had a fierce antipathy for racial distinctions and racism, having been briefly involved with the shameful Japanese internment program during World War II, and he was still very active in the local Japanese-

American Citizens League. He gloried in being detested by the Salt Lake City business community for his successful fight with realtors and property owners to break the invisible "bamboo curtain" that prevented Japanese-Americans, many of them well-to-do, from living on the east (or better) side of State Street. A popular lecturer, constantly attacking Mormonism and lacing his lectures with off-color stories, he was well known not only in the university but also in the community at large.

The other was Charles Dibble, whose courtesies I've already mentioned, and who for years was a continuous delight. He and I soon began to go out to lunch together and continued to do so for many, many years (he loathed the brown bag as much as I), and we talked of many things. I learned about the quirks and foibles of many key people at the university from his pithy, sometimes oblique, comments, which were not only amusing but also accurate vignettes of the various individuals. However, he shunned confrontation, rarely taking a dissenting view in any discussion. He, too, had a local M.A., with a Ph.D. from the National Autonomous University of Mexico in Mexico City, making him essentially an ethnologist-linguist with a primary interest in Mexico. By the end of his career, he and Arthur O. Anderson had translated the twelve volumes of Sahagún's, "General History of the Things of New Spain," from the original Aztec, a self-imposed task that proved to be about a thirty-year project. Much to my disappointment our relationship cooled after about twenty years, for reasons I never knew.

During that first year I also met Henry Frost, a sociologist, and his wife, Ruth. Jane and I both took to the family, and we had many drinks, dinners, and pleasant conversational hours with them, and we remained close friends until his death. After that, Ruth began declining invitations, and we rarely saw her after the funeral. Sidney Angleman was one of the most stimulating persons I had ever met. He was associate dean of the College of Letters and Science, but was charged only with the general education program. He was also a professor of English, and kept up with politics, music, and the contemporary scene; but primarily he worried about the "health" of the university. He viewed with vocal alarm any action that seemed to him to lower standards or otherwise weaken the school's academic intellectual strength; I suspect some of that concern with standards may have rubbed off on me. Any discussion with him was certain to be lively, probably argumentative, often loud, but always interesting. We were often at the Anglemans' and they at ours. He was socially the soul of gentleness, but a grim, inflexible martinet—almost sadistic—administrator of the general education program, a paradox I never understood.

Among the things I had been told at my interview with the dean and the president was that they wanted an ongoing university archaeology program started. They also emphatically mentioned that a museum would further enhance the department. In view of my long interest in museums I took their interest as a kind of invitation. They recognized that the prehistoric riches of the state were neither widely known nor understood and that the department should capitalize on that vast resource. I welcomed both the opportunity to think museum and the injunction to begin study of the state's prehistory. As already mentioned, my interest in museums stemmed from my conviction that the museum is the best way to translate the ponderous prose of the scientific monograph into something lay people (who in final analysis pay for the archaeologists' work) could understand, appreciate, and perhaps enjoy. Moreover, the opportunity to design and direct a long-range archaeological project would in large measure replace the two such research activities I had already planned at the Trace and the Plains but had lost when transferred away from them.

Accordingly, I went to work on a statewide survey design. By then I had read the skimpy literature, which consisted of site reports by Julian Steward, John Gillin, Elmer Smith (who had salvaged some material from Dead Man's Cave west of Salt Lake City), Noel Morss's work on the Fremont River, and J. O. Brew's Alkali Ridge; Neil Judd had two short papers covering two surveys, and Jesse Nusbaum had a report of DuPont Cave near Kanab. The library was little more than a suitcaseful. Although the southeastern corner of the state where the Anasazi had been concentrated was already known, or at least well enough known that people were confident of the sequence and the contents, there was no information, except in the Virgin Valley, for the southwestern quadrant and none of any importance for the northeastern or central portions. My plan was quite simple: first, look where we know the least, then go to the other areas in order. Probably, left to my own devices, I would never have gone into the Anasazi area. Although I always picked a spot for the field school, the assistant who ran the survey, as soon as I acquired him, searched various sections of the state reasonably well from the last snow to the first, for several years. Therefore, in three years I had a pretty good idea of the extent of and the variation in the Fremont culture, but with my own digs I continued to stay for several years in the northwestern part of the state, where Danger Cave, Hogup Cave, and Swallow Cave all yielded much information completely new and complete unexpected. Obviously, I hardly need to say that as we learned more about the state the selection of sites became more rational because, in most cases, we were trying to extend our knowledge of one or another of the now-recognized cultures. The seven-year break in my plan, caused by the later Glen Canyon work, was actually quite useful in that Glen Canyon contributed much knowledge about the distribution of the Anasazi, Kayenta, and Fremont cultures that we had not possessed earlier. The rationale behind all of my selection of areas for research was quite easy since there was no well-controlled archaeological work except in the southeastern corner of the state. Whatever I did was probably useful in that it added another bit about the overall prehistory of Utah.

I went directly to Dean Meredith Wilson with my plan, who quickly approved the ideas and promised the full-time man, who I think was employed by 1950, about a year after I presented the plan. Wilson also approved the establishment of a field school in the summer of 1949. The summer school was continuous from then until the mid-1980s, except for the years of the Glen Canyon project (about which, more later).

In preparation for the survey I acquired all the U.S.G.S maps that were available as well as county maps for the whole state and attempted to pinpoint on them all of the sites reported by anyone up to then in publications and the few mentioned in notes kept by Smith and others. I renumbered all of them in the Smithsonian Institution trinomial system which I had learned in the Plains. I also simplified and extended the recording systems Spaulding and I had utilized in Lee County work for the Trace, using and teaching the system from then on.

By now I had come to believe that good fieldwork was learned by doing fieldwork—essentially an apprentice approach—because, in addition to digging, fieldwork involves learning to observe phenomena and their relationships, developing a reasonably clear descriptive writing style so that the relationships may be accurately recorded; the recognition of soils and their textures and colors and some intangible attitudes are slowly learned as well. So, I thought: Why not teach a field technique class before students go into the field? Why not? Harvard, I had heard, used to bury a skeleton under a pile of sand and require the students to find and expose it, an exercise that captured nothing of the archaeology I had learned; rather, it was sandbox play, usually and properly reserved for toddlers.

But the germ of an idea came from that sandbox, leading me to decide to create some miniature sites, modeled on a scale of 1:24, that were simplified replicas of already excavated and reported sites. Tiny artifacts such as metates, axes, milling stones, pipes, pots and broken pottery, and other things could be made, structures built to the same scale, or nearly so, could be re-created and placed in proper relationships in the various layers of the earth of which the sites were made. The soil used was colored with mineral pigment so there would be good visual contrast between the layers, and actual wood, charcoal, charred sticks, ashes, and red earth (simulating burned earth) were used as appropriate. Each site contained three or four cultural layers: some of the simulations I created were a small Plains village, a Hopewell mound, a Mississippi mound, a Kentucky shell heap, a Southwest pit house—all simplified, of course. Building the sites sounds like a lot of work, but I did little of the actual labor, having already learned much earlier never to do anything that someone else could do as well. So, student assistants gathered materials, made the artifacts, mixed the soils, and did whatever else was needed. When all was ready I put in six or eight hours building the sites (with several "gofers" helping), finding that the sites were far easier to build than I had expected.

After a few three-hour lecture sessions and explanation of the recording system I wanted to develop, the students, in teams of three, were turned loose on the sites with one person in charge, laying out strategy and keeping notes, while the others "labored." After two weeks the "boss" dropped back to laborer, while one of the others assumed the supervisor's role, with another change of supervisors in another two weeks. The usual field situations and problems, such as intrusions, superposition, reuse of the same area by subsequent cultural groups, and other fitting cultural changes were built into all the sites. To my surprise and great pleasure, the exercise worked in that the students became just as involved, experienced the same frustrations, and made the same mistakes as happened on a real site and, gratifyingly, with *no loss* of scientific information. When the dig was completed—when the last crumb of earth had been swept away—each student wrote a straight-faced report of the site exactly as if the location actually existed, identifying the cultures involved and explaining, if they could, the unusual and incorrect chronological sequence they discovered.

Even more to my surprise, after I reported the exercise in the journal *Archaeology,* my colleagues jeered at me for being a fool, seeing no merit in the exercise whatever. Nonetheless, I continued to offer the class nearly every other year until I quit teaching at Utah, and I remain convinced that one tabletop dig allows more learning and makes a better apprenticeship than one summer at the average field school, including my own. One or two people have used the same system; whether on a continuous basis I do not know.

During that first year I was in a continuous wrangle with the purchasing department. Why did a professor want so many maps? Why did I want raw mineral pigments? Why did I need gallons of DDT? Why? Why? Why? The purchasing officer was also the manager of the bookstore, a holdover employee from prewar days before the university expansion began; he labored under the apprehension that if left to his or her own devices any prof would fritter departmental monies away, which came to mean that the purchasing officer saw his role as saving money, not facilitating departmental functions. After several visits to his office, I finally got better service, but it was two or three years before I convinced the buyers that I only ordered what I needed and that I needed it when ordered, not thirty to sixty days later. That office would, for example, put out a requisition for one-half dozen number 2½ shovels to bid, with a thirty-day award date! Eventually all that passed.

During that first year I also had to plan a self-sufficient field school, which I had decided to conduct at two caves on the west side of the Great Salt Lake. Obviously a camp or field school for twelve to fifteen people for eight weeks required tents, stove and cooking gear, cots, digging tools, first-aid supplies, hand carpenter tools, and much, much more. When I learned that the university had a surplus property department that contained thousands of classes of surplus war materiel, I went crazy. Here were tents, stoves, iceboxes, cooking gear, plywood, hand tools, cordage, all for the asking. I made a list and carried it to Mr. Malone, the tough little custodian of the gold mine, but from him I learned there was a committee which allocated the surplus items, so I went to it with my list. The chairman, also a miser, I suppose was appalled and set out to require a specific justification for perhaps 200 items, a request that led me to blow up, demanding to know what experience he had that qualified him to weigh my needs. He, a civil engineer, acknowledged he knew nothing of archaeological fieldwork, so I suggested (with some heat) that he simply assume I was competent to do what I'd been hired for—just okay the list and let me go do something more important than bicker with him. Surprisingly, he did, and even more surprising, he became a friend, helping me later in various ways such as lending me a plane-table and alidade, even assigning one of his staff to teach the rudiments of plane table mapping to two of my students.

I was to have that first field school during the summer of 1949, and, of all things, I wanted it to go well because I had several goals, which together would establish a pattern for future sessions. First, there had to be a reasonably comfortable camp. That requirement translates into adequate housing, good water, good food in ample supply, a clean camp, regular work hours which include cleaning and sorting artifacts after dinner along with occasional seminars, and a semblance of order in day-to-day behavior. Second, I regarded teaching as important as but no more so than research, so I felt that any dig must generate new useful data or the whole exercise would have been only an exercise—in short, an expensive failure. Students must have an opportunity to learn as many skills and procedures as they had the capacity or desire to learn and achieve some understanding of what record keeping and all the other necessary procedures entail. On a purely personal level, I wanted to establish that the field school was the effort-equivalent of any other teaching quarter and that I would get the autumn quarter free to study the collections and other data we had amassed. I was also determined that I would report one project before the next was started. I felt, and still believe, that an unreported excavation or any other piece of research is wasted money, time, and effort. New knowledge not made public does not enrich the discipline for which it was generated and is, therefore, lost. In my view, an unreported site would be better left undug. I know the history of archaeology is studded with individuals, frequently highly respected, who left mountains of raw data behind them, usually never to be reported. I didn't want that kind of irresponsible negligence on my record.

Funding the field school was never easy, which surprised me; in fact, in my innocence I had thought *all* universities *always* supported research. For the first two years Dean Wilson, after persuasion, found the funds, although he violently disapproved of not giving credit hours for the summer work. Nor did he understand why I wanted money to feed the troops. I argued that food and shelter were small rewards and relatively inexpensive for a summer of strenuous and free labor by the students. At first my arguments prevailed. Later, after Wilson left, I was finally forced to offer credit and charge for board and tuition; with the tuition and board money I paid the cook and bought the groceries and gasoline, while salaries for one or two graduate assistants and other expenses I usually could get from the University of Utah research committee or the Department of Anthropology or both.

That first season of 1949 was only moderately successful from the research point of view. We established the camp just east of Wendover, Utah, which lies on the Nevada line, and began work in the caves of the Pilot and Desert Range where we excavated Jukebox and Raven Caves and sampled Danger Cave. None was very informative. Jukebox and Raven had had little occupancy, and at Danger, as the season closed, we merely cleaned out the holes made by Elmer Smith in earlier work. We did learn that the Danger deposits were deep, clearly if complexly stratified, and worth a season of exploration; actually, we spent the summers there for several more years.

That first year, and often thereafter, I organized junkets for the administrators to whom I was obligated in one way or another. That first year I invited President Olpin, Dean Wilson, Dean Angleman, Dean Geerlings, and my chairman, Hoebel. They stayed with the crew, slept on cots in the dormitory tent, climbed to both Jukebox and Raven Caves to watch the crews at work, and ended the day hot, tired, and thirsty. After dinner I took them across into Nevada to the bar at the Stateline Motel, where the Mormons drank Coke and the others took beer, while I alone had bourbon. They expressed great interest in everything, but seemed most impressed by the orderliness and discipline of both the camp and the dig—discipline that I took for granted because I had made it clear to the students that listening to whining and complaining about conditions was not part of my job. They had two options: either endure and carry out instructions in silence or go home. I offered the same options to all subsequent students or hired crews. Although I am fully aware that *sotto voce* complaints and much moaning went on when I was not around, the public face was a quiet, if not contented, one.

In all fairness, I must say that I felt that any and all moaning was entirely justified. The caves were very dusty. The southwest wind blew until sundown, leaving dust on everything in camp, which lay on the edges of the Great Salt Lake Desert. In the daytime the heat got as high as 110 degrees Fahrenheit. The crew members, both men and women, were soft, several never having done physical labor, so they developed sore muscles and blistered hands within hours. Several had never used a shovel and had to be taught the energy-saving rhythm that experienced laborers used, letting the back and legs, not the arms, do the work.

We also took one or two short trips. One, I recall, was to Robert Heizer's dig in the Humboldt Sink in Nevada which proved to be a bad experience. Heizer's camp was dirty and littered, his digging techniques were casual and sloppy, and the food was execrable, being prepared by complaining students on a daily rotational schedule. Dinner that first night was overboiled potatoes, undercooked rice, and badly scorched unseasoned hamburger patties. To return to our wholesome balanced meals, with homemade breads, pastry, and breakfast rolls thrown in, was a privilege. Crew morale was very high after we visited Heizer, and I noticed, too, an added effort at cleanliness and careful work on the dig. Overall I felt the field school format I had forged was workable and effective. With variations in detail depending on circumstances, I retained that format for the remaining years.

As mentioned earlier, work at Danger Cave was continued for several seasons. Although the working conditions were bad—blinding, choking dust was a major handicap—we partially solved the visibility problem with strong lights and the breathing problem with industrial masks that kept the dust out of our lungs. The dry cave site had preserved everything from beetle wings to textiles and even human coprolites (desiccated fecal matter). The random deposition of the fill made digging more complex and challenging, while the many artifacts kept the troops interested. I finally analyzed the data with student help during the winters and a six-month leave from teaching made possible by a grant from Wenner-Gren Foundation for Anthropological Research. As I recall it, I was able to hire Ed Norbeck to teach for that six-month's leave period. I was department chairman by that time and was able to add him to our faculty when the grant monies were gone. He was a congenial colleague, good teacher, and good friend, and later together we organized a symposium on American prehistory for a Rice University semicentennial which was published and widely used as a text for several years.

As I labored through the Danger Cave data I, of course, read widely in order to develop some sense of how Danger fit into the dim outlines of the western desert prehistory as it was then known. In the meantime, I had sent samples from every major stratum to Willard F. Libby at Chicago for a C-14 assay. I was certain the cave was old because, according to my reading of the evidence, its occupancy had begun almost immediately after Lake Stansbury had fallen below the cave's threshold. But the age of Stratum 1—over 11,000 years B.P.—truly surprised me.

Perhaps a digression about the location of the cave is needed. The Great Salt Lake lies at the lowest point in a huge basin without external drainage called the Bonneville Basin. Throughout the Pleistocene epoch a huge lake, Bonneville, covered most of western Utah and impinged upon eastern Nevada and southern Idaho a short distance. The lake stabilized three times and cut three major beaches, or deeply etched strand lines—called Bonneville (the highest), Provo, and Stansbury—on the slopes of the ranges in and surrounding the basin, still plainly visible today at many places in the Salt Lake Valley. The latest and lowest of those long-lived lakes and beaches—called Stansbury—was some 200 feet *above* Danger Cave. Danger itself lay at just above the fourth, almost imperceptible strand line called Gilbert of a still smaller and later lake; it was obvious that if the cave had been fit for human occupancy it was free of the lake water, meaning that the lake had dried up considerably. Inasmuch as the disappearance of the last lake (leaving Great Salt Lake as a remnant) marked the end of the Pleistocene, I expected considerable antiquity for the earliest or deepest material in it, but the extreme age of more than 11,000 years ascribed by the C-14 analysis made the site more important because its age exceeded all but a few of the excavated sites in North America.

Although it was exciting to learn the cave deposits were so old, the excavation process itself was even more exciting to me for several reasons. For example, the thirteen-foot-deep deposit of trash—the debris of living—that had accumulated from 11,000 years ago to 2,000 or less years ago was entirely random. Because each layer was related to a single event, placed accidentally, not purposefully, where we found it, each had to be traced, one at a time, over its full extent.

Some of the dozens of layers had been spread as a result of winnowing of tiny but nutritious seeds of the plant burroweed (*Allenrolfea occidentalis*) that thrives in the salty soil of the Great Salt Lake Desert. There were also layers of windblown sand, and a few zones of rock spall from the ceiling of the cavern. The extremely dry conditions of storage meant that *anything* left or lost in the deposits was still there—leather or buckskin scraps, pieces of rawhide, tools and implements of wood, a thousand pieces of string, as well as one or two nets of twine, coarse fabric, many basket fragments whose manufacture changed through time, tools made of bone, even human coprolites. Of course, the tools—knives, weapons, and millstones, both broken and intact—were found as well.

One of the most amazing things was that we recovered identifiable fragments of sixty-eight plant species which grow yet today within ten miles of the site; historically all those plants had been used by the Gosiute of western Utah for food, tools and utensils, or medicines. Of the more than one hundred animal species found historically near the cavern, over thirty, ranging from bison to wood rats, were used as food by the Northern Paiutes; the bones of most of these species were represented in the debris within the cave. The coprolites proved to contain evidence of single meals—*Allenrolfea* seeds, which had not been fully crushed in the milling and had survived the passage through the alimentary tract; hair and small bones of rodents; the skin of prickly-pear fruit and leaves—and even the eggs of intestinal parasites!

The fascination of such varied finds—entirely new to me—finally was transformed into the realization that we had come upon a full and intimate glimpse into an entire lifeway geared to an ecosystem we could visualize and understand. I later learned that the same adaptation to the desert environment was documented in the ethnological record of the historic Shoshone-speaking tribes of the West.

Although we eventually excavated three other informative and exciting caves (Hogup, Cowboy, and Sudden Shelter), each of which was different and therefore challenging, none equalled for me the thrill of Danger Cave. Moreover, each of the caves extended and expanded our knowledge of the early cultures.

Given the wealth and extreme age of the early deposits, I naturally felt I had to learn more about the geology of the lake and particularly Bonneville Basin while I read further in the literature of western archaeology. The result of this reading was to further convince me that the terminal Pleistocene had occurred here earlier than was believed at the time. It made me more and more aware that, based on the widely scattered data then available, there had been a very ancient, uniform way of life blanketing the dry steppes of the west for several thousand years from Mexico to Oregon and from the Rockies to the Sierras. I therefore suggested that idea in the Danger Cave report, which I finally finished late in 1955. It was published in 1957 as a memoir of the Society for American Archaeology and simultaneously as the University of Utah Anthropological Paper No. 27. Because of its great age and the richness of the cave's contents, I published the data in both journals because I thought the site was important enough to be brought to the attention of as many of the profession as possible. It was the largest mass of data I had ever worked with, and I was afraid I couldn't or didn't do it justice. I did the analysis with the help of two student assistants, as well as I could and called it quits.

The report was well received. My suggestion of the existence of a long-lived, widespread Desert culture (I later called it the Desert Archaic) aroused both criticism and support, but ultimately, as more and more research was done, the concept became less controversial and the furor largely abated. The only reason there was such excitement over such a simple idea was that it flew in the face of current belief. I understand that even the geologists now accept the Danger Cave data as valid. I suppose that the Danger Cave report helped me get the Viking Medal for Archaeology award in 1958, an honor I neither expected nor suspected; to receive any recognition or an honor without any warning is a wonderfully exciting experience, a warm and pleasing shock. But awards can be taken two ways: The recipient can say, "Right. I am fulfilled. This is the capstone of my career," and relax as some do. The other reaction is, "This is wonderful. I am grateful. But why me? Do I deserve it? Probably not, so I had better do something to earn the continuing confidence of whoever gave me the award." I opted for the second course. Honors seem always to stimulate me to further effort, in that rather than boast of them I set out to prove I was worthy to receive them. Possibly because of the Viking award I was elected to the presidency of the Society for American Archaeology, in itself a modest kind of honor.

To my surprise, I learned that honors sometimes have a monetary value in academia. The Viking medal got me a $1,000 permanent raise in university pay. Later I was named a University of Utah Distinguished Professor. That netted me a $500 raise. Many years later (1977) I was elected to the National Academy of Sciences, possibly the greatest honor one's professional colleagues can confer. Instead of a raise I got a short letter from my dean and from the president of the university. I'd readily have traded the dean's curt letter (there was little accord between us) for a monetary token of notice. Probably I should have tried negotiation.

Having survived the first twelve months of university life by teaching, starting a field school, and, at least on paper, establishing a statewide archaeological survey, I moved on to the second chore: the creation of a museum that I had promised during my initial interview. Obviously, it would be small and in my mind, at least, temporary. It would be a trial or pilot run to see whether I could do it, and if it succeeded, I would take on a larger one. I decided that I would, first, attempt to define anthropology (it was 1949, when anthropology was by no means a household word) and, second, present what I could of Utah prehistory. I was already aware that museums were moving from endless displays of similar objects toward conveying concepts and ideas exemplified by fewer objects in more attractive settings. I had also been deeply impressed by the brilliant work of George Quimby and Donald Collier in remodeling the North American Archaeological Hall at the Field Museum of Natural History in Chicago. The exhibits were colorful, lively, well lighted, and with short clear labels. I modeled the style of my exhibits after theirs as much as was possible, given the difference in our resources.

From Dean Wilson I got the funds to build a little museum (fifteen cases, as I recall) where I would carry out my grandiose scheme. In the echoing empty half of the mess hall that had not yet been utilized for department offices and a classroom, I built a room within a room. The interior room had fifteen windows with slanted glass behind which was space enough to tightly attach fifteen sealed boxes or cases that contained the exhibits. I was particularly proud of the cases. They had ground-glass tops, were tightly sealed and clamped with a seal onto the wall, and thus they were essentially dust-tight. Being lighted from above with external light fixtures, they never "breathed" to bring in dust to dim the colors and objects within. I was so pleased with the cases that I gave a blueprint of them to Marie Wormington of the Denver Museum of Natural History. A year or so later I visited her, and she showed me several cases she had installed, telling me proudly that she and her staff had designed them, but they were indistinguishable except in size from the Utah ones. I'm sure she thought the idea had come from her shop; equally I'm sure that others have designed comparable cases before and since, but I designed mine to meet problems I knew were common in the cases of that day.

With hired student labor, one being a biologist-artist named Don

Hague, we created and installed the cases between January 1 and April 1, 1950. The finished product was nice. There was no overhead lighting in the hall, all light came from the bright, colorful exhibit windows, so no external reflections blurred the contents. It was so striking, so pleasing to me that I decided to hold an open house/grand opening, with punch, tea, and cakes at the ready, so I invited some fifty university officials and profs to be the first visitors. The viewing was a great success; at least I was showered with compliments. The little museum, although housed in an out-of-the-way spot in an old World War II temporary building, was highly successful. As an estimate, my guess is that an average of 8 to 10,000 school children visited it each year, and I was more than pleased with its impact, limited as it was. (The exhibits stayed in place until about 1966 or 1967. They were then cannibalized, and some of the objects were included in exhibits in the Utah Museum of Natural History, which opened in 1968. With the debut of the Utah Museum of Natural History I managed to get the museum obsession out of my system, and have rarely visited one since.)

After the little museum was completed, I went to work to found the Utah Museum of Natural History, a task, as it turned out, that went through many phases. I had naively assumed that it would be easy. I would simply ask the university for the money, draw up some plans, and start building. When I got an appointment with President Olpin and explained all this to him, he was stunned and even indignant. He said somewhat belligerently, "You've got your museum. Why do you want another?" I explained why what we had was nothing, simply nothing, pointing out temporary versus permanent, limited use versus statewide involvement and impact, a highly focused museum versus the complete natural history presentation, the great need for a natural history institution in the face of no proper museum between Denver and California, and on and on and on. He said "no" again. There were important things in his life: a new engineering building, a new law school, and several other important things. I deplored his warped sense of values and withdrew, an act that ended the first phase—but I did not retreat.

I regrouped after I had another idea. Although Olpin had given me short shrift, he surely would listen to several professors in coalition. I asked the dean of the College of Letters and Science, the philosopher Sterling McMurrin, to appoint a museum committee with me as chairman, which he did. McMurrin had—and still has—more brains, probity, and vision than most of any faculty, and his espousal of my natural history concept remained strong long after he moved on to higher positions in the university and ultimately became U.S. Commissioner of Education, among other accomplishments. So, I met a few times with the heads of biology, geology, art, and architecture, as well as other departments, but after a year or so I gave up. The geologists wanted geology and paleontology to be dominant. The biologists wanted bugs, plants, and animals to be central. Art simply said "To hell with it; we have an art museum already," while architecture began having students draw plans for a second Smithsonian Institution. My concept of a proper approach in which man, land, and other species were shown in a balanced and intertwined way appealed to none of them; in fact, I think few of them even understood the ecological foundation I was proposing. And they even bickered about who was to direct it when it was formed. The director problem, in my mind, being long since solved, I simply let the committee die on the vine. I called no more meetings and it simply went away; meanwhile, I sulked for a while. That was the end of phase two.

By then, it had become clear to me that I had to be the only proponent and would have to create the museum through harassment. After a year or so of talking to anyone at the university or anywhere else who would listen, I met Neal Maxwell, a smooth, persuasive vice president who had many jobs, including working with the state legislature, softening relations between the faculty and the administration, and generally oiling any troubled waters he spotted. He was superb at his job. He went on to become a power in the Quorum of Seventy in the Mormon church. I convinced Neal that the museum would be a powerful public relations tool for the university and that within the university there were extremely good collections in every field of natural science as well as the expertise to create a first-class natural history museum from scratch. He promised to write a bill authorizing a state museum of natural history to be located on the University of Utah campus. After he wrote it he tried to lobby it through, but he failed for a number of reasons, primarily because some legislators did not like the university, others wanted the museum in their districts, others asked, "Who needs it?" and to all of them it was a new and, therefore, suspect idea. Neal then told me I first needed a grass-roots demand. Fortunately, by that time the Statewide Archaeological Society existed, with a few scattered chapters over the state, and, more important, there was one *special* member. That man, George Tripp, was a pharmaceuticals salesman who was frighteningly enthusiastic about archaeology, had boundless energy, and was fanatically interested in the museum concept I was peddling; Tripp went to work on the problem. Since his work took him all over the state, he hunted up every legislator and senator and gave each of them the museum pitch whenever he was in their towns. He also interested other members of the society, who I understand also lobbied their own representatives effectively. When the next legislature met, Tripp haunted the halls, reminding legislators of his interest, while Neal reintroduced the simple bill. It went through in February of 1963, but with only authorization—no money was included! This ended phase 3.

As soon as I had a copy of the signed bill I took it to the academic vice president, then Jack Adamson, with whom I had a good working relationship. I think he read me correctly as direct, candid, more or less honest, and with no hidden agenda; "what you saw was all there was." I asked him to appoint me as director of the Utah Museum of Natural History. He said, "What? I don't know what you're talking about." I showed him the bill, and he said, "Sure." I wrote the letter for him, including in it a paragraph about university support of the creation and operation, but I did not mention finances, naively believing that support included money. (As it turned out, the university never intended more than moral and material support; however, the university support eventually came to include a fine, suitable building—the George Thomas former library building—some remodeling, heat, light, janitorial service, and the salary of the associate director, leaving me in the final analysis no cause for complaint.) Adamson signed the letter, thus giving me a new job, no money with which to do it, and no extra salary, nor any relief from teaching, a situation that never changed. Although I never had any extra salary for the museum work I did, I pressed on; whether to credit my persistence to stubbornness, stupidity, or public spirit is not clear. This marked the end of phase 4.

Since I had given up being head of the anthropology department in 1960, I only had the normal teaching, research, and other chores on my schedule. I had time to push museum matters, but I didn't really yet know what or where to push. But here again, I note it's better to be lucky than smart. Out of the blue, a Salt Lake City stockbroker, then head of the Salt Lake City office of Dean Witter, Inc., named Calvin Gaddis, a man I had never heard of, walked into my office with a question. He had a wealthy client, a Mrs. Cooper from Monticello, Utah, who wanted to do something for archaeology! What should he tell her to do? I think it was $25,000 she wanted to dispose of. Not surprisingly, I suggested the museum as worthy of support. Gaddis, capable of intense, if sometimes short-lived enthusiasms, steadfastly helped with money raising and friendly advice for several years. He also introduced me to Leland Swaner, an extraordinary, public-spirited man, with cattle, real estate, and other interests, who, before his untimely death, soon came to share my concept and helped mightily, going with me to make sales pitches to many local citizens as well as donating several very large amounts of money personally.

As soon, however, as I had the Cooper money, I hunted up Don Hague, who had helped me on the little departmental museum. He had long since finished school and after a series of design jobs had wound up at the Fort Worth Children's Museum for some years. I found him back in Salt Lake City working in design for the Sperry Corporation, so I offered him a job as curator of exhibits, which he immediately accepted and was installed in an office. We then went to work crystallizing my ideas and reducing them to more tangible form. We worked on themes, halls, individual exhibits, planning to install the exhibits in two or three sizes and shapes of standard cases. The cases were to be large and sturdy, embodying all the features of the highly effective experimental pilot ones I had designed in 1949. (I presume they are still in use today.) To Hague I stressed three prime controlling concepts for the exhibits: accuracy, simplicity, and dignity of execution for all exhibits. Some time after Don was hired, probably within a year, I formed a committee of technical advisors—William Behle, ornithologist, Daniel Jones from geology, and perhaps one or two others to ensure accuracy of the exhibits. I myself took responsibility for the anthropology material.

After Don had spent months at the drawing board, and I had reviewed what he did, we began to construct exhibits in another vacant barracks building that I had gotten permission to use indefinitely. As each exhibit was finished, it was carefully wrapped in plastic or otherwise protected and stored. The artists and technicians continued to build the exhibits Hague designed after we had decided on a theme or concept. Thus, when we finally got the library space assigned, most of the exhibits were ready to install. That way we had almost "instant" museum.

The next year or two were, in retrospect, nightmarish. With only the help of Gaddis and Swaner, I made dozens of sales pitches, finding that begging for money was very distasteful. It also took much time and taxed my patience to the utmost. Over the years, however, we raised perhaps $200,000 from the downtown businesses. I applied for and received a small National Science Foundation grant for a series of traveling exhibits, and faculty friends gave unsolicited small amounts. I would do anything for money. Once I even went to the gala opening of a new McDonald's, where I was presented with a toy McDonald's made of cardboard containing dollar bills. I duly took the little building and all the money (it proved to be $103) to the bursar's office and deposited it with fanfare amid much laughter and a few jeers. One way or another we raised and spent, as I recall, nearly $300,000 in creating scores of exhibits and in paying the staff. That amount was augmented when Governor Calvin Rampton, without my knowing it, put a one-time item of $60,000 in the state budget for the museum. Evidently his wife, Lucy Beth Rampton, a former student of mine, had nagged him into it, a fact I only learned at the dedication of the museum in October 1969, where he gave the dedication address. He said, "Jennings is a hell of a good politician; he even planted a lobbyist in the governor's bed."

Early in 1967, during the creation of exhibits that were being wrapped and sealed in plastic and stored in the firetrap barracks, construction of a new library was begun, and the old one, a grand, honest old building with an enormous reference and reading room, would soon stand vacant. There was the answer to the problem I hadn't yet faced—a building for the museum. The infighting for the building was intense; the university's TV station wanted it and needed it; the School of Architecture coveted it badly. The geology department wanted all of it. But I *had* to have it. I made my pitch to everyone in administration, the planning department, buildings and grounds department—anyone I thought could help. I spent the most time with the then academic vice president—the third with whom I had dealt. He was a law professor named Alfred Emery with whom I felt very easy. The reason we were comfortable with each other was that for several years we two had fought long, hard battles side by side for worthy projects that came before the university's research committee, of which we were both members. While there were perhaps a dozen committee members, Emery and I were the only two not involved in such *real* subjects as chemistry, geology, pharmacy, or medicine—the other members, in short, were not interested in such *minor* things as law, social sciences, English, or geography. He had learned during our association that I did pursue goals, that I made good use of such resources as I had, and that I was, within limits, to be trusted. Bucking for the honor of being first in line for the library building space went on for months.

Finally in late August 1967, just before I was to leave for a year as visiting professor at the University of Hawaii, I heard that a decision was to be made early in September, the date not specified. From earlier conversations with him, I knew that the campus planner handling the disposition of the library was dead set against wasting the space on my crackpot scheme and had vowed to kill my ideas in conference; therefore, I arranged a thirty-minute appointment with Emery so as to make one last frantic try for a commitment. I took a tiny scale model of the reading room and its projected contents which Don had had made for me. It was a little gem. The central exhibit of three dinosaurs, the earth models, geological panels, the biology section—all were represented. The miniature conveyed the feel of the displays in the huge hall very effectively. In a folio I had also had prepared were fifteen or twenty artist's drawings of key cases so that the fully developed treatment of several of the concepts to be purveyed could be viewed in detail or even, one might say, could be experienced. After I had gone over the entire library building and my plans for both the first and second floors with Emery, he laughed and said, "Jess, you are wasting our time—you are arguing your case before it is called," and ushered me out. But the big meeting was called the *very next* day for late afternoon—and all the claimants were there. Each made his case except me. Emery listened and finally said, "All of you need this space, but Jennings needs it the worst. Jennings gets the first two floors and biology gets the rest," then saying to his assistant, "See to it." I waited around after the meeting and asked Emery to pay Hague's salary out of his account. He agreed, thereby firmly attaching the museum to his office, an action that removed the museum from future interdepartmental or intercollege budgetary disputes. Although I obviously felt very good about having managed to get prime space on campus for the exhibits, there remained a couple of years of work before we were quite ready for the opening; there were a few necessary modifications to the building; there were cases to build, exhibits to install, dinosaurs to assemble, and other countless tasks to be performed.

I've already indicated two or three enormous strokes of luck that had marked my efforts to build the museum. After I returned from Hawaii another incredible piece of luck came when I was approached by the Junior League of Salt Lake City. Several—three or four, as I recall— elegantly dressed, nice-looking young women called on me to request that they be *allowed* to help me with publicity, supply docents for the many school groups, and pay the salary of a head docent whom I would select!! Their support, including the salary of the head docent, was to run three years. This indeed was manna from heaven. The league also staffed and paid for needed equipment for the Junior Science Academy for per- haps five years. In a few years the docent program perpetuated and ran itself, but for those first few years those wonderful women were the edu- cational staff. I believe some forty women volunteered; although a few dropped out, the Junior League staff remained at full force for the three years. Moreover, a year before we opened, leaguers took a propaganda film that we had made, announcing the coming of the museum, to every school in Salt Lake and Davis Counties. The film (created by a mad ge- nius whose name I can't recall, who volunteered to do it) was a thirty- minute masterpiece called "Frozen Moments in Time." I had three copies made. The league organized the schedule, sent out its teams, and thus as- sured that there would be thousands of eager young patrons the day we opened, a campaign that almost guaranteed high attendance from the opening day. No one today other than I knows how much the museum owes that group of fine young women. Some people tend to denigrate the Junior League, but I certainly do not. To those women we owe the inter- pretive program in place today as well as the early strength of the mu- seum's youth educational program.

But a problem yet remained—no money for the operational budget came from the state nor from the university. I finally learned that one rea- son for the lack of funds was that Neal Maxwell, in his lobbying back in 1963, had assured the legislature that no money would be requested—all that was needed was an authorization. Had I known about that at the time, I would surely have dropped the whole idea. For reasons I never understood, the university wouldn't ask for funds in its own budget. So there I was, with no funds other than gate receipts for operation. At one point I was hopelessly behind with the payroll, so I asked the university for help. The president, at the time, James Fletcher, later of NASA fame, gave me $60,000, but made me sign a note for it! A couple of years after Fletcher went on to greater honors the note was canceled by Fred Emery, who, as it happened, had given me the building and was then acting president. As director I had built up a small staff, tried to establish broad, sensible policies; mostly, however, I scrounged, scrimped, and begged with Swaner's help for downtown funding. But mainly with the help of George Tripp and others, I continued to hound the legislature. I held two open houses with catered luncheons for both legislative houses, and I testified endlessly before committees. Several times during those years the bursar met the payroll for the staff for me; I always paid it back eventually from some source or another. Finally, and again because Emery was acting president during one of Fletcher's frequent absences, the university requested and got line-item money in the budget for the museum from the legislature. That was authorized, I vividly recall, on the last day of February 1973; with relief flooding my entire being, I could now quit. There was a museum, it was funded so that the director could be a museum person, not a scrounging beggar worrying about meeting payrolls; I had started and finished the job, the circuit was closed, and I was burned out. I had enjoyed building the museum much more than trying to finance it.

At about 8:30, then, on the morning of March 1, I handed Emery my resignation, almost exactly ten years since Adamson appointed me director. I asked him to appoint Don Hague, who had labored alongside me, to the directorship; and, as can be imagined, I thanked him profusely, even tearfully, for his unwavering support over the many years. In those years I, with much help, had pushed through to the creation of a sparkling new natural history museum which displayed Utah geology, paleontology, biology, and anthropology, arranged against a background of general knowledge in those fields. Its quality earned it accreditation by the American Association of Museums during the second year after it opened. I was, and remain, very proud.

While I was still director (and in my second hitch as departmental chairman), I transferred all the archaeological collections to the museum for curation and attempted to acquire all the geological, paleontological, zoological, and botanical collections at the same time. But I failed to achieve anything beyond the promise that they would be transferred some time in the future. A letter of agreement to that ultimate exchange was filed with the academic vice president, probably in 1970 or 1971—I can't recall exactly. By 1985 the entire building—all floors—was administered by the museum and all the collections were in its custody. While I can take credit for that much, Hague acquired and displayed a valuable

mineral collection, created several large exhibits including a enlarged dinosaur group and a Pleistocene mammal group. The educational activities
have experienced a phenomenal growth from the three Academy of Sciences classes originally offered for children by the Junior League. There
are now a lecture series and travel packages; continuing education classes
for adults; and field trips, classes, and workshops in natural science for
children. The museum is now an educational force for the entire Utah
community. As is proper, its main audience remains the children. I am
proud of it and what has been accomplished. It is interesting that in Utah
and even at the university, the part-time task I undertook of founding the
museum is far better known than my efforts at scholarship.

The above account of the development of the Utah Museum of Natural History is as I experienced it and remember it—from 1949 until I resigned as director. Except as mentioned above, no one but I was involved
in the effort until Hague came; of course, after 1965 he was fully involved
in design and other exhibit work. Rarely, if ever, did I include him in the
financial end of things other than to put limits on what he could spend.
Since his job was on the creative side, I followed my usual tendencies and
spared him the financial realities. Until he became director I doubt he
ever fully realized what a shoestring operation he had taken over.

With the museum diversion recounted, I can now shift the narrative
to my major interest—professional contributions to the discipline of
American archaeology—the field where, by chance, I had done nearly all
my work. Any reader who has come this far has discovered that my professional life has been shaped by no personal "life plan," the courses I followed being all opportunistic. Chance or luck or circumstances brought
me interesting jobs, which I took as they opened up and merely did what
seemed necessary or appropriate or possible within the context of the situation. I also squeezed all I could out of whatever data I had generated.
In retrospect, I presume I was fortunate in always working alone. Because of my earlier jobs I was acquainted with and competing with the
many good archaeologists whom I continued to meet and enjoy at meetings, but there was no daily give-and-take. Probably I deserved the loner
label often applied to me. If by loner one means I made my own decisions
and took either the credit or the blame, then the label is appropriate.

Although I won't dwell on it, I think the single event that helped me
the most professionally was my election in 1950 to the editorship of
American Antiquity, the journal of the Society for American Archaeol-

ogy. My election brought me again in contact—conflict is more accurate—with Robert Wauchope. As mentioned, we had met in Georgia, and he had preceded me by one season at Kaminaljuyú, but this time we were both candidates for the editorship. Apparently I won by a slim margin, and the secretary of the society drew me aside and said I could decline to serve if I wished, with Wauchope declared the winner. Naturally, I refused the offer and said I would serve. Wauchope was furious and would not speak to me nor acknowledge my presence for two or three years. Evidently, he was so sure of being elected that he had arranged for a reduced teaching load, a full-time secretary, and a separate office at Tulane University where he taught, having apparently assured them that he would be the next SAA editor. I fancy he was embarrassed at the way things turned out. Actually, the incident proved valuable for the society, because upon my recommendation only one candidate was nominated thereafter, meaning that the nominee was elected.

I inherited the office from Irving (Ben) Rouse, who was most courteous and helpful in explaining all the logistic and procedural steps I needed to know to get an issue from manuscript to the members' mailboxes. When he had finished teaching me the "business," he then casually remarked that the printers had terminated the contract for the journal; I now not only had a new and unfamiliar job but I had also to find a printer! The University of Utah Press, with some misgivings, undertook to print the journal and actually kept it for something like twenty years, long after I had served my term.

I greatly enjoyed the people at what had been until then a university printshop, but which soon became the University of Utah Press. They worked to very high standards because the boss of the printshop was a Swiss craftsman working to the standards he had learned as an apprentice in Switzerland. As a result, all the printers, whatever their specialties, were competent, all were interested, all were friendly and helpful, and they responded surprisingly well to my effort to use the printshop language, dredged up from my long-ago experience with printing the college annual back in the '20s. The boost it gave my professional career came from what I learned as editor, because I saw all the hottest news, being, except for the author, the first to read any of the many discoveries or new ideas that appeared between 1950 and 1954. I refer to such things as Spaulding's reintroduction of statistics into the archaeologists' analytic repertoire and Giddings's announcement of the Denhigh Flint Complex (now subsumed within the Arctic Small Tool Tradition) as the oldest culture then known in Alaska. More important, I thought I saw vague outlines of system and order in the archaeological record—knowledge which helped me greatly when, by 1965, I decided to attempt a college textbook for American archaeology; it was first published by McGraw-Hill in 1968 and went through two more editions. McGraw-Hill published the second edition in 1974; Mayfield Press published the third edition in 1989.

TEN

On Being a Professor

IT MUST BE REMEMBERED that no matter what else I was doing after 1948—editing, teaching classes, promoting the museum, administering the department, or running the summer field school—I was primarily a university professor in a university environment with all the advantages and disadvantage that may imply. I learned that there is more to survival as a professor than meets the average eye. It requires more diplomacy and political maneuvering than I had expected, but I presume that was merely my naïveté showing. I retained student memories from Chicago, where teachers taught, offered encouragement and directions, and at the same time exposed laziness and sloppy class performance to scathing comment. Based on my own experiences, I even supposed that university presidents were kind, courageous, and wise, as were their deans and fiscal people.

At the University of Utah, however, I soon came to know there were those who were favorable to ideas and actions and those who were timid, or feared change or even action. Because I was impatient with delay and obstruction, I came to deal less and less with the subordinates, always going when possible straight to the top. Thanks to the basic western informality prevailing at the university, where very few well-defined administrative channels existed, or possibly due to my lack of awareness of procedural protocol, I succeeded in moving my projects along well enough. One example will suffice. When I was tooling up for the Glen

Canyon project, I needed four Jeeps, in the larger version then available of the famous wartime workhorse. Although the contract monies would cover the purchase, university policy at that time was to own no vehicles other than those needed to operate the university physical plant. Research vehicles were rented, departments not being permitted to own them. I found that Jeep rentals were exorbitant, a six-month lease costing about the same as one vehicle, given the university's discounted price. After vainly trying to secure clearance from the president's timid assistant, who monitored requisitions for any equipment, I went to see President Olpin himself so I could ask for a waiver of the rules in order to make the purchases. He listened and said the rental company was trying to rob me, whereas he could get a decent price. As I sat there, he called the city's largest Chevrolet dealer, evidently a personal friend, asking what that company's rental charge for Jeeps was, and told him to call back. We sat for a few minutes while he aired some personal troubles, and eventually the friend called back, quoting exactly the price I had had quoted by the other rental people. The president turned to me and said somewhat impatiently, "It will be cheaper to buy your own. You should have known that. Go buy what you need and stop bothering me. Why you people bring such simple matters to me I can't understand. Can't you handle your own affairs?" I thanked him, excused myself, and left, marveling at the presidential mind. I never thereafter went to any of the successive presidents, however, unless I had to or was called—being called was rare. President Olpin thought slowly and brooked no new ideas, although often later thought of them for himself.

Despite the intense frustration I always felt when dealing directly with President Olpin, I wholeheartedly admired his vision and tenacity. Well nigh singlehandedly he changed the university from its original status as little more than "Salt Lake City College" to a leading western university, known especially for the excellence of its medical, engineering, geological, physics, and chemistry schools and departments. Moreover, while supervising the continuous growth and upgrading, Olpin was obsessively protective of the teaching staff and the concept of academic freedom. The state of Utah owes him a great debt.

Upon his retirement in 1964, Olpin was replaced by James Fletcher. Fletcher, if I went to see him, listened, took out his slide rule and manipulated it, then asked, "What's the cost? What are the trade-offs?" and then, "Why should I say 'yes'?" When Emory took over for a year as interim president after Fletcher departed, Emory listened, and as always, approved whatever I wanted. David Gardner from California was finally selected to replace Fletcher after a long search and many visits by several applicants for the president's position. Gardner was like a softly padded juggernaut. Everything he wanted happened. Nothing of which he disapproved did. I seemed to have Gardner's confidence, but I didn't particularly need it. By that I mean that by the time he came, the museum was open and functioning, and at long last we were getting fiscal help from the legislators.

During a short orientation visit by Gardner to the campus after he had been selected and was deciding whether to accept, I earned both enmity and chuckles from the entire administrative echelon. I had learned that no visit to the museum was included in Dr. Gardner's visitation agenda; I felt I had to "sell" the museum, however, because if he didn't see it on that trip he might not hear of it for months. I therefore had a caterer bring crab meat, ham, and roast beef sandwiches and drinks of all kinds and staged an impromptu lunch for him at the museum with me and the staff in our so-called boardroom. Then I hung around the administration building all morning of the first day of his visit until I spotted him and his entourage at about 11:45 A.M. I edged up to the group and introduced myself, saying quietly, "There are no formal luncheon plans, so I'm inviting you to lunch at the museum to get acquainted with its potential." He stared hard at me, hesitated, excused himself from the group, and came along. Once there, we took a quick look at a few exhibits, he heard my story of its creation, ate his lunch, and then asked, "All right, why am I here? I could have learned this any time." My response was short: "I am deeply involved with the success of this place. I merely wanted to show you its value to the university, let you quietly savor its quality, and solicit your strong support when you take office." He looked at me for a long moment and said, "Well, if you are done, we'd best go back."

We went back to a storm of censure and verbal abuse, if not actual vilification, directed at me. It seems the kidnapping had been done so quickly that no one realized the man was gone and would be gone for over an hour; indeed, no one even knew where he was. Later, one of the secretaries, laughing, told me that the escort group had panicked, had run here and there searching the building, and had called the campus police, and was on the verge of nervous collapse when we strolled in. Naturally, her story delighted me, although I already thought it had been a neat and successful venture. So far as I know, Gardner supported Hague, the new director, and his programs. Perhaps he would have anyhow, but I didn't want to leave that to chance.

I learned that a university, like a democracy, has a life and momentum of its own, surviving budget cuts, poor leadership, venal and incompetent administrators, program cutbacks—everything. Its quality may suffer, it may not attract bright new faculty, it may win fewer grants for research, but in regrouping and picking up such pieces as it can, bumbling and rumbling along, it seems to continue unperturbed. The whole process is mysterious to me. One impressive thing is the speed with which the university changes; its inertia is awesome—everything takes time. In fact, academic decision making is so leisurely it makes a glacier seem to be sprinting. All decisions take a year because of the committee system, a device widely used by administrators to avoid making decisions. If they can wait a year, the decisions come ready-made in a report containing the recommendations of the committee, after which, if they are not too outrageous, the recommendations guide some form of action. Committees consider anything and everything. A major problem, such as dividing the College of Letters and Science into separate parts—science, humanities, and social science, for example—obviously would and did require a committee. Whether to change the color of the exam booklets from blue to canary yellow also called for committee deliberations. A committee has a chairman who convenes the group, explains the problem to be solved, and appoints subcommittees, if needed, for a series of meetings over the academic year. The reports are presented, after which everyone speaks, but action is not always taken. Finally, after several sessions at which each committee member makes the same speech several times for or against, there at last is a move toward action. The language of the report is now debated and amended several times. Finally, a vote is taken. If the report, as amended and emasculated, is submitted, it's over; if it fails, the committee tries again or resigns and a new committee starts anew. Committees routinely take a full academic year to decide any matter; hence, change is slow.

The most prestigious committee, of course, is the faculty senate, to which (usually) older scholars are elected. It is seen as governing the university's administrative and academic policy, but its actions, like those of the student body government, are subject to administrative review; in fact, the chain of command extends all the way to the regents. Senate decisions are in effect only suggestions which may or may not be accepted by the real owners of the university—the administrators and the money handlers. This leaves much room for persuasion and horse trading when there is conflict between the senate and the power. At best, the senate can and does influence university policy. At worst, its power is illusory.

Over the years, I served several times on the senate and a few on the executive committee of the senate, where most decisions were made. Usually I held a minority view because I fought against anything I saw as diluting academic standards, as "coddling" students, as cutting programs, as inconsistent with academic freedom, or as unfair to any segment of the university. Some issues I won; some I lost. In the process I was awarded the nickname the "Old Curmudgeon." I was flattered by being compared to the stalwart Harold Ickes, secretary of Interior under Roosevelt, but I felt it was unfair. I did not heckle for pleasure; I am certain I was always defending some obsolete or obscure principle or other. In any case, I think that most committees are a great waste of time. Quick administrative decisions or a flip of a coin would take care of 90 percent of the questions passed on to committees. What do we pay the administrators for? To skulk behind the anonymity of a faceless committee? Above all, committees are boring. I discovered, too, that many professors make a career out of committee service, feeling, as I once did, that committee membership brings prestige.

After a few years I found myself on eight committees, including the senate. Most were dealing with what I saw as trivia, but I thought, "This is great. People want to hear my ideas. I'm an important man on campus." But one evening after a particularly dull session, I awakened. Next day I consulted my appointment pad and calculated the time I had spent in meetings and traveling to them on our sprawling campus. To my horror the hours added up to ninety for the quarter. That is the equivalent of 2¼ forty-hour workweeks. I went that day and told the academic vice president, then G. Homer Durham, that I felt I was more valuable to the university writing a report or studying to improve my classes or reading journals or even talking to students than dozing or arguing ninety hours a quarter. He correctly, for once, gauged my outraged mood. Then and there he accepted my resignation from all committees except the senate, the senate being a forum to which I was elected and which I quite enjoyed. Crossing swords with some of the quicker minds on the faculty sharpened my own wits. I was never again on more than one committee per year and the university ticked along somehow without my help.

In the senate, of course, there was constant debate on matters grave and trivial. Of the dozens where I participated, I only remember a few. One I particularly enjoyed was about an amendment to the faculty regulations to consider whether moral turpitude was a cause for discharging a professor, tenured or not. The proposal came from the administration following three or four juicy sex scandals on campus: one was a physics prof who flaunted his affair with his secretary; another was a philosophy prof who flagrantly preferred the wife of a drama professor to his own. The amendment was wordy, full of circumlocutions, and at no point did it define or clarify what moral turpitude was conceived to be. After the debate had gone on for a long while, I gained the floor and said, "I can't find out for sure what moral turpitude is. I can't vote either way when I don't know the issue. I can't tell if it's good or bad. For all I know, I might enjoy it. I hereby move that the amendment be rejected." Amidst howls of laughter, my motion was seconded and the vote to reject was unanimous.

About my years at Utah I have one great regret: I neglected the state-wide archaeological society after I had helped it off to a wobbly start; I suppose I simply didn't have the interest. Only a few chapters had been established and their existence was due largely to the untethered enthusiasm of George Tripp, whose help I've already mentioned. Bud Peterson of Logan was also a faithful backer. I did speak at a few chapter meetings, and nearly always at the annual meeting, but I felt ill at ease with most of the members. For one thing, they all had collections and wanted to show them to me and did show them to me, a tedious exercise for me. Moreover, they always seemed to take more interest in expanding their own holdings than generating data for the statewide survey. I tried to coerce the several successive survey supervisors into promoting the society, but for various reasons none of them expended any great effort in that direction. One, David Pendergast, did organize a volunteer dig near Ogden one weekend, but his ardor cooled quickly when he discovered that the crew members expected to keep whatever artifacts they uncovered. I'm sure the finders-keepers attitude would have discouraged me as well.

Despite neglect, the society lived and with the advent of a permanent state archaeologist, a position for which I wrote the criteria and job description and worked hard to establish, has grown into a strong support base for several archaeological firms and agencies and university departments now in the state. Most of the government agencies added archaeologists to their staffs after 1975. I am still embarrassed by my neglect of the amateur archaeologists' potential. Now, as I did then, I justify it by thinking that the other things I was involved with were more important over the long haul.

One of the more important things (I think) I did was establish a "scholarly" series—the University of Utah Anthropological Papers. I started it by publishing several passable term papers on Utah archaeology that Elmer Smith had earlier duplicated and distributed as University of Utah Museum of Anthropology Ethnology and Archaeology Bulletins. Until my arrival he had had a kind of loose cognizance of the museum collections on the upper floor of the administration building. Later, after reprinting the Smith material, I reprinted two more important articles by Smith. The reprints were labeled *University of Utah Anthropological Papers* and were paid for with departmental funds. Thus the series was born. It was created because I had just edited the proceedings of the Sixth Plains Conference, which had resulted in a fairly worthwhile collection of forward-looking papers containing new material and I needed a way to publish the volume. At that time, vehicles for publication of regional materials were almost nonexistent, but by having "published" ten papers I now had a place for the Plains material, which became number 11.

Keeping the series alive was a continuous struggle. I took departmental funds, I forced authors to defray some of their own costs, I sought grants from the University of Utah research committee (although I was not yet on the committee); all I didn't do was steal from widows or orphans. Somewhere along the line, perhaps in the late 1960s, the University of Utah Press, under a new director, took over the account and fully supported it thereafter. By now there are about 120 separate volumes, several of which had been useful enough that they have been reprinted— some more than once. Reports of nearly all University of Utah anthropological and archaeological research have appeared in the series.

Somewhere along the line, when there were probably seventy-five or eighty volumes, G. Homer Durham, the academic vice president, heard of the series. He had not known of it before, so he asked questions and looked up old records to discover that no one with administrative authority had approved the series. Since I was editor from the beginning, he presumed I would know something about the matter. He was quite upset, calling me on the carpet, condemning the papers as an illicit action that had no university standing whatever and was, therefore, disgraceful. In great detail I outlined every step of the history of the series, emphasizing the value the papers had for western scholars, that the press took pride in the series, and insisted that he was picking at a pointless technicality. To create a storm about it would result in orders to stop publication, an event which would rack up distinct losses for the Department of Anthropology, the university, and the press. He mumbled about proper procedures, he didn't like irregular activity, and so forth and so forth and so forth. After perhaps an hour of my arguments, he agreed not to pursue the matter. As I left I promised to start no more scholarly series except with explicit authorization from a proper source.

Although I thought the incident very funny, privately I freely admitted that he was right; an unauthorized series could well have embarrassed the university, depending upon its content. But I insist that in starting the papers I was neither devious nor deceitful, I was entirely innocent of guile. I was simply too ignorant to even suspect permission was needed to do something so obviously worthwhile.* I fear, however, that even had I known permission was required I might have ignored the knowledge, because I had already, much earlier in my life, learned that asking permission for anything inevitably led to unnecessary delay, explanation, and, hence, frustration, and maybe permission would not be granted. Better, I had found, do whatever you wanted and, if no one noticed, no harm was done; if someone objected, you apologized, promised to do better, and then asked permission to continue whatever it was you had started. The important point is that most often no one ever notices.

For reasons I have never understood, many university colleagues and administrators frequently and openly expressed reservations about proposals of mine because they could not exactly identify my motive, my hidden agendum, what I stood to gain from the idea. That still troubles me, because any proposal I ever made was to do whatever I said I hoped it would do. Every move I made was one I hoped would benefit or strengthen or in some way improve the university or the department. My

---

* Archaeologists often express their gratitude to the University of Utah Press for continuing to publish a monograph series that contributes more to scholarship than to monthly sales figures.

hidden motive, if any, was only for personal satisfaction in case the proposal made some procedure easier or more effective or guarded against loss of values or standards of excellence or other worthwhile things.

One result of my preference for quality was that I was seen as an educational elitist. Although I believe I am an egalitarian in most things, I am not a fool, and I can easily see that some people are smarter, can run faster, are more talented, more motivated, are kinder, or have stricter moral and ethical sense than many others. I thought, and still believe, that the brainiest and the most talented deserve an education from the most able teachers available. I see the teacher not as an infallible oracle, but as a guide helping people through a morass of facts and ideas; the teacher does not so much teach as show an active mind what there is to learn, leaving the student free to learn what he or she wants to learn. Believing this led me continuously to support high university entrance standards and limited enrollments battles. I lost on all counts. Through the years I watched what I thought was an erosion of standards and of excellence, a phenomenon evidently noted throughout all of the American system of education. However, my teaching remained the same, so I came more and more to be known as a "tough but fair" (I prefer "demanding but fair") teacher. Although I am, in fact, a most genial fellow, with a warm and roomy heart, that does not prevent my thinking that students should learn something under my guidance.

Because I had run many digs, directed research, and been a chairman of a department for about ten years, I developed an effective, if somewhat abrupt and direct, administrative style. I consistently followed the advice of some Civil War general whose name I forget. He said, "When in doubt, attack," which I interpreted and modified to be, "Do something—no matter what, do something." Thus, when any problem came up, I made a quick—or at least early—decision, took the action, and rarely reversed it. I also promulgated as few rules as possible for the personnel working for me. When rules were necessary, I tried to frame them positively.

When someone did question a decision or a set of instructions, I merely said, "That is not a debatable subject." In field schools, when the group was in camp and I was responsible for not only the field research but also crew health, safety, cleanliness, and camp comfort, I was even more curt. When any student resisted the routine or any rules or decisions, I made a quick offer: "Either shut up and do it, or pack your gear so I can get you to the bus station and ship you back to Salt Lake City." In all the years, only one person chose the bus.

I learned that quick, even snap, decisions were as good as if one dithered for weeks about a problem. Employees liked to know what to do, so the administrator should do something sooner rather than later. On the whole, I think the successful administrator only has to decide correctly 51 percent of the time. That way, the organization hangs together and runs well enough and people tend to forget blunders if things bumble along with no great problems. Of course, the decisions which clearly carried distant consequences should be among the 51 percent made correctly. But most decisions are trivial or on trivial matters anyway, so the important ones tend to identify themselves quite clearly. Decisions on important questions must be delayed until the implications and consequences of any action can be sorted out and weighed. Finally, the wise administrator never talks about mistakes and readily forgets them.

In the mid-1970s I was invited to help establish the minimum professional standards that archaeologists should meet before doing independent research, an activity that was of direct benefit to the archaeological profession. The need grew out of the existence of the Environmental Protection Act which made it necessary for federal agencies and private companies working on federal areas to determine in advance whether archaeological values would be jeopardized by the proposed construction or modification of the landscape. A committee, of which I was a member, was formed by the Society for American Archaeology in the hope that it would partially solve the newly recognized problem of how to deal with incompetent individuals doing archaeological work for private or public agencies as required by the EPA; many such individuals were not doing their job adequately or even accurately.

The committee was chaired by Robert McGimsey, who had been involved for decades with what he called "public archaeology," a term I never fully understood. Ed Jelks acted as moderator of the sessions, where, after a day or two of debate, a code of ethics, a minimal training and work experience requirement, penalties for rule violation, and a grievance procedure were worked out and forwarded to the society that had requested it. The SAA, then under Ray Thompson as president, recoiled in horror, not wanting to dirty its hands with policing or enforcing or involvement with sanctions and told us so. The work of the *ad hoc* committee on standards was thus completely wasted unless something else was done.

Naturally, the committee members thought some action was urgently needed or they wouldn't have met and debated, so the original group incorporated the Society of Professional Archaeologists in 1977, I think, thus establishing a new semiprofessional society. The term "semiprofessional" is used advisedly, because the small new society could not generate the same kind of power to compel compliance as could, for example, the American Medical Association or the chemists' organization. Regardless of society clout, the action was highly beneficial in that some government agencies began to select only SOPA members (or those with comparable qualifications) as employees, and some private companies began insisting that the archaeological firm awarded contracts must employ SOPA-qualified personnel. Thus, it would appear that the effort was beneficial.

One of the disappointments I personally feel about SOPA is that most academic archaeologists have never joined, and many of the people involved in administering the archaeological programs for numerous governmental agencies also have not joined. The reason may be as simple as that joining the society is just one more annual professional assessment; or it is equally possible that many of the academics know they couldn't meet the requirements; or perhaps since so many private firms employ only SOPA members, the taint of commerce is repugnant to the academics. I simply don't know. As it stands, for whatever reason, most SOPA members are today working for private or institutional contract agencies, but the very existence of the society and its standards have brought about a vast improvement in contract work, which in turn has led to improved data collection and reporting. I therefore think the founders of SOPA made a distinct contribution in enhancing the professional stature of all archaeologists.

I found that one of the more enjoyable aspects of teaching was the occasional invitation to fill a visiting professor slot at another university. I had five such opportunities: Northwestern, University of Minnesota (1960–1961), University of Hawaii twice (1969 and 1973), and a Fulbright Lectureship to the University of Auckland (1979). At any new school I had, of course, no local reputation, meaning that I had to attempt to capture the attention and interest of students who were complete strangers to me, and at the same time I needed to show them I knew my business and would require certain minimum accomplishment on their part. I welcomed the visiting assignments, therefore, because at those times I strengthened and improved my notes, made crisper lectures; I also felt that I improved my teaching overall because I was able to extend the lecture material when I had no local administrative or other responsibilities. I simply saw it as an opportunity for focused reading and study and at Northwestern actually began to write the text, *Prehistory of North America*, which first appeared in 1968.

ELEVEN

Polynesia

M Y FIRST HITCH AS a visitor at the University of Hawaii gave me a new interest. There I met Roger C. Green from the University of Auckland, who was also on a visiting assignment to the Bernice P. Bishop Museum in Honolulu; from him I learned about the ferment and new developments that were transforming the understanding of Polynesian prehistory. The key to the new thinking was the highly distinctive Lapita pottery described during the early 1900s from the Bismarck Island chain. As a ceramic complex from the Bismarcks, it was merely interesting; but discovery of the same pottery in Fiji and Tonga hundreds of miles to the east created a problem to be solved, especially when C-14 assay showed the Lapita culture to be over 3,600 years old in the Bismarcks and slightly over 3,000 in Fiji and Tonga. It should be noted that in Tonga there was no local knowledge of pottery, nor was there a tradition of pottery ever having been made. The rapid eastward expansion of Lapita and the unexpected age of the complex made it the probable founder population of Polynesia at a time much earlier than scholars had suspected or even speculated about. The proposition that Lapita provided the Polynesian founder population is now generally accepted, I believe, by Polynesian scholars.

After many conversations with Green I resolved to try to participate in the research if possible, and managed to arrange an orientation trip to the major island chains, so that Jane and I visited Hawaii again. This time we were only looking at the archaeological features, then on to Tahiti, Fiji, Tonga, and New Zealand, visiting as many prehistoric sites as possible on each chain. While there I also called upon the few resident local archaeologists on Tahiti and Fiji and in New Zealand, suggesting that I would like to work with them on problems they would set for me. I met with varyingly negative reaction, ranging from indifference to downright hostility, except from Green and his student, Janet Davidson, both of whom already knew of my interest.

Soon after the interisland trip, Green, because he knew I wanted some island action, asked me to go to Western Samoa to investigate a putative Lapita site submerged under six feet of water on the north coast of Upolu Island. The site was discovered during the enlargement of the berth for the interisland ferry that connected Upolu with Savai'i, the larger of the two islands. I found the site to be as it had been described, yielding many distinctive Lapita sherds that were eventually dated to 3,000 ± B.P., the date being derived from associated shells. Moreover, the site was the farthest east of any reported Lapita material and from an island again without either ceramic remains or any local knowledge of an earlier pottery tradition. However, Green and Davidson had found early ceramics on Upolu during their long-term study conducted in the late 1960s. The pottery was not decorated; it was probably a plain Lapita ware, but at the time was not so identified. The age of the pottery Green and Davidson found was only about 2,000 years with none younger being found by them or later by my party.

During my study of the ferry berth material I, of course, met with members of government including Secretary to the Government Tuala Karanita Enari, a highly intelligent, charming man who was quite sympathetic to my desire to work there and encouraged me to initiate research on Western Samoa. I gratefully acknowledge Enari's support through all our time in the country.

Accordingly, I applied for and received a National Science Foundation grant, enough money to take Jane and three students with me to conduct a survey and test excavations on Upolu from August through October of 1974. Fortunately, the best digging season in Samoa coincided with my usual autumn quarter off, I having already spent the summers in the field school situation. We received two more grants, so we went three times to the field—in 1974, 1976, and 1977—for a total of nine months' fieldwork. We investigated fishing camps, abandoned villages, and many house mounds, establishing a fairly firm local chronology from 3,000 to 300 B.P. There was a suite of over thirty radiocarbon dates, which provided a fairly firm basis for the island chronology. Our reports were well received, especially the last one, which dealt with settlement patterning in the period prior to European discovery.

Although the Samoan research was successful in that we did come up with new data, particularly with respect to the inland villages, I was dissatisfied with the exercise. My dissatisfaction lay with the complete lack of interest the students showed in the work, either while in Samoa or later. Their performance was perfunctory rather than zealous, and none continued in Polynesian research as I had hoped and expected. The failure of the students to respond was, I now think, largely my fault; rather than "camp" in the public eye in one of the villages as the New Zealand excavators had done, I put the party up at Aggie Grey's Hotel in Apia, the capital of the country.

How the hotel started is told (correctly?) in James Michener's *Tales of the South Pacific*, in which Aggie was known as "Bloody Mary." While we were there Aggie, who was by then terribly crippled by arthritis, but still visible on important occasions—feasts, Sunday night movies, etc.—had given over management to her son, Allen Grey. Today, I'm told, the manager is little Aggie, Aggie's granddaughter. We knew her as a shy, quiet girl being educated at the convent. I met her later as a freshman in one of my classes in New Zealand. As I recall it, she earned a grade of A. The hotel (where we were charged only 40 percent of what the tourists paid), known all over the Pacific for its charm and quality, was primarily a resort—people came there to rest, relax, loll under the palms or in the crystal pool, sit in the famous bar, eat the excellent food, and continue to relax. The example set by the tourist guests infected the crew each year, rendering their interest casual and their efforts bordering on the languid. Of course I, too, enjoyed the moist heat of the tropics and the civilized surroundings, which were in sharp contrast to the usual field situation. So it is possible that I set a less energetic example than I would have at a field school in southern Utah. In any case, I discontinued research, if not my interest, in Polynesia.

Polynesia, however, was later the scene of one of my most pleasant experiences when, in 1979, I was awarded a Fulbright scholarship to the University of Auckland. Roger Green, now the dean of Polynesian scholars and a man whose research I greatly respect, had asked me, in 1977, to apply for the Fulbright. After I was selected, Green picked my name off the list and I was invited to teach for six months—February through August—at the university. Jane and I both enjoyed the city, which is studded with open parks, playing fields, and a profusion of near-tropical plants and flowers in the many well-tended gardens, called "domains." The leisurely pace of life was infectious. We took a few tours (Cook's) and were enchanted by the rolling, always green hills, where thousands of snowy white sheep were always grazing or ruminating. We lived in a stately old building that had been the Government House, where for a century colonial government had been administered. When a new building was built, the old one became the university faculty club, with the upper stories devoted to apartments for visiting professors and the occasional dignitary. The house was surrounded by gorgeous gardens and parklike plantings of trees and shrubs which gave us continuing pleasure.

We lived there only three months—the extreme limit for transients—so we moved to an attractive first-floor apartment at a hotel a mile or so from the university. Being "forced" out of home was fortunate as it turned out. Jane had broken her leg on our between-term trip to Australia—as guests of Jack Golson at the University of Australia at Canberra—and couldn't have negotiated the stairs anyhow.

One part of my commitment to the Fulbright was to lecture at other New Zealand universities, if invited. Both Otago, at Dunedin, and one of the schools at Wellington invited me. I gave several lectures at each school. At each, I gave an evening public lecture about our recent work at Samoan; both were enthusiastically received, with questions following the lecture for an hour or more, until I begged off pleading fatigue.

I taught only two classes: one was for freshmen that met only once a week, and I spent a lot of preparation time on that one because it was a survey of world prehistory, a class I hadn't taught for several years; the other class for upper classmen was easier, since it dealt with American prehistory. With only two classes there was plenty of time to work with the proofs of the book I edited, *Prehistory of Polynesia*, published by Harvard University Press. I was flattered by the fact that two of the young professors in the anthropology department attended all sessions of the North American class. One, Geoffrey Irwin, sometimes came by my office to discuss the material. I thought him bright, easy to be with, and have kept in touch with both him and Green, exchanging notes and reprints. Geoff Irwin, as I write, has advanced to a professorship and head of the department, after a stint at the University of Australia.

In closing this section on the New Zealand experience, I should like to report my reaction to the New Zealand students, some of whom I grew to respect very much. In general, the New Zealand students were more conscientious in doing the assignments. I discovered early that many of them had good vocabularies, so I tended to use essay-type examinations. My teaching and grading techniques were very unusual as far as they were concerned. I gave quizzes every two or three weeks; and in order to help them understand the few concepts I offered, I gave problems or exercises which made various points about archaeological survey work, sampling, reading evidence in the soil, and such things. In addition, of course, there were periodic quizzes on the material covered in the past two or three weeks. Neither of those procedures were familiar to them. The New Zealand system simply has one endless final examination at the end of the school year and the student performance on those examinations establishes their grade for the whole course over the entire year. It was necessary that I get departmental and then college approval of my procedures, but I was able to do so, and we went along on that basis.

For the upper classmen I offered a course in North American prehistory, while my huge eight-hundred-student freshman class dealt very sketchily with world prehistory as I understood it. For the undergraduates, of course, I merely gave true/false and completion examinations administered by half a dozen graduate teaching assistants. I particularly enjoyed the questions, which were good, but rare, that I got from the upper-division people. But I was most impressed by the freshman class which included twenty to twenty-five or more older women. In fact, I commented on the number of older women starting in their freshman year and opined, "I'll bet some of you are grandmothers." The following day one of the finer looking old ladies stopped me on my way into class and said, "For your information, sir, there are nine grandmothers in your class." Naturally, I enjoyed some give-and-take with even the eight hundred.

The upper-division class was perhaps more stimulating, but one of my fondest memories of that class came on the last day when I was giving a final quiz on the last two weeks' work and exercises. After the quiz was about half over—perhaps an hour or an hour and a quarter had passed—three or four or five of the students folded their exam books, got up and filed quietly out of the room. There had been some preset signal, and they just quietly left. I was amazed and didn't have time to say anything, but I was certainly puzzled. The other students went ahead with what they were doing. In a few minutes, the door opened, the missing students returned pushing a trolley and with their hands full; with no comment and no talking, they walked over to the side of the room where there were some folding tables stored, opened two or three of them, put them end to end, and began to lay out one of the most unusual buffets I had ever seen. There were, of course, perhaps half a dozen four-liter cartons of wine and paper cups; there were smoked oysters, jellied eels, pickled pigs' feet, some scones, some jams or preserves. In fact, an enticing brunch was laid out. Just as arranging the table was finished, another one of the students walked in bringing Jane. He had gone to the apartment and brought her, so we had a riotous wine-soaked celebration of the end of class. Obviously I was deeply touched. A similar experience happened to me many years later when I began teaching part time at the University of Oregon, but I was stunned by this first of the events. When I asked the other members of the department about it, they said to a man, "It certainly never happened to us," so I presume it isn't surprising that I think fondly of my tour of duty in New Zealand.

TWELVE

The Glen Canyon

MY LARGEST RESEARCH opportunity came in 1956, just when I had decided my edge was blunted and that I should try to move to some other school. I was then nearly forty-eight years old, an optimum age for hunting and starting a new job, perhaps at a better university. As already narrated, the museum wasn't a viable idea at this time, so I figured I would simply forget it. But then I was invited by the National Park Service to take a contract for the emergency archaeology made necessary by the creation of a huge lake behind Glen Canyon Dam on the Colorado River (eventually quite properly called Lake Powell, after John Wesley Powell, who discovered and named the canyon). The lake, when full, would be 186 miles long, running diagonally northeast from the Utah-Arizona line to Hite's Ferry in Utah. The dam itself was to be located in Arizona only a few miles below the Utah-Arizona line. The lake would drown some of the greatest scenery in the Southwest, scenery that included near-vertical red and buff sandstone cliffs as much as 800 feet high in places, the wooded downstream portions of dozens of tributary streams containing lush riparian vegetation and attendant fauna, and hundreds of archaeological sites reputed to be spectacular and valuable. It promised to be a tremendous research and student training opportunity that would come only once in a lifetime.

Naturally, I accepted with no hesitation, but many misgivings.

Could I handle the planning, administration, and production of results in a credible manner? Just how complicated would it be? For one thing, I knew I had to think bigger than I yet had at Utah. Fortunately, the seemingly huge sums involved were no problem thanks to my Ocmulgee and Natchez Trace experience, where I had learned to think in tens of thousands of dollars rather than in the hundreds I worked with in Utah, so for this program I figured I could upscale without trauma.

The Glen Canyon project was but a portion of a larger, highly publicized Upper Colorado River scheme involving the Glen and four more reservoirs upstream from the Glen Canyon. Before I was approached, the Museum of Northern Arizona had been invited to survey the left or south bank of the Colorado and the San Juan Rivers, leaving the University of Utah to be concerned with the right bank of the Colorado, the triangular area between the Colorado and the San Juan, and the left bank of the Colorado above the confluence with the San Juan. Work on the damsite had already started by the time I became involved and the coffer dam which would shelter the dam construction and the two diversion tunnels were under construction, which meant that soon the coffer dam would be closed and the lower reaches of the river would be flooded; therefore, the downstream work had to be done first.

Although the University of Utah committed itself and me to the project in 1956, a contract was not expected until a year or more later, leaving a year for badly needed planning since the job promised problems I had not yet dealt with. The Glen Canyon is that part of the Colorado that runs through southeast Utah, splitting the Canyonlands section of the Colorado Plateaus. For anyone familiar with the country as it was, the Glen runs from the lower end of Cataract Canyon past Hite's Ferry and on downstream to Lee's Ferry in Arizona, a country known then only to a few cattlemen, river runners, a handful of early explorers and adventurers, and one or two Eastern artifact collectors who had visited over the years, but left few or no records of their finds.

As always, I prepared for the new venture by consulting books, maps, newspapers, explorers' journals, and anything else that offered detailed information. Before I attempted to create a six- to eight-year research strategy, I needed to collect all the background information I could find, because it soon became clear that the Glen Canyon project was special, with its remote, uninhabited wastes posing unusual logistic, supply, and communications problems. It was not even clear whether search of the area could best be done by surveying from the river, going up each tributary in turn, or whether the work should be done from land-based camps on the tributaries. In the end we employed all these strategies, being river-based for two years, then working the tributaries downstream from the headwaters. In either case, it was obvious that while the fieldwork might be fun, it would be no summer's lark.

Early in 1957 I had decided on the following basic elements of the project design: (1) the excavation units would be small; (2) one competent crew chief would be fully responsible for ensuring the safety, day-to-day living, archaeological strategy, records, and supervision of a crew of six or eight men; (3) there would be two to four parties, each self-sufficient and autonomous; (4) I would have no crew, but would move from party to party all summer, visiting each for a few days perhaps three or four times each season. I reasoned that if I were responsible for total results, I wanted to be present and participate in site choice and at least observe some of the site exploration throughout the project operation.

A plan based on library study is not enough; therefore, between March and June I spent nine or ten days in reconnaissance. During that period I flew the project area twice, maps in hand, identifying and following all the few roads in the area, paying particular attention to the area nearest the damsite. I then drove all the roads, which were either sandy or stony trails and which were sometimes barely negotiable. Unexpectedly, when I had barely finished the reconnaissance of the area in June 1957, money became available for a small beginning on the archaeological work and initiation of both the historical and ecological studies. Hurriedly, I negotiated for the ecological and historical work with the appropriate university departments, which they effectively carried out as planned. I concentrated on the archaeological survey of the Escalante River, the Kaipairowits Plateau, and the area in between.

Only one survey party, three or four men under Robert Lister, went into the field that year. I wanted Lister, who had the experience I knew was needed in the beginning, because it was imperative that there be an experienced and resourceful man managing the "pilot" study, one who would perform conscientiously, finish the assignment, and then prepare a professional report. He did what I expected, setting a high standard for the younger, less experienced personnel to come in following years. He

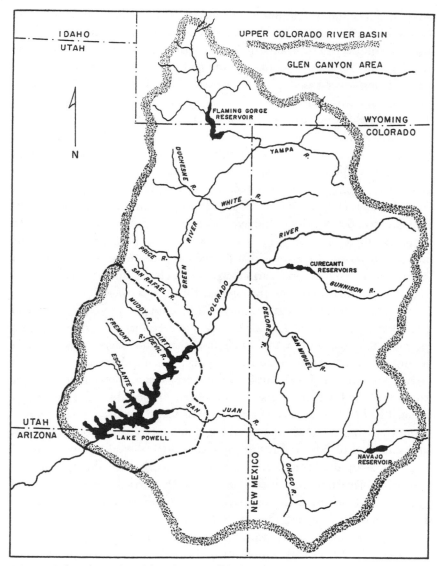

Upper Colorado Basin with Lake Powell behind the Glen Canyon Dam.
(University of Utah Anthropological Paper No. 81)

used the town of Escalante, Utah, where I visited him, as his base. Through my visits to him I was able to get acquainted with key people there in the town. Escalante became our outfitting and rest and recreation base for two or three years after Lister pioneered it. The next year, at my request, Lister took a year's leave from the University of Colorado, to run a large summer excavation at the Coombs Village site at Boulder, Utah, and to write what is one of our best reports the following school year, the first year of all-out operation. I was, and remain, deeply in his debt, both for his work and for his example for, and his influence on, the younger group of crew chiefs I assembled for the second year. The second year truly tested the design. After the first year, Lister had supported my view that streamlined and portable camp gear was essential. I continued to allocate two tents per party, one for the office, personal gear, and supply tent, the other was the cook tent. Cooking gear was scanty, but always included one or two Dutch ovens for bread, stews, and whatever else was needed. I had small, ten-by-twelve-foot tents specially made with four-foot-high walls so that all the interior space was usable.

In every way I tried to envision all that could go wrong with an isolated group in wild country—today it would be called "worst case scenario" planning. I devised a first-aid kit that included a snakebite kit for every man and a supply of Demerol and hypodermic needles to be kept by the crew chief; bottles of salt pills, diarrhea remedies, halazone tablets (water purifier), aspirin, and laxatives were also standard items. I did not include cooks in my personnel roster, leaving the crew chief to make his own arrangements with someone on his crew. When someone volunteered, he got credited with three more work hours daily and cooked in addition to his regular crew assignment. This procedure was less hazardous to the health than might be supposed in view of the wide variety of canned and packaged foods even then available. Almost anyone can open cans, and almost anyone can make a cake or bread from a box of mix. In two instances when I went out on the first dig of the season with a new crew chief, I did the cooking, having, as noted, had previous experience. In both cases some unsuspecting youth hung around the stove, acting interested in cooking, and I immediately apprenticed him, gave him my six or eight basic camp recipes and a cookbook, and designated him the cook when I left. After all, I had come along not to cook but to coach, instruct, and assist the new crew chief.

In only one case did I let the crew chief go—my recruiting had been reasonably successful. Because there were but few qualified students at Utah, I recruited both chiefs and laborers from other schools. By 1965 I could identify thirty-three Glen Canyon alumni from other schools who had continued and won advanced degrees in anthropology, many of whom continued in anthropology and professional archaeology. I had determined at the outset to use the project as training for my own and other students, but the digs were emphatically not mere training exercises. Instead, the excavations were honest efforts to acquire new data as accurately, as cheaply, and as quickly as possible. Living conditions were primitive, the work was arduous, the heats were intense, the students were working for very modest pay, and there simply wasn't time for a teaching dig *per se*. It is, however, obvious that a trained person who can do several things is more useful to the employer than an unskilled helper, so I instructed all crew chiefs to teach technical skills to anyone who wanted to learn something beyond the basic ones of moving dirt.

Between the 1958 and the 1959 seasons, I designed a laboratory and field manual, drawing as I indicated earlier upon my hypothetical research center for the Plains. It was planned that notes, films, and artifacts would be transferred from field to the laboratory every two weeks during the summer. At the lab the records would be checked for completeness, the objects cleaned and labeled and otherwise prepared so as to be ready for analysis as soon as the field party came in. Ideally, the crew chief who generated the data was to analyze and prepare a descriptive report before the following June when he would return to the field on the next leg of the research. Thanks to a uniform recording system already devised, the notes were understandable and usable by persons who did not experience the actual dig. The system, as envisioned, worked well enough. In one or two cases field chiefs left after the fieldwork, but others used their notes to create acceptable, if not superlative, reports. Dee Ann Suhm set up and managed the lab for two or three years. When she tired of the task, Norma Mikkelsen took over. Both performed conscientiously and efficiently; the few glitches that developed were not due to their negligence.

The years of full-scale project operation, 1959–1963, were exciting, sometimes tense, and the exact chronology is today somewhat blurred in my memory. I do recall that 1958 was entirely survey work—land-based with Jeeps or pack-animal trains. The years 1959–1963 were full-scale excavation projects done by two or three scattered crews. The 1959 and 1960 years were handled from the river; 1961 and 1962 were entirely land-based with Jeep transport; 1962 and 1963 were devoted to the two largest left-bank tributaries, Lake and Moqui Canyons.

When it became evident that in the beginning, at least, we would be forced to use the river as our travel and communication line, I again sought personal experience before the season began. As a matter of course, I ran the Glen Canyon twice with Frank Wright, a famous river runner from Blanding, Utah, before I put the green young men on the job. As best he could he taught me the river, how to read shoals, how to run the rapids, and showed me vital landmarks, although I did not enjoy the trips because I was, and remain, terrified of water. I was tense and nervous on both trips, and I suppose my fear intensified my perceptions, but I learned a great deal, which in turn I passed on to the troops. I survived the trip with one deep concern: I wanted no wrecks or capsizings jeopardizing either people or gear. Of course, I later learned that in summer, with low water, probably no one would drown because they could walk ashore, but most certainly I did not want tools, notes, and cameras lost in the river. The fear of upsetting boats was, therefore, less a concern since any men who were dunked merely got wet, but I wanted to avoid the expense of replacing equipment, the loss of time, and the loss of irreplaceable data—they were my overriding worry. After all, we were there to gain archaeological information, not to have adventures and learn survival skills.

Acting on Frank Wright's advice, I acquired two aluminum flat-bottomed scows called Arkansas Travelers—large, stable, flat-bottomed load carriers. Because I was afraid of shipwrecks with the heavily laden boats, I added a high shield on the bow to help cope with the waves when going upstream or up a rapids. No uglier craft ever floated on the Colorado, but when equipped with two big outboard motors they served us very well. Today I would probably use the more usual launches and carry more freight more safely, except that during low water the Arkansas Travelers rarely shoaled as more conventional boats would have. Thus, I felt my choice of watercraft was sound. There were, however, many broken shear pins and bent propellers, with one motor burned up because no oil had been added to the gasoline, and there were sundry other incidents; but no accidents occurred.

For the river years our usual base was Kanab, Utah, with Padre Creek our point of entry, some seventy or eighty bumpy miles to the east of Kanab. If not Kanab, we used Blanding, Utah, where we entered the river several miles below Hite; both towns were good outfitting towns, and we were made welcome. From the outset I had established a ten-day-on, four-day-off work pattern so that every two weeks the crews came in, resupplied, did laundry, took on whatever beer and spirits they wanted, and ate restaurant food that someone else had cooked. I had outlawed alcohol, even beer, in the camps, not for moral but for safety reasons, reasoning that it was easier to fall off a cliff or drown in a river when intoxicated. If there were violations of the restriction, I never knew of it.

My own schedule was fixed before the season started. Each party had my itinerary, where I would meet them, how long I would stay, and so on—a plan that never broke down, although it was stretched once or twice. I hired planes (later the University of Utah had one I could rent), used my own Jeep, sometimes used a horse, but managed to make nearly every rendezvous on time. I got a very particular charge out of the time when, in one single day, I used two different boats, a Jeep, an airplane, a pickup truck, and walked, all but the pickup by prearrangement to a time table. It went like this: I joined the river crew in Kanab at the end of their R and R break, leaving my Jeep with their vehicles at Padre Creek; from there we went by boat upstream to their riverside camp; I, of course, always had my own bedroll and duffel bag along. After three days with them at their two digs, I planned to get on to Escalante, where I was due to meet two crews in that area. To do this, I had planned to be taken by one of our own boats back downriver to Padre Creek, but Frank Wright passed camp late in the afternoon with a load of tourists and offered me a ride downstream. He was to camp about two miles downriver from our camp, so at about 5:00 A.M. I was taken down there and rode with him to Padre Creek, from where I then drove to Wahweep Creek to the airstrip, took the plane I had arranged to be waiting there, and flew north to the Escalante airstrip some two miles from town. I asked the pilot to pick me up two days later at the airstrip, shouldered my gear, and began walking to town. In a few minutes a pickup unexpectedly came by to give me a lift the rest of the way. We reached Escalante by 6:00 P.M., thirteen hours after I had left the crew's camp. I suppose my kick came because all the elements in the complicated scheme clicked into place so neatly. On no other occasion did I complicate things that way. Usually the visits required only driving to the camp or flying to isolated airstrips left over from the earlier uranium prospecting fever of the early '50s, where a crew member waited for me with a Jeep. I spent about 60 percent of each summer in transit or at digs and still managed to keep up with the departmental and laboratory work.

One unexpected aspect of the project was the tension it induced. I spent every summer afraid there would be an accident, with injury to someone or lost time or both. My position was that the entire project was inherently dangerous. Jeeps can break down and strand a party far from help or water in killing heats. Of course, I took all reasonable, perhaps unreasonable, precautions. All Jeeps carried two spare tires, extra gas, extra water, extra rotors, extra points, a spark-plug pump, and a sizable tool kit. Most important was that at all times, too, the buddy system prevailed, or so I hoped; at least I had ordered it. No exploring, sightseeing, or wandering, and certainly no work party with less than two people. As far as I know all crew chiefs except one supported this rule throughout the years, realizing that all rules were calculated to promote efficiency and safety. We were there to recover information, so any lost time was time wasted, that is, diverted from our goal, which was to spend all the money on research. I didn't want to lose time waiting for something to be fixed or replaced or for someone to recover from an injury.

All the precautions I established seem to have been effective—most of the time. I am aware of only four accidents in the six years of operation. One, possibly the worst, was to a man who tried (against instructions) to reach a tiny alcove high on a sheer cliff in Moqui Canyon. As one would expect he fell, breaking his ankle in the process, but the buddy system worked; his companion was waiting below and helped him onto his horse. They had been surveying about midway down the canyon from the base camp. They returned the several miles upstream to camp, where the injured man was given a shot of Demerol; the administering of the Demerol by hypodermic turned out to be the most difficult aspect of the operation, because everyone declined using the needle until one man put the needle through a hole in the man's Levi's, closed his eyes, pushed, and administered the shot. Again on horseback, a party of three or four went another few miles upstream to the only trail out of the canyon—the trail was no more than a massive falling dune that sloped up to the slickrock where the vehicles were parked. With the injured man padded and braced with sleeping bags, the party started to Blanding. On the way they passed Natural Bridges National Monument, where they awakened the park ranger, who radiophoned for an ambulance, which met the party somewhere west of Blanding and took the injured man to Monticello, the nearest hospital. Altogether the injured man traveled maybe 150 miles in about twelve hours, eventually being flown to Salt Lake City, where his ankle was patched up. Within a year he was walking well.

Another accident, apparently unnecessary, involved a Jeep which ran off the road and rolled a few times because the driver was looking at a spectacular view and just drove toward it. While no one was injured, the Jeep was mangled, thereby causing the loss of two weeks' time for one crew while the vehicle was rebuilt. Another incident which caused no particular damage actually pleased me, because it emphasized my rule against adventure for its own sake. It involved a crew leader who, seeking thrills after work, attempted to traverse a long, steep, slickrock exposure alone. There was no reason for the move, there was nothing on the other side; he just wanted to do it. As one might expect, he lost his footing and slid down perhaps 200 feet of sandstone, fortunately on his back. During the slide he lost skin on his legs, back, and buttocks, and landed with a terrible thump. I wasn't there, but I saw his scab-encrusted body later. No better object lesson in the results of reckless derring-do could have been devised and, of course, I told the story to all the other crews that year and in successive years, so I think the incident actually helped the safety record.

The fourth incident was much more frightening. On one visit to a river crew, I found one man literally dying of poison ivy infection; his entire body was covered with blisters oozing serum in heat that was intense and inescapable. He would soon have died of dehydration, so I simply turned the boat around, loaded him aboard, returned to the landing, and rattled the Jeep to Kanab faster than I ever had before. We caught the doctor just leaving his office, but he took time to shoot the man full of cortisone, telling me to put him in an air-conditioned motel room and force fluids continuously—every kind but alcoholic. I tended him for two days, bringing food and drink until he was better, then left him to recuperate until the crew's next supply visit.

There was, however, an epidemic that frightened me terribly. We were initiating work in Lake Canyon, camping near the head of the canyon, in a pleasant sandy spot near a spring. Of course, it was hot as always, and there seemed to be more wind than usual. One or two crew members began to complain of symptoms vaguely suggesting some form of flu. Although I can't recall all the complaints, it was clear that people were ill. As they dropped, I took them to the Monticello hospital, where

X rays showed their lungs badly congested, but there was no fever or other signs of pneumonia. The doctors were stumped, but released them as soon as they felt better, while I brought in others. One man from Pennsylvania was so sick he went back home as soon as he could travel; he was the son of a physician, who advised him to leave. One Utah student was so frightened that he, too, left, although he had not been afflicted. The crew was in a state of panic, and I was only a little short of it. Naturally, everyone wanted to know what had hit us. In Monticello I spent much time on the phone with the M.D.s at the university, trying to find someone who understood the mysterious plague. Finally, the director of student health identified the disease, explained the short and rarely fatal course of the infection, and told us to relax—this, too, would pass. To cut the story short, we had experienced an epidemic of the well-known, but rarely discussed, desert fever *(cocccidiomicosis)*, which varies in its severity. Westerners apparently all have had it early in childhood, when it is usually diagnosed as a mild, short-lived cold; they are thereafter immune. The crew experience fit the syndrome perfectly in that only eastern or midwestern students were sick, with the locals or those from other western states unaffected. When we returned to campus in the fall, the doctor interviewed most of the crew and I believe reported the incident in some journal of epidemiology.

The Glen Canyon experience was all that I had expected and more. Scientifically it was a success in several ways. Over all of the area, the surveyors found and recorded over 2,000 archaeological sites, of which about 80 or 85 were fully or partially excavated. About thirty monographs were published and distributed as University of Utah Anthropological Papers. Three or four papers covered the basic ecological studies made by the biologists, and three reported the extensive historic data, most of which dealt with abortive gold-mining ventures in the canyon. Perhaps the most important discovery we made could be called negative. The rumors of large rich sites awaiting discovery were false—mere fables. The major occupancy was during the period of A.D. 700–1250 by Anasazi small farmers, with slight evidence of earlier preagricultural use and fairly heavy historic Navajo and Paiute presence.

After completion of the project I wrote a brief summary of the archaeological findings, whereas I had written only part of one seasonal report during the life of the project. I did not and still do not approve of the common academic practice in which the professor signs, as senior author, any report of research done under his or her direction. In my case, the men who did the work, the analysis, and the writing were shown as the authors; as a result, several crew chiefs had respectable publication records by the time they received their Ph.D. degrees. (A publication list is a distinct advantage when first seeking academic employment.) Thus, I thought the effort had met all my goals—a good safety record, useful scientific data, considerable training of students.

I wrote the summary after the work was completed and the annual report was written in 1963. I actually undertook the summary three times, finding it much harder to write than expected. When it finally appeared in June 1966, I utilized data from Alexander Lindsay's report of the work done by the Museum of Northern Arizona as well as our own, so to some degree my account became a summation of the findings of both institutions. I mentioned only a few sites such as Creeping Dune (University of Utah) and Beaver Creek (Museum of Northern Arizona), where two unusual irrigation systems were discovered; Slick Rock Canyon, where good evidence of the cultivation of wild plants including prickly pear *(Opuntia)* was recorded; and several where unusual architectural features were found. Perhaps most space was devoted to my argument that the emphasis on the big late ruins and the accompanying elaborate crafts (pottery, textiles, and lapidary work) had tended to distort the true genius of the culture, which had been created and developed by many generations of small farmers who harvested many wild foods and skillfully exploited scant water resources near small areas of rich arable soil. They were essentially desert foragers who had learned to farm both wild and domesticated plants.

Much later I learned that the project had been regarded by many as a model operation and that several other scholars had used those parts of my design appropriate for their situation. Gratifying and flattering news; and I have heard that my summary, which contained some new ideas about the Anasazi, had been for a time in unexpected demand and had to some degree influenced thought about that culture. On the personal side, learning the Glen and working in and near it for six or seven summers was a rich, emotionally charged period of my life. The vastness, the isolation, the stillness, the overwhelming beauty of the land, even (especially) the heat, the still starlit nights, the blue or brassy midday sky, all combined to make me constantly aware of my good fortune. To be sure, I never forgot that it was a dangerous land and that poor judgment or forgetting the water could bring disaster. However, if one accepted the conditions and respected them, it was a privilege as well as a challenge to have seen it and worked in it and returned with indelible, pleasant memories. In retrospect, to coin a phrase—tension or not—I fear I loved every minute of it.

Today the twisting tributaries, the willow-covered sandbars, the flashing rapids are all deep beneath the waters of Lake Powell. The area is still beautiful with the same colors except for the green vegetation along the banks; and the water now laps the cliffs, which don't loom as high today. The millions of vacationers who each year fish, swim, water-ski, windsurf, and camp in the tributaries and some spots on the lake itself see and enjoy much the same natural beauty as I once did. But the intimacy of the river and the side streams is gone, and all my hard-won knowledge of the sandbars, the shoals, and the camping sites is now obsolete, but remain bright in memory.

Just as the Glen Canyon project was completed I began work on the museum as already described and also resumed the summer field schools, trying to learn the full prehistory of the state, working at both Archaic and Fremont locations. The Fremont, dating from about A.D. 500 to A.D. 1200 or 1300, is characterized by good ceramics, permanent housing, and limited agriculture. The culture covered most of the state and provided the preponderance of the sites recorded by our surveys. By the mid-1970s the students and I had established the sequence and content of several regional variants of that culture.

Although the variety and richness of remains found in dry caves like Danger, as well as the complicated strata, kept me in pleasurable suspense each working day, the simpler Fremont sites attesting the success of those farmers in a country too dry for farming filled me then and now with wonder at their tenacity. Of course, we knew from the findings of meteorologists, climatologists, and palynologists that the climate was moister during the 800–900-year life-span of the Fremont and that food resources—wild and cultivated—were more abundant. Nonetheless, when today one tries to visualize fields of maize and squash in the arid valleys of the Great Basin, the Fremont survival there for many centuries remains remarkable.

To be sure, our research showed that the balance between the wild subsistence resources and the horticultural products varied greatly from west to east. The villages on the Wasatch Plateau and westward tended to be larger, often located where streams from the plateau emerged and fanned out over the valleys, with the evidence of cultivated food plants more abundant. There may have been some floodplain irrigation, but that is not well demonstrated. East of the Wasatch in the Colorado Plateaus the settlements were smaller and more numerous, with the subsistence base apparently weighted more toward wild food than to cultivated species.

Between east and west there were other differences. Along the western edge of the Wasatch and out into the basin the above-ground structures, usually labeled granaries, were made of "coursed" adobe mud. "Coursed" means that the walls were made of six- or eight-inch-high layers of mud, as much as one foot wide. The basal course outlined the structure. When the mud dried and would support the weight, a second layer was added, and so on until the wall reached the desired height. To the east, although coursed walls occurred, stone and mud masonry as well as vertical posts, plastered with mud, were common for storage and granary structures as well as occasionally for residences. However, over all of the Fremont area, the semisubterranean pit house was the preferred dwelling structure.

In both zones the carefully modeled, elaborate little unfired clay figurines, of unknown purpose, were found. For most people these little gems are regarded as the hallmark of the Fremont—equalled in excellence nowhere in the west. Pottery everywhere was almost always a strong, durable, undecorated greyware, but was occasionally adorned in well-executed designs in black paint. The Fremont, then, were a hardy people who, despite a somewhat hostile environment, practiced a sound, efficient, and unspectacular lifeway that still commands respect and admiration.

Analysis and reporting of the data recovered each summer by the field school was done the following winter by students working under my supervision. This was done by a volunteer Student Individual Research Group (SIRG), where students were given the opportunity to do data analyses and in some cases to write reports. The SIRG concept was nothing but an extension of my conviction that gaining experience under instruction is the quickest way to learn archaeological skills. The SIRG students met with me once a week, outlined what they had done, and what if anything their lab work had taught us about the site since they last reported. In this way all students knew what all the others were doing and discovering, and they also learned a little about how to build a report from the raw data. More advanced students were invited to write sections of the final report, subject to my rigorous editing, and their sections were published under their names. I operated the field schools and SIRG until 1978. That was my last field season because my arthritic knees were bothering me too much for all-day, active fieldwork. The field school was offered for a few years after 1978 by James O'Connell and Duncan Metcalfe, but I gather it is now discontinued.

Mouth of Danger Cave. Note dumps to right of portal. (Department of
Anthropology, University of Utah)

Danger Cave stratigraphy. (Department of Anthropology, University of Utah)

Sue Price beside one of the six little fireplaces on the beach sand at the base of the Danger Cave deposits. (Department of Anthropology, University of Utah)

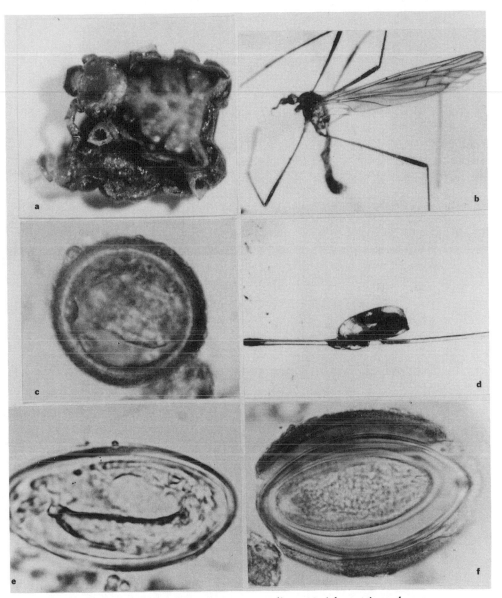

Evidence of parasites from Danger Cave coprolites: (a) tick, species unknown;
(b) mosquito; (c) taeniiform tapeworm egg; (d) human head-louse egg case;
(e) pinworm egg; (f) thorny-headed worm egg. (Department of Anthropology,
University of Utah)

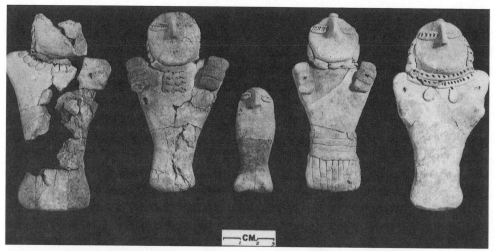

Fremont figurines from Old Woman site, south of Price, Utah, on Ivy Creek. (Department of Anthropology, University of Utah)

First day of a three-day junket for University of Utah administrators and a few Utah State Highway and other officials. Taken at Coombs Village site, Boulder, Utah, Glen Canyon project. Remainder of trip was to the desert and Hole-in-the-Rock, south of Escalante, Utah. (Department of Anthropology, University of Utah)

One of the Lake Canyon crew's camps, in typical canyon country. Cook tent and tarp on left; office and storage tent on right. Although pleasant and comfortable with a strong, sweet-water spring nearby, it is a stupid and dangerous location for a camp. Following a thunderstorm upstream, a typical western flash flood filled the canyon and roared down past the camp. The cook and wrangler succeeded in getting tents and all gear up to the flat area (left center) with no losses of life or property. They returned to the lower terrace in a few hours when the water receded to the channel. The crew, working upstream, heard the flood coming, retreated into a side canyon, later returning to camp unharmed. (Department of Anthropology, University of Utah)

With sons David and Herbert, leaving Lake Canyon after a visit to the camp that later was threatened by flood. Herbert, the younger, is riding one of the pack animals, using the pack saddle rather than the usual and normal, more comfortable western saddle. (Department of Anthropology, University of Utah.)

Fence Ruin. Note trees in present stream bed far below. This photo nicely captures the beauty and rugged nature of the Glen Canyon tributaries. (Department of Anthropology, University of Utah)

Talus Ruin, Glen Canyon, 1959 season. (Jennings)

Defiance House pictographs, Glen Canyon. (Department of Anthropology, University of Utah)

Native cotton seed in pouch from Benchmark Cave, Glen Canyon. (Department of Anthropology, University of Utah)

In Glen Canyon with Bureau of Reclamation party. Jennings talking with Frank Wright, on his right. (Department of Anthropology, University of Utah)

Smith Fork pictograph, Glen Canyon. Note kissing *Ovis canadensis* (mountain sheep) just left of center. (Department of Anthropology, University of Utah)

Informal office photo, late 1970s. (Richard Howe)

THIRTEEN

Personalities

I HAVE ALREADY RELATED at some length the learning I experienced and how much I enjoyed the Glen Canyon project. Glen Canyon was funded by line items in the federal budget, a relatively new thing in the late 1950s. It was due in part to the Moss-Bennett bill which established by law the policy of including in any federal construction budget of facilities on public lands a 1 percent set-aside to be used for historical, geological, paleontological, archaeological, or other scientific purposes. The Glen Canyon funds were administered by the National Park Service, in my case represented at the Region III office at Santa Fe by Archaeologist Charlie Steen (not to be confused with the uranium king of Moab, Utah). As already described, he invited three institutions to participate in the Glen Canyon program: the Museum of Northern Arizona at Flagstaff, the Laboratory of Anthropology at Santa Fe, and the Department of Anthropology at the University of Utah. As mentioned before the University of Utah was to do the right bank of the Colorado River from damsite to Hite and the Colorado River–San Juan River triangle. The Museum of Northern Arizona was to do the left bank of the Glen Canyon up to the San Juan River and the left bank of that river. The Laboratory of Anthropology was to work the headwaters of the San Juan, which included many tributaries far to the east. In this way I again met Steen, whom I had known from earlier casual visits to Santa Fe and

233

the National Park Service headquarters, where I had first met him; Fred Wendorf of the Laboratory of Anthropology, whom I had met once before; and Ned Danson of the Museum of Northern Arizona, whom I had also met once. (I had met the latter two in 1953 at the Pecos Conference held that year at Emil Haury's field school at Point of Pines in east-central Arizona.) Steen I had come to respect as a slow, deliberate thinker with a good brain and high standards of work, so developing cooperative agreements (contracts) with him and meeting his requirements was easy since he was fair but firm in his demands. I came to trust him, and I think he knew he could rely on me to fulfill any commitment. As the work continued for several years I met his deadlines and enjoyed the frequent meetings with him, whether in business or in social settings. Jane and I even went from Salt Lake City (believe it was in November) to Pecos, New Mexico, for the almost orgiastic retirement party the National Park Service staff at Santa Fe gave him.

Wendorf, a slender West Texas youth with the characteristic accent or brogue (which he has never lost), was very bright, aggressive, even brash, and he needled me frequently during a lecture I gave at the Point of Pines meeting about Danger Cave and what I thought it meant. Wendorf, along with most of the Southwesterners, always seemed to resent me, primarily, I think, because I had never attended a Southwestern university, had never (to their knowledge) worked in the Southwest, and was not therefore a member of the fraternity or clan or cult the Southwest has always been. And it's entirely possible I was a trifle cocky—not overly impressed with the casual ease with which their excavations followed masonry walls while I had always been forced to puzzle over the more ephemeral data of an earthen mound. I also sensed in Wendorf the supreme political animal he has proved to be; the certainty that he was a slick and opportunistic operator left me a little leery of dealing with him. At the time of the Glen Canyon work he was the director of the Laboratory of Anthropology, so in our contacts there I was guarded and non-committal in my dealings. Wendorf left the laboratory to head up an anthropology department at Southern Methodist University, where he has built up a strong department with a good staff. At the same time, however, he has himself achieved international fame for his work on the Nile, he has been elected to the National Academy of Sciences, and awarded the Distinguished Service Award by the Society for American Archaeology. Moreover, I am reasonably certain that Wendorf, while still at Santa Fe in the 1950s, single-handedly established the concept of salvaging archaeological sites ahead of construction on federal highway projects. As I understand it, he did it working with the director or chief engineer of the New Mexico Federal Bureau of Public Roads (I think the federal highway agency then had that name). Between them they worked out this idea, and it soon became a nationwide policy long ahead of the Environmental Protection Act with its many constraints. As a matter of fact, highway contracts supported several of my larger projects in Utah: Snake Rock, Sudden Shelter, Median Village, and other lesser ones. In my view, Wendorf deserves his many honors.

Ned Danson, a dedicated Southwestern cultist, received a Ph.D. from Arizona, and went from there to become director of the Museum of Northern Arizona, inheriting a long-established private institution with a capable staff where there was also a tradition of archaeological fieldwork, with one or more archaeologists always on the staff; in all, it was a comfortable, undemanding place to be. Danson was a charming host and easy companion who was evidently totally uninterested in pursuing any personal research. He hired and fielded crews for his part of the Glen Canyon program who, as near as I could tell, worked at the leisurely pace characteristic of the full-time staff throughout the previous years. I think of Danson as passably competent, but a person who had no pretensions of scholarship. My contacts with Danson were limited to the Glen Canyon program, as was true with Wendorf.

Writing the above made me realize that, although I was never a card-carrying Southwestern club member, I knew the Southwest scholars because, I suppose, I spent nearly forty years in Utah dealing with a Southwestern-related culture, the Fremont. And, of course, I knew a few because of my earlier hitch as a ranger at Montezuma Castle, which eventually came to be administered by Region III of the National Park Service at Santa Fe.

Of all the archaeologists I met in the NPS, possibly I most respected the late Erik Reed of the regional office. He had, it seemed to me, the best grasp of Southwestern literature—even then extensive—of any of the people I met. Moreover, he was great company, with a flashing wit, and was generous with his time, his knowledge, and his ideas. Once, Jane and I stayed at his guesthouse during the two-week seminar (mentioned earlier) that he had helped me organize at the invitation of Robert Wauchope; his grasp of Southwest material helped that seminar succeed.

Our seminar was, I thought, successful—I heard later that it had served as a basis for graduate seminars at several universities. Later, I twice invited Erik to Utah as a one-quarter visiting professor. After he retired from the Park Service, however, we lost touch.

Reed was capable of intense concentration, also. Once while we were there, I went over to his house as the family was finishing breakfast. Eric had just finished putting sugar and milk on a bowl of oatmeal, and was stirring it when his son asked a question. He leaned toward the boy and began to answer the question, gesturing with the spoon in his left hand, he being left-handed. While he talked, one of the two huge cats that shared their home jumped to the table and rapidly emptied the oatmeal bowl and quietly left. Eric eventually finished his answer, turned to his oatmeal, saw it was gone, and laid down his spoon, finished his coffee, and we went out to the Laboratory of Anthropology where the seminar met. As far as I know, he never knew he had failed to eat his oatmeal.

Another person I admired was Robert Lister. As already related, I invited him to take leave from the University of Colorado to lead my first Glen Canyon survey party, along the Escalante River. He was a wonderful companion, a good excavator, entirely competent, a good leader, and a diligent worker. Personally he was relaxed, witty, never complaining, but he was infrequently subject to moods of deep pessimism—depression, perhaps. At those times we simply left him alone until he regained his normal cheerfulness. Jane and I visited the Listers at their Salt Lake City apartment, and they were often at our house. His wife, Florence, was a bright, attractive woman who helped with ceramic studies in the lab, ultimately writing a general report of the Glen Canyon ceramic complex and its probable Mesa Verde affiliations. Robert's death in 1990 was a great shock to many, including me.

For me, as well as for most archaeologists, the late Emil Haury is the dean of Southwestern archaeologists dating from the early 1930s until today. My relationship with him always puzzled me. He was senior to me in every way, and I had no intent to challenge him in any area. Nonetheless, I felt a reserve in our rare meetings at the occasional Pecos Conference I attended. I do recall differing with him at one session on some long-forgotten point, but that should not serve to generate hostility on either side, happening as it did at a professional meeting. However, during the life of the Glen Canyon program I was in Flagstaff to learn what the

Museum of Northern Arizona crews were finding. There I was told by Alexander Lindsay that I was mistrusted (if not even despised) by all the Arizona graduate students because I was hard and ruthless and difficult. When I asked how this was known (since I had never yet been in Tucson, to say nothing of at the university), he said it was widely known that I had tried to sabotage the Pecos Conference. On the surface that belief was justified.

It happened this way: In 1953, in order to hold the first Great Basin Anthropological Conference, I had sought and received a small grant from the Wenner-Gren Foundation for Anthropological Research to cover expenses—some travel, mimeographing, mailing and postage, and so on—and I invited the then few Great Basin scholars to come to an organizing session. The Pecos Conference was scheduled to meet probably late in August or early September at Gila Pueblo in Globe, Arizona. The chairman that year was Dale King, whom I knew from the National Park Service days of the 1930s, and I asked to be given a one-day session on the proposed Great Basin conference *before* the Pecos sessions began, reasoning that some of the Southwesterners might also want to participate. I gave King $50 to help defray the costs of printing and mailing the announcement of the meeting and however else it could be used. So King scheduled our meeting *simultaneously* with the first day of the Pecos meeting and used the $50 to put on a free barbecue, for which he named me host! Expectably, there were complaints because many people, as did I, wanted to attend both sessions. So I presume the older heads, which would include Haury, felt I had done it deliberately, whereas I had carefully specified that I wanted no conflict—that I wanted a separate day.

When I taxed King with the mistake, he shrugged, saying essentially, "I thought this way was better. What difference does it make, anyway?" Years later I asked Haury about it; he said he had thought nothing about it one way or the other. I continued to hear, however, from other people that he thought it was done deliberately. It was not my doing. It was a stupid blunder by King. In any case, and for whatever reasons, there was always a little stiffness in the Haury-Jennings exchanges until quite recently. I very much regret that state of affairs because I have always regarded Haury as a man of high professional standards, a scientist and an administrator of great ability from whom I could have learned. I won't attempt to catalogue his many well-deserved honors or his many contributions to American anthropology. His warm personality and a touch of the patriarch in his dealings with students leave him a well-loved and respected friend of hundreds, and I regret we were never close.

But something good comes out of everything. Among the six or seven people who helped organize the Great Basin Anthropological Conference in 1953 (over 400 attended the 1990 sessions) were Clement Meighan and Richard Daugherty, who were supportive then and have remained friendly, generous with information when it is solicited; they are men I respect greatly. No two men, however, could be more different. Daugherty was a dapper, almost foppish dresser, and a politician second only to Wendorf. His relations with the Washington delegation to the Congress insured his great success with grants of federal money. His discoveries at the early Marmes site and at the Ozette Village site were of immense importance in clarifying the prehistory of the Northwest. His findings all over Washington during his thirty- to forty-year career were usually reported by students. Those findings, while less spectacular than some of Daugherty's own, are equally valuable in understanding the prehistory of the Northwest. Daugherty's own writing has been minimal.

Meighan, on the other hand, is a tall, lanky boy from the farm; dapper would not describe him. He speaks with a twangy accent I cannot identify. He favors one leg; evidently in World War II he was in combat some five minutes, took a slug in his thigh, was discharged as disabled, and began school on the G.I. Bill. As he puts it, "I traded an inch of femur for a Ph.D." Now retired, he is one of the respected elders of California archaeology, having made important contributions toward understanding the California story, ranging from Paleo-Indian discoveries to historic times. We were associated only once. I invited him to participate in the Southwestern seminar already mentioned which we called, "The American Southwest: A Study in Cultural Isolation." There he contributed data, shrewd insights, and a running fire of clever one-line comments. Also, over the years I have enjoyed his papers at the Great Basin conferences and at other meetings. He has been supportive and generous with information when asked.

The longest time I ever worked directly with another archaeologist was the seven or eight months Albert Spaulding worked for me at the Natchez Trace Parkway mentioned earlier. He had just finished class work at Columbia with some previous field experience, although I can't recall the area where he had worked. We worked well together. He was cooperative in every way, took meticulous notes, and helped with an improvement in the recordation system we were using, as I have already mentioned. He had a biting, sarcastic wit, was very bright, wrote well, and was fun to travel with on our trips to the Delta and to sites in the Natchez area whenever the WPA crew was shut down.

Many years later, probably 1950 or 1951, when the National Science Foundation anthropology program was being developed, and it became apparent that a full-time program head was needed, I was invited to fill the position. After trying and failing to design a part-time arrangement with NSF which would permit me to be in Washington for part of the year and in Utah the rest of the time, I recommended Spaulding, who was then at the University of Michigan at Ann Arbor. He was selected and served very effectively for two two-year terms, after which he joined the staff of the University of California at Santa Barbara. To him, archaeologists are indebted not only for his influence in enlarging the National Science Foundation allocation for anthropology but also for his reintroduction of statistics into our arsenal of analytic tools in 1952 or 1953. His seminal article appeared in *American Antiquity* while I was editor. It was among the several important papers I accepted and published in my four-year editorship. Perhaps I should mention that in those days the editor had no assistant (I dragooned Jane into proofreading for me for the four years); the editor made the decisions about which papers to publish and got credit for mistakes, although rarely credit for guessing right. Today, of course, all manuscripts are subject to peer review, although the editor can still reject the paper should it not meet his or her standards of scholarship, writing, and so on.

As mentioned earlier, I was associated with Paul Cooper in Tennessee for a while. Actually, we worked together three different times. He was the photographer at Kincaid for one season, my next-to-last season there, and was highly skilled. Then he was on the Chickamauga job as a supervisor when I arrived. While we were there he became very ill with kidney stones. Lewis was there at the time but refused to take the illness seriously. Jane and I managed to get Cooper from camp to a Chattanooga hospital, where the doctors mangled his kidney but finally found the stones. Jane and I thought him too ill to leave alone in the hospital, so we sent him back to his home in Wisconsin, we feared, to die. There the surgeons removed the kidney and Cooper recovered. Later he even repaid the cost of his train fare. We next met in Lincoln, Nebraska, where he was in charge (assistant director) of the Smithsonian Institution office of the Missouri River Basin program. Wedel (also mentioned earlier) was the director, but he spent only the summer in the field; the rest of the year he was in Washington. I found that Cooper had changed greatly. He had attended Columbia University, where he worked under Duncan Strong, but was permanently embittered after some kind of disagreement with Strong that lead to his leaving school. Cooper was himself a bright man, knew a great deal about Plains prehistory, but was miscast as a director in that he disliked confrontations and imposed no discipline. It is true that at the time he had a motley crew of misfits (and one or two incompetents) as crew leaders and analysts, so he is not entirely to blame for the disorganized nature of the Smithsonian laboratory at the time. He was an unhappy man and left Lincoln sometime after I left the National Park Service.

I retain a fondness for the people at the Laboratory of Anthropology in Santa Fe because of the help and encouragement they gave me at what I think was a critical time. I was teaching at Hope, and, as I've said earlier, they supported my little dig at Peñasco Bend. They also impressed me as being very learned: Sid Stallings, a dendrochronologist; Stanley Stubbs, who knew a great deal about ceramics; Dr. Harry Mera (I thought him to be a Ph.D., but he turned out to be a retired M.D.), who knew little but Navajo blankets and late Rio Grande Valley ceramics. The lab was directed by Jesse Nusbaum, who was not an archaeologist at all but an ex-superintendent of Mesa Verde. I held them all in great awe when I first met them, but I soon came to realize that Stubbs was the only scholar there. Nonetheless, I owe them a lot for their encouragement and the confidence that I derived from that brief period of support. I, along with many others, mourned Stubbs's death which occurred sometime in the early 1960s.

Two people who have continuously cropped up in my life are Richard and Natalie Woodbury. I first met them in Tucson at one or another of the meetings I attended there. Later, I saw them at Flagstaff and Taos at Pecos Conferences, at Washington after Dick left the University of Arizona to join the U.S. National Museum, and at countless Society of American Archaeology and American Anthropological Association meetings. Nat is direct, sees through sham and pretense, has a flow of quick and witty comment. We hit it off well and had more than one gossipy hour at meetings or cocktail affairs. Dick is far less outgoing and aggressive, but equally capable of pungent and penetrating commentary on the passing scene. I suppose one would call him a conservative in most matters, particularly fiscal ones. Both are deeply committed to what I presume could be called "civic participation" or "civic activism" as far as anthropology is concerned. Dick has been president of SAA, editor of *American Antiquity* (he took over directly from me after I finished my stint), held offices in AAA, and has served on many committees. Nat, since she hasn't taught for many years, has been even more active on many thankless organizational jobs and committees. After doing good field-work in Guatemala and Arizona, and perhaps elsewhere that I don't know about, Dick began teaching at the University of Massachusetts at Amherst, where he built a strong department of young people. The two Woodburys are perhaps the nearest thing to long-time professional inti-mates that I have. Fortunately, Jane shares my feeling for them, and we have been able to entertain them once or twice in Salt Lake during their almost continuous summer travels. Once Dick kept me from getting a job I had been interviewed for at the University of Wisconsin at Madison. Chester Chard, who later left the profession, was then chairman of the Wisconsin department and asked Woodbury for his opinion about my fitness for the position. Dick told me that he told Chard that I was com-petent, but if anyone gave me trouble, I would rattle his cage. Possibly in one sense it was a compliment, but it may have helped me not get the job, although I am reasonably certain that I had already lost the invitation with no help from Woodbury. Chard and I didn't hit it off.

Speaking of Wisconsin reminds me of David Baerreis, a professor there whom I barely knew except through his published works. I had the highest respect for his views and his innovative work with climate and blending climatological with archaeological data and his incredibly pains-taking work with land snails—microscopic creatures so sensitive to cli-matic conditions that they provide an accurate and fine, as opposed to coarse, record of past climates. In the late 1970s, when I had just finished digging Sudden Shelter (which he had heard about), he volunteered to come to the site, collect his own samples, and give us a detailed analysis of the climatic variations as revealed by the changes in the snail species at the site, which we already knew dated to about 5000 B.C. Of course I urged him to come, met him at the site, helped him collect samples, and later re-lied heavily on his conclusions in the interpretation of the data from the dig; his findings confirmed and refined the coarser conclusions we had reached on subsistence (based on floral and faunal evidence), alluvial and colluvial records, and the artifactual data. Shortly before his death I saw him honored by SAA with the Fryxell Prize, annually awarded to those archaeologists who venture effectively into other fields in order to strengthen their archaeological conclusions, as Baerreis had.

Alex Krieger was a gifted, if erratic scholar, from whom I learned a great deal, partially because I didn't believe some of his most vigorously defended views. He had two major handicaps to overcome: he was extremely deaf, requiring what looked like a powerful hearing aid, and he had a speech impediment which made him almost unintelligible at times. Sometime after his death I learned that his problems were related to a World War II injury, but I had never heard that before, so whether it is true I have no idea. I also heard that his deafness was a rare sort of continuous internal head noise which prevented him from hearing signals from outside. In any case, it was difficult to converse with him for long periods. He may also have been difficult to work with; at least he seems to have lost his position with the University of Texas, where he had, along with Dee Ann Suhm's help (Dee Ann Story after she married), prepared an excellent handbook of Texas archaeology that is, I believe, still a standard work. He ended up teaching at the University of Washington at Seattle after losing an excellent place at a museum in California—at Riverside, as I recall. Evidently he had little field experience, because he supported (in the preface to one of the reports) the dubious claims of Phil Orr and Ruth Simpson as to the extreme age of the Tule Spring materials, and as mentioned elsewhere he agreed with Orr's claims about the Santa Rosa mammoth claims. As far as I know, the only dig he was actually associated with was with Luther Cressman at Roaring Springs Cave in Oregon. His major interest was in the Paleo-Indian. He was convinced, if not obsessed, with the idea that humans were present in the New World during the Late Pleistocene. In support of that notion he traveled extensively in Mexico and South America, visiting all the sites where finds leading to claims for great antiquity had been made, after which he wrote an article hypothesizing an extensive human presence before recent geological times. He called the presumed early culture the Pre-Projectile Point Stage—a concept never accepted by his colleagues. But as I've already said, his work influenced me greatly, both when he was right and when I thought him mistaken.

Although we were never close associates, I learned early to respect George Quimby for his intelligence, quick wit, and industry. Although he seemed in conversation to be interested only in the ladies, he wrote several sound and useful articles and at least one book about the late Paleo-Indian population of the Great Lakes region. I salute his innovative museum designs created at the Field Museum and his later complete and effective overhaul of the antiquated display at the Thomas Burke Museum at the University of Washington, Seattle, where he still lives. He was first employed at James Ford's laboratory in New Orleans during the closing years of the WPA program. When I first met him at a Southeastern Archaeological Conference meeting, I asked for, and received, assistance with my analysis of the ceramic materials from the Chickasaw area digs. He compared the potsherds with those in the Louisiana collections, assuring me that there was little or no similarity between the ceramics of the two areas. I relied on his judgment in my final report.

I must also acknowledge my debt to Charles B. Hunt of the U.S. Geological Survey. A student of the famous Richard Foster Flint, once the dean of American geologists, Hunt spent most of his professional life in the West, unraveling the origins of the Colorado Plateaus and Henry Mountains of Utah. I knew of his work through Ernst Antevs, the Swedish geologist who established the three major climatic regimes that characterized the United States in recent time (the last 10,000 to 1,000 years).

I had invited Antevs to view and react to the Danger Cave relationship and past geologic events; he spent two or three days in the vicinity during the first year (1949) before all the Danger Cave strata had been exposed. Soon after his visit I invited Hunt, who brought a younger colleague, Roger Morrison, and they also spent a couple of days viewing the cave and environs. Antevs was, as I recall it, noncommittal as to the possible age of the lower levels and never provided a written reaction to the site.

Hunt and Morrison, however, wrote a long, lucid statement summarizing what they saw and their interpretation of it. Later, when C-14 samples were analyzed and the great age of the lower level was known, Hunt totally rejected the dates and my interpretation of the deposits. He and I remained in close contact and debate for some years; he continued to question the reliability of C-14 dates—a position for which he became well known. As indicated earlier, I ignored his advice and used my own evidence in reporting the Danger material. I owe Charles Hunt my once-extensive education in local Late Pleistocene–Recent geology (I read everything he recommended and listened when he talked). And I'm equally grateful for the many hours he and I spent in vigorous bickering and debate about both geology and archaeology. Charles may have been often wrong, but he was never in doubt!!! We had good times together, the last being 1978, after he had retired from the U.S.G.S. to live in Salt Lake City near his son.

FOURTEEN

Outside the Ordinary

Dᴜʀɪɴɢ ᴍʏ ʏᴇᴀʀs at Utah I was involved a few times in what I called "fantasy" archaeology. I refer to extraordinary claims for early human activity in North America made by people apparently lacking in formal training and any knowledge of archaeological techniques, unskilled in reading soil conditions, and evidently unfamiliar with the concepts of context and association which archaeologists rely upon so heavily. One of these was the famous Tule Springs project initiated by Willard F. Libby of C-14 fame (who was archaeologically incredibly naïve). After he learned of the shaky claims by Mark R. Harrington and Ruth DeEtte Simpson of the Southwest Museum, of a late Pleistocene presence in the Tule Springs area north of Las Vegas, Nevada, Libby called a meeting of well-known scholars in several fields to explore ways to better understand the "application of radiocarbon dating to archaeological problems." Just what that meant I never did understand.

Among the many conferees were J. Desmond Clark, Robert Heizer, Phil Orr, and an enthusiastic friend of Simpson's—an amateur collector and engineer—named H. C. Smith. The upshot of the meeting was the decision to mount an extensive excavation program at Tule Wash. After receiving a grant from the National Science Foundation, the work was initiated in late summer of 1962 on a grandiose scale.

Through the efforts of Smith, several pieces of heavy earth-moving equipment, skilled operator labor, and fuel for the machinery were all donated to the project by different firms. Then, a series of exploratory trenches twelve feet wide and as deep as thirty feet were dug across the wash. Although a number of trenches (totaling two miles in combined length) were dug, creating clean, cross-sectional exposures of Late Pleistocene sediments across the whole valley, no evidence of either Paleo-Indian or earlier occupancy of the area was discovered.

Despite the hoopla publicizing the event, and the air of carnival that hovered over it—Smith was quite a showman—the effort came to naught, archaeologically speaking. However, the Ph.D. dissertation Vance Haynes based on the geological data revealed by the trenches and Peter Mehringer's analysis of the fossil pollen recovered were very valuable contributions. The nominal director of the project was Richard Shutler, although at the time of my visit Smith and Simpson were much more visible and vocal. Many others had been invited along with me to hear the project outlined and to observe the work and findings in progress. I knew several of the other guests and met many more whose work I knew. Most notable were possibly the British scholars Kenneth Oakley and J. Desmond Clark, but I was particularly pleased as well to meet Yale's famous Pleistocene geologist, Richard Foster Flint. Flint was with his equally famous student, Charles B. Hunt, whom I had known for many years thanks to his help at Danger Cave. Robert Heizer was there as well, as was Al Spaulding, who was then director of the Anthropology Section of the National Science Foundation, who had come to see how the NSF money was being spent. Archaeologically, the project proved little except that evidence of human presence was lacking. Everyone I talked with shared my view that there was nothing of archaeological value there. We also agreed that the earlier Harrington-Simpson finding, which led to the project, had been ephemeral at best.

Oddly, Simpson's faith was in no way weakened by the Tule Springs episode. Later employed at San Bernardino County Museum, she continued her search for ancient sites, surveying the Calico Hills area northeast of San Bernardino, California. There she found literally thousands of fractured rocks on and in an ancient mud flow. In her eyes some of the stones resembled the Paleolithic tools of Europe; she therefore got in touch with and discussed her finds with the famous Louis B. Leakey, whose discovery of *Zinjanthropus* and his widely successful lectures about his work had made his name a household word in the 1960s and 1970s.

When I was chairman of the Department of Anthropology at Utah, I had been able to twice schedule lectures by Dr. Leakey. In Salt Lake City, the headquarters of the Mormon church, which denies any possibility that human evolution occurred, his lectures, not surprisingly, drew standing-room-only audiences. Leakey was a gifted speaker, showman, and ranconteur. On one of his visits I held a reception for him at our house, where he kept a score of students and faculty mesmerized for hours. When the last guest had finally gone, some time after midnight, he then settled down to entertain our two sons with African string figures while he told the tales the figures illustrated. During the evening he (having taken a bottle with him when he sat in one corner of the floor of the room to talk with the students) consumed nearly a fifth of bourbon while he talked. I marveled at his capacity, to say nothing of his creating, after several hours of drinking, the intricate string figures with his still-nimble fingers. My sons both speak of him today.

But to resume the Calico Hills story: Leakey at one point received an appointment to lecture, perhaps for a semester, at the University of California, Riverside, and visited both the Manix Lake and Calico sites with Simpson. Despite his total ignorance of North American prehistory and local geology, he confidently pronounced the Calico site to be ancient and drove stakes precisely where Simpson was to dig (or so she said).

With financial help from several sources, including the National Geographic Society and the Wenner-Gren Foundation for Anthropological Research, and the labor of hundreds of volunteers, a multiyear project was begun. Several trenches and two very deep pits were painstakingly excavated, a centimeter at a time. From the thousands of fractured chert and chalcedony fragments thus excavated, Simpson segregated those few which seemed to her to show purposeful chipping and were, therefore, human-made artifacts. Later Leakey re-sorted the "keepers" and saved those he was sure were artifacts. After five or six years of intermittent work at the site, the claims for antiquity and even the artifacts were viewed very skeptically by most American experts; the geologists questioned the ages ascribed to the sediments containing the artifacts, while the archaeologists denied that the specimens being saved showed human handiwork.

Thereupon, in 1970, the San Bernardino museum, with the help of several other institutions, staged a huge conference where qualified scholars from around the world could "evaluate" the site location, the technical quality of the excavation procedures, and the objects themselves. Nearly one hundred experts were invited; presumably all of them came because of the publicity Leakey's interest in the site had stimulated. The three-day inspection trip included a visit to the site, a viewing—but don't touch—of the artifacts Leakey had selected, and finally speeches by Leakey and others. Of the scholars present, I knew about one-third. Among them were the same people I had seen at Tule Springs, and I also again met José Cruxent from Venezuela, whom I had entertained earlier at Utah. After the second night's dinner, twelve or fifteen of us met in Clark's room, at his invitation, to work out what we thought about the situation. Consensus was that the stones were not artifacts, but naturally fractured fragments. Glynn Isaac, a compatriot of Clark's, was dragooned for the task of reporting our negative view on the following day when speeches, questions and answers, and any conclusions were to be presented. He succeeded in presenting such a brief, vague, although negative review that the hosts weren't particularly offended—at least not publicly. Most of the visitors expressed similar skeptical conclusions. The group then disbanded, and Calico Hills has rarely been seriously thought of since in other than geological terms. Perhaps another day.

Even earlier, in 1960, I had my first evaluation visit at the invitation of Phil Orr, a paleontologist from the Santa Barbara museum who later was involved in both the Tule Springs and Calico Hills work as has been mentioned. He had discovered and excavated one or two or more pygmy mammoth on Santa Rosa Island off the Santa Barbara coast (the name "pygmy mammoth" has always given me a chuckle, being a combination of such contradictory terms) which were radiocarbon dated at over 20,000 years. Orr claimed that one lay in a zone of fire-reddened earth which he regarded as a fire pit, especially since the mammoth bones were black, Orr assuming the black color meant they were burned.

Orr invited several small groups to view one of his finds, which he had left exposed for inspection. The group of which I was a member included Emil Haury, Norman Gabel of the University of California, Berkeley, Dr. F.-C. Cole, my one-time department chairman, now retired to Santa Barbara, and a couple of local geologists whose names I cannot recall. Alex Krieger had been to the island on one of the earlier visitations and had assured Orr that he was interpreting the site correctly as being an elephant roast. I had never seen a roasted elephant before, but I had seen a great deal of burned bone. In my opinion, the bones lying there were not burned. After being shown all the sites and sights (the island is windswept and barren, but mightily attractive in some ways), Orr asked us what we thought. I should say first that Orr had taken time to show us the beach cliffs and other natural features on the island. In viewing the beach cliffs we had all noticed that there were extensive red strata from top to bottom and isolated red lenses in all the perhaps forty feet of accumulated strata exposed in the cliffs, so I, at least, felt that any reddened zone could be the result of wildfires any time during the Pleistocene era. There were even a few places that could have been created by the smoldering of tree roots. Therefore, given the facts that throughout the strata there were areas of fire-reddened clay, that the mammoth bones were not burned or charred, but in my view merely superficially blackened, and that there was neither charcoal, ash, nor a single flint chip associated with the "mammoth roast," I opined that the association of the mammoth and burn zone was entirely fortuitous or coincidental and that no human agency was involved. I even suggested that the blackening of the bones was probably manganese stain deposited when the mineral had leached down through the sediment once covering the scattered bones. Orr was apoplectic, and our relationships were forever thereafter strained when we occasionally met, as at the Calico Hills event. Later in 1990 a qualified geologist made an extensive study of the Santa Rosa sediments and, like our party of 1960, decided that wildfires had caused the reddening. But more important, to me at least, there was in the 1980s a chemist's detection of manganese on the mammoth bones, thus sustaining my twenty-year-old hunch long after I had dismissed the Santa Rosa Island from my mind. I am indebted to Jon Erlandson of the University of Oregon for telling me about the recent study on the island; he even lent me reprints of the relevant materials.

Less exciting, perhaps, but also worthwhile learning experiences were the two summer institutes in which I participated. I don't recall who funded them or organized them, but from some source there was money for departments of anthropology to organize short, intensive study opportunities lasting about two weeks for, I think, both high school and college teachers wanting a little college credit and wanting to learn more about anthropology. When once the group gathered it was exposed to a concentrated two-week introduction to the several fields of anthropology. As I say, I have no idea where the money came from or how long the programs lasted. The first one I was involved with was at the University of Colorado in Boulder, Colorado; the other was at Fairmont College in Fairmont, West Virginia. At the Colorado session, directed by William Kelso, I was to give five two-hour lectures summarizing current thought in archaeology, cultural anthropology, physical anthropology, and linguistics, with the fifth day focusing on a review of North American archaeology (I should point out that in the 1960s it was *possible* to keep abreast of the five fields, and I had made every effort to keep up with major developments; but after preparing those five lectures, I knew I must pull back and therefore concentrated thereafter on North American archaeology). I had plenty of warning, so I worked one week each on the five lectures and felt that I had done them justice. I was a little surprised, however, that my inspiring words seemed to fall on deaf ears. I later learned, in fact only the day I left, that Kelso had told the group they would be thoroughly examined on the lectures by Leslie White, Peter Murdock, and by Kelso himself, but there would be no exams covering my presentations! Although I learned it after the fact, the knowledge did partially explain the vacant stares and listless note-taking that characterized the student response to my remarks. Not that I blame them—all were enrolled in the institute for college credit, perhaps to keep their teaching certificates in force for another year, and if no exam threatened, ignoring the material seems the right response.

A year later, at Fairmont, my assignment was simpler and easier. It was to survey world prehistory with emphasis on North America. Again in the 1960s, less was known in any field of anthropology, so outlining what was known with a little detail here and there was easier, and I'm sure I did it better. One or two of the Fairmont College group had also been at Boulder, and they welcomed me, promising at the same time to pay more attention to my words. There were also in the group two nuns who were bright, deeply interested, and quite witty. On one occasion at lunch I asked them to discuss how their order, a recently formed one, differed from the more traditional ones. After they had outlined the mission of their own order—teaching—I remarked that I would, if I were younger, have liked to have joined their order. The eldest of the two, in her soft, gentle voice, said, "Dr. Jennings, we would like to have you, but you would have trouble passing the physical," eliciting loud guffaws from our tablemates who teased me about taking vows for the rest of the session.

Leslie White was also present at this institute and was expressing his usual view that culture was the key to human existence, that God did not exist, and that individuals had little or no real role in human affairs; he was a source of much discomfiture among the students. Although he was softspoken and calm, his words were searingly disruptive of the beliefs and expectations of most people, so he was much discussed and even resented. He was also a bit of a bully, so he often spoke directly to the sisters when he was assigning God to a minor or nonexistent role. One day at lunch after his lecture had been most eloquent on that topic, he asked the sisters if they were enjoying his lectures. Again the eldest answered, saying, "We are enjoying your lectures; your viewpoint is new to us. Every night we discuss your class, compare our notes, and make sure we understand you. Then we pray for you." Again there was a gale of laughter, this time at White's expense and to his great annoyance.

Perhaps the most interesting and unusual opportunity that came my way was to join Edward Norbeck of Rice University in organizing a symposium on new world archaeology as part of the semicentennial anniversary of Rice University. It came about this way: As mentioned earlier, while I was chairman of the department at Utah, we hired Norbeck for a six- or nine-month temporary stint of teaching. He was well liked by students, fitted into the departmental group very well, and we were able to raise the money to keep him for three or four years, until he was offered a better position at the University of California, Berkeley. Later he accepted the chairmanship of the Department of Anthropology at Rice, where he had volunteered to organize one of the many symposia planned for the Rice celebration. He called and talked with me about it, and we thought that a summation of all that was known, area by area, about New World prehistory would be worthwhile. As we discussed the symposium, it seemed likely that such a gathering would attract a great many already established professional archaeologists from all over the country, perhaps some from Central and South America, and that the whole affair might be very beneficial for all of us. We were pleasantly surprised at the number of professional American archaeologists who did come for the event.

Since he and I had hit it off well, having coauthored a paper in 1955, he invited me to select the topics and the speakers, to review and accept their papers, and eventually he and I would be coeditors of the book that would result. His part would be all the scut work at Rice on the local arrangements which a gathering of this size entailed. The one condition he imposed upon the list of speakers was that I must use Ignacio Bernal and Alfred Kidder II as two of the speakers. I never understood, nor did I ask, about his insistence on these two men, but I would assuredly have selected others. However, we conferred by phone about areal coverage and eventually, with a free hand on all other matters, I selected the fifteen other best qualified persons to summarize the then-available data, relevant theoretical views, and the status of archaeology in sixteen areas, giving Kidder the South American High Cultures, with Bernal asked to come up with some brief concluding remarks with which to close the symposium.

Everyone accepted. One or two of my speakers violently objected and very reluctantly rewrote their original papers when I rejected their first efforts. Nonetheless, the symposium was held on November 9 and 10, 1962. Attendance by students and lay people was excellent—the speakers had been constantly reminded to write for essentially a popular, rather than a professional audience (write simply, in other words), and most cooperated fully.

Rice University, as could be expected, gave the group VIP treatment; we were put up at the Shamrock Hotel, then one of Houston's finest, given luncheons and dinner, and on the last day were provided with a lavish party at the hotel after the last paper. A good time certainly was had by all. But the best part came last: the papers were of such quality that in one book they served for many years as the only introductory text covering both North and South American archaeology, serving thousands of students; it was actually easy to teach from the book, titled *Prehistoric Man in the New World*. Moreover, it made quite a bit of money for Rice University, which had paid all the authors a modest but fair honorarium for their labors, thereby acquiring all rights to the book and all rights to whatever royalties the book generated. All in all, I think it was one of the most interesting and satisfying activities I've been involved in, particularly when one considers the usefulness and longevity of the book that resulted from the affair.

FIFTEEN

Retirement

I LONG AGO NOTICED that retirement means different things to different people. Some look forward eagerly to retirement, so they can pursue their hobbies or avocations full time, sometimes even as second careers, while many others, after a few months of idle tedium, return to their old jobs or similar ones. For those who return to their original work, retirement is merely a part-time or reduced level of intensity in a familiar setting. Such reduced effort may lead to lesser recognition on the job, resulting in an erosion of peer esteem, and the retiree may slowly do a phase-out once more, this time into full rather than semiretirement. Or at least this is how the retirements I have watched, as well as my own, have struck me. My own retirement, since I have no particular avocation or hobby, has been only a gradual, more or less unstructured reduction in my normal work and a relaxation of work habits. I would include here, unfortunately, considerably less professional reading than before retirement.

Although we left Utah in 1980 to a house we had built in Oregon, I continued to teach autumn quarters at the University of Utah. I finally resigned as of June 30, 1986, with thirty-eight years (not the forty years I had planned) as professor there. However, in 1981 I began offering a spring-quarter seminar at the University of Oregon in Eugene; this opportunity disappeared after 1992 when funds became scarcer. I believe my seminars were better since retirement because I devoted more time to preparation before class sessions began, rather than dipping into the material during the course of the class. In general, I find retirement to be a pretty boring situation: there is no great action and little pressure. I know that statement may seem odd to many; few people realize that a university professor's life is full of quiet action and that there is often pressure, both of which have always stimulated me. Thus, I now miss the pressure of deadlines and the writing of research reports—having done no field research since 1978 when I conducted my last field school. As mentioned, I stopped fieldwork because of widespread arthritis which had finally become quite troublesome. All told, in my first decade of retirement I've seen more scalpels and stitches and hospital beds than in all my previous years. In 1981 I experienced a carotidectomy, in 1983 a total right knee replacement, and in 1986 the left knee was replaced. The right one was perfectly done and has served well; the left was only a partial success, so I still limp. A cataract was removed from my left eye in 1990; nine months were required for good vision to be restored. The right eye was done in July of 1991, with vision apparently okay in about six weeks. Otherwise, except for the loss of hair and the lethargy induced by retirement, I remain healthy if creaky.

What is most interesting about retirement for me has been the wonderful and unexpected honors. In 1983 I was honored with the Distinguished Service Award from the Society for American Archaeology. In 1985 I was invited to give one of the plenary addresses at the fiftieth anniversary of that same society. Naturally, both events lifted me to emotional heights equal to being elected to the National Academy of Sciences in 1977. Those three honors were most important to me because all three represented a judgment—a favorable judgment—of my career by my professional peers. Very heady stuff. A similar honor, I felt, came in 1990 when the Great Basin Anthropological Conference, which I had founded in 1953, established a Jesse D. Jennings prize to be awarded at intervals to a person with a record of productive anthropological research in the Great Basin. This, again, was a great lift. Another honor, with perhaps less emotional impact although an equal honor, was the 1986 publication of a volume, or *festschrift,* in my honor, containing papers by several of my better students. I was delighted with the papers which I thought were far better than those in the average *festschrift*—but I may be somewhat prejudiced.

Also in 1986, Jane and I had the biggest adventure of our lives—a two-and-a-half-week trip to China. We were invited by Verne Huske of Newport, Oregon, the best travel agent we have ever dealt with, to join a group of local people he had assembled for a tour of China. It was to visit all major cities in the east, north, west, and south, beginning and ending in Hong Kong. I was apprehensive. I had never been anywhere that I couldn't speak a few words of the local language, but my worry was wasted. Our tour director was a highly competent and experienced Chinese-American woman named Ellen who, with an interesting mixture of patience, humor, and firmness, shepherded us through unscheduled changes of plans, airline delays, and other hazards with great grace and poise. I hold great admiration for her skill.

It would be foolhardy to describe China after seventeen days' experience, especially when that experience was gained in a sanitized tour, insulated from any contact with Chinese other than the local guides picked up at each new stop. It is enough, I presume, to say that China (and all its many faces) is fascinating, fulfilling all our expectations and all we had heard or read. The expected throngs were there; we have all heard of Asia's teeming millions. The beauty and squalor, side by side; the endless temples, shrines, and gardens; the vast scale of Beijing and Tiananmen Square and the government buildings; the rich gardens of the Yangtse delta supporting the Shanghai metropolis; the awesome China Wall, 2,300 miles long; the misty crags and spires that line the river Li; and much more were there to be savored and appreciated. Albeit crowded and rushed at times, as all scheduled tours are said to be, one finished the tour exhausted, sated with successive visual, even emotional, experiences of a deeply satisfying nature. Given the chance, we would take the same tour again.

Actually, we did get back to China again because while our first tour was in Xi'an, where the incredible army of terra cotta soldiers was unearthed, I was able to meet Professor Shi Xing Bang, one of the investigators of the site, whom I had met earlier when he was the guest of Melvin Aikens of the University of Oregon. He and his wife were able to have dinner with us, and we visited for a long while with the aid of one of the tour interpreters. Two years later in 1988, to my surprise, Professor Shi invited us to return to Xi'an for the thirtieth anniversary of the founding of the Xi'an Archaeological Institute where 15 or 20 foreign (non-Asian) and over 100 Asian scholars would be in attendance. I gathered it was one of the first—perhaps *the* first—scientific meeting of that nature in the area despite the archaeological riches. Three days of meetings alternated with three days of all-day field trips to regional archaeological landmarks and treasures. While the papers given varied from poor to excellent as is always true, things went slowly because the use of interpreters, of course, required that each paper be given twice, once in each language. I gave an evening lecture using exactly 100 excellent slides (my own, as well as many acquired from friends and colleagues), in which I visually summarized North American prehistory. It was interesting that, although a one-hour lecture on North American prehistory is undoubtedly skimpy, the lecture stimulated a surprising number of excellent questions so that the total time spent was about two hours. Maybe I should speak to the Chinese oftener; I have never had such a response in the states.

The most interesting and time-consuming thing I undertook in my retirement years was the extensive revision and rewriting of the most successful textbook *Prehistory of North America*, which was solicited by the Mayfield Publishing Company of Mountain View, California. I had been intermittently working on that revision, but with the signing of a contract and the establishment of deadlines I became much more interested in it and made the deadlines so that the book appeared within a few days of the date anticipated by the contract. I did read a great deal of professional literature at that time and the response to the volume has been most gratifying. I count that as a productive retirement activity.

SIXTEEN

Retrospect

Having spent (after retirement) so many pages reliving the eighty-plus formative and professional years of my life, I suppose that something like a summary is in order. No doubt others would evaluate my career quite differently. I will deal with those years on both a personal, that is, nonarchaeological, level, as well as on a professional. On the purely personal level, I would reckon that the Utah Museum of Natural History, with its impact—whether inspirational, stimulating, informative, educational, or boring—upon thousands of children and many adults annually, is the most important project that I undertook. It will, I hope, continue to prosper, playing a socially valuable role in the lives of Utah youngsters long after I and my archaeological achievements have been forgotten. But what is more interesting to me is that my obsession to create a modern museum purveying ideas and concepts rather than merely displaying rows of pots in glass cases was born during my first visit under John Fagan's wing to the Field Museum of Natural History in Chicago in June or July of 1929, an event I have already mentioned. The Utah Museum of Natural History finally opened in October 1969—a forty-year gestation period for one idea seems ridiculously long.

I presume that teaching also is personal rather than archaeological. If one can gather and organize material, present it coherently, and is interested in the subject, he or she can teach. If there is some smattering of critical thought or at least a skeptical stance—what's the evidence or how do we know?—the quality of instruction is, I believe, improved. If the teacher is something of a ham and can leaven the ideas being purveyed with an occasional twist of humor, so much the better. Through the years enough students, both graduate and undergraduate, have told me years after leaving school about the value of what they learned from me to make me think I was a capable teacher. A few very vocal students insist I couldn't teach, but then contradict themselves by saying they learned a great deal in my classes. Very little of how I behaved in class was consciously contrived except that I tried to speak from notes, rather than read, made many blackboard sketches and diagrams, and tried never to stand still very long.

In seminars I usually only asked questions. However, I did consciously attempt to organize seminars in a way that would force graduate students into behaving like professional scholars, even though the students may not have realized it. I "tricked" them into reading widely on an assigned topic, then they were to prepare a short outline which presented a coherent report on the assigned topic, an outline which synthesized data they had drawn from the many sources. Some students succeeded in learning to sift and select relevant material from many sources; some did not.

To evaluate my contributions to archaeology is much harder and probably is a waste of time because any contribution to any field of knowledge is judged by others, not the individual. Any contribution, whether it be an idea or a corpus of empirical data, if it survives testing and proves to be useful soon sinks into the vast reservoir of common knowledge and is taken for granted. Rarely does an identifying label as to authorship remain after a few years. And as time passes and new generations of scholars appear, the ideas or data often become obsolete or even irrelevant as the directions of research change or the emphases of thought shift. Thus, most contributions, it seems to me, are ephemeral as far as the origin of the contribution is concerned.

I further fully realize that any accomplishment must be timely and accepted by others if it is to be useful. The general state of knowledge must have reached a point that an idea or a discovery can be seen to be relevant, that the concept utilizes existing knowledge in a new way or possibly extends it or explains the phenomenon in a new or simpler way. Since I am neither a philosopher nor a historian of science nor much given to introspection, it perhaps behooves me to forego further efforts to explain the reasoning behind the choices I list below.

I count as still valuable three regional cultural sequences that I noted and first reported. The first was in Georgia; it was the simple Macon Plateau to Lamar sequence at the Lamar site, where clear stratification existed. Today the units would have been called an Early to Late Mississippian sequence. The next similar discovery was in northeast Mississippi. I noted a cultural sequence from what I called Pre-Pottery through Miller I, Miller II, to Chickasaw. Today they would be called Late Archaic, Early and Middle Woodland, and finally, Protohistoric and Historic Chickasaw. That general sequence—Archaic to Historic—is still applicable over most of the Southeast.

Perhaps the major contribution I made resulted from the Danger Cave work. In view of the depth of the deposits, I assumed an age of several thousand years; my wildest guess was 5,000 or possibly 6,000 years old. But the 11,000-year radiocarbon assay, making it then and now the oldest documented culture other than the Clovis in North America, amazed me. After analyzing the artifacts and reading extensively, I hypothesized that there had been an ancient foraging culture, exploiting about the same resources through time, that continued until historic times over most of the desert west and down into the Mexican Plateau. I first (1957) called it the Desert culture, then the Desert Archaic, and finally (by 1963 or 1964) I simply called it the Western Archaic. The suggestion from the beginning was, of course, *apparently* quite new, although many earlier authors (whom I cited) had voiced similar views without advancing much proof. Nonetheless, the idea drew attention and extensive criticism (still continuing) and stimulated much research and discussion. It is reckoned by others to have been a useful theoretical concept.

A few years later I reread some of the material I had consulted before I offered the Desert culture idea. I discovered again that in the thirty years before the publication of the Danger Cave report no less than ten prominent archaeologists had published their view that an early, basic, preceramic culture had preceded both the Anasazi-Hohokam sequence of the Southwest and the Shoshone-speaking tribes of the Great Basin. The hypothetical culture they described was what we found at Danger; even many of the same suggested resources were harvested there! Yet at the time I wrote the Danger Cave report, I had come to believe that *I* was the first to notice. This incident reinforces the notion that an idea *must* be timely; if it comes too early, no one notices. To me the interesting thing is that, although I had read the earlier authors, I honestly thought I had arrived at the idea simply by studying the data from the cave as carefully as I could and cited the conclusion to which the data led me. Certainly I had no intent to come up with or claim a new idea. Actually, I guess what happened was that the Danger Cave evidence proved their point.

Other things I am proud of involve others, largely students. This list begins with the Glen Canyon project. I was deeply flattered later when directors of other similar projects adapted my field and operational manual originally written for the Glen Canyon supervisors and crew members. Fred Wendorf used much from my manual (and gave me full credit). Others, without giving credit, used it extensively as well, especially the laboratory organization. At least one other, George Gumerman, credited the manual with helping with his overall design for the famous long-running Black Mesa project. As for project operation, I've already mentioned my pride in the safety record as well as the largely descriptive reports of each year's work, which were prompt and complete. Actually, our scientific results were unimpressive. We discovered scattered Archaic and more abundant Anasazi materials, with considerable evidence of modern Ute and Navajo use of the area. However, we did destroy the apparently deathless myth of many rich and extensive ruins rivaling Mesa Verde rumored to exist in the canyons tributary to the Glen. We found the scattered farmsteads left by Anasazi subsistence farmers, not extensive towns.

Another item I would include is the results of many summers of field schools as well as contract and National Science Foundation-supported research into the unique Fremont culture of Utah. Gathered from all over the state, our data led to recognition of five regional variants. Later, students using the same data but different interpretive values reduced the number to two variants. Our facts have been augmented, of course, by later research; interpretations will continue to change as they are guided by new research interests.

Probably I should cite the results of the Samoan interlude as extending the time depth of the human occupancy of that island group by about 50 percent (from 2,000 to 3,000 years before the present), and I think my later analysis of the shifting Samoan settlement pattern through time added a bit of information lacking up to then. Both of these results have merely merged with the many new findings in Polynesia, and are no doubt already forgotten by the numerous students now doing finer-grained research there.

Although we who did the work and established the Society of Professional Archaeologists are already lost in the crowd, I feel that the opportunity to be part of the crafting and incorporating of that society was a privilege and that our group, headed by Robert McGimsey of Arkansas, performed a service important to the entire archaeological profession.

Perhaps I should mention as an accomplishment the textbook, *Prehistory of North America*, which I wrote and have twice revised and updated. Before and between these editions I also edited three volumes purporting to fill the same need. The first, in 1964, was *Prehistoric Man in the New World* (with Edward Norbeck); *Ancient Native Americans*, in 1978; and the two volumes, *Ancient North Americans* and *Ancient South Americans*, in 1983. These books, whether edited or authored by me, have been used by several generations of students. While most of the data used comes from the research of others, textbooks do represent *some* effort by authors as they sift from many articles and monographs what is needed to develop a coherent account of the regional cultural sequences, their geographic extent, and their slow change into something else. Textbooks also give authors the opportunity to record their own viewpoints on prehistoric events and their positions on controversial points. Therefore, while cheerfully acknowledging the huge debt to many others, I think I can legitimately add these several texts to my claimed accomplishments. In any case, I was, and am, very proud of the chance to pass on to thousands of young people my interest in, enthusiasm for, and the deep enjoyment of the patterned changes I perceive in the story of human conquest of the New World.

Finally, again in a personal vein, I am very pleased with the system that I installed at the archaeological laboratory at the University of Utah for identifying and retrieving artifacts in the archaeological collection my students and I generated. All curated materials are identified by the Smithsonian trinomial site designation, a number that gives the site its eternal identity. Any material generated by the recovery—artifacts, notes, photos, maps, sketches, tabulations, work sheets of any kind—are keyed to the site number. Such materials as the original notes, work sheets, analysis, tabulations—anything on 8½" × 11" sheets—are filed with the original site recording form that describes the site location and

bears the identifying number. Artifacts from a site are similarly stored together as much as possible, and because the site designation number is
keyed to the notes it serves to preserve the provenience of the specimen.
There are a few details in the system not described here, but its consis-
tency and simplicity as opposed to many other curatorial and retrieval
systems makes it easy to operate. Visitors from other institutions who
come to study the University of Utah collections quickly and easily learn
how to use the files and retrieve the notes and objects; often they express
surprise at how well the system facilitates their research. As far as I know
the system is still in use at the university for any new acquisitions. Naturally, I am delighted that it has worked satisfactorily over so long a
period. Obviously, this is not an earth-shattering accomplishment; nev-
ertheless I am quite proud of it.

Finally, although it was the object of laughter and some jeers from
my colleagues, I still think the miniature site as a vehicle for teaching field
problems and concepts is an excellent notion. Perhaps if I had patented
the idea it would have been in greater demand.

SEVENTEEN

Archaeology without Theory

An Innocent at Work

T HESE CLOSING REMARKS, which continue to be autobiographical in tone, result from a remark by a student during a seminar I conducted at the University of Oregon, Eugene, spring quarter of 1991.
During the discussion following a paper given by the student I pointed
out what I thought were inadequacies in one of the sources he had relied
heavily upon. Out of the blue he then asked: "I'd like to know what you
think about before attempting to mount an archaeological excavation,
and how you do it." Weeks later, I recalled his words and realized that I
had never analyzed my attitude toward, or my thoughts about, recovering archaeological data through excavation. In fact, I didn't realize I
ought to have thoughts about it. I presume I thought that if fieldwork was
fun, filled with challenge, and something I enjoyed doing, it required no
further justification from me. Later, I came to realize that my "fun" was
publicly supported and was interesting to many people (for the same reason I was involved, that is, curiosity about the past) and that my findings
should be available to those who footed the bill; in short, those who paid
my salary were entitled to know what I found and what I thought about
it. To this latter awareness, I credit my strengthened interest in natural
history museums and their function as interpreters of technical data.
Later herein, I attempt to answer the student's question.

Then, while I was pondering the student's question, I happened to read Bruce Trigger's *History of Archaeological Thought,* published in 1989 by Cambridge University Press—a book given to me earlier by another student. From Trigger I learned that in order to function as an archaeologist I should have a theoretical base; evidently, one needs a theoretical stance or perspective in order to interpret the new data one generates in the field. If Trigger's view is correct, one must filter the data (either old or new) through a perception of reality acquired *before* dealing with the data. It seems to me, however, that the analyst with a "stance" has donned a mental straightjacket or a set of mental blinders; either of these will warp or distort or limit the analyst's objectivity in varying ways and in varying degrees. However, I recognize that I, too, as suggested by Trigger, perhaps have a materialist, middle-class bias which colors and controls some of my thoughts, and I must also agree that total objectivity cannot be achieved. All of us, teacher and student alike, have some unconscious or subconscious biases influencing our choice of objectively observed facts and how we deal with them. One can only report all the "facts" apparent in the data and strive at all times to retain or acquire objectivity toward them.

In his analysis of archaeological thought through the centuries, Trigger also sorts the hundreds of authors he consulted into labeled slots or pigeonholes. Many of the authors would be surprised, perhaps even dismayed, to learn that they are antiquarians, Marxist materialists, neo-Darwinists, linear and multilinear evolutionists, culture historians, processualists, functionalists, post-processualists, imperialists, and even New Archaeologists. Although I have, I thought, been an archaeologist since the 1930s, I seem not to fit comfortably into any of Trigger's slots as far as I can see; possibly I am a culture historian. Certainly I profess no scientific goals, having wearied during the 1950s of attempting to follow the sterility or the speculative dead-end paths or the convoluted mazes that lie within the tangled forest of theory upon which "scientific" archaeology is based.

Because Trigger's erudite and sometimes tortured prose had left me much depressed, deeply conscious of my shortcomings as a scientist, I decided to consult others who seemed to know what archaeology is about. So, among several others, I consulted the Sharer and Ashmore version, *Archaeology: Discovering Our Past,* published in 1987 by Mayfield Press, and then the shorter *Discovering Our Past,* by the same authors (in reverse order) published a year later by the same press. The latter volume, essentially a primer for undergraduate students, was written in simple, nontechnical style which I felt I could understand. It contained both an exposition of scientific archaeology and a section on how to do field-work. As an aside I mention that there are scores of "how to" or "cook-book" volumes, usually called *field manuals*, about conducting surveys and excavations. The authors of one such book (Hester, Heizer, and Graham, *Field Methods in Archaeology*, 1975, published by Mayfield Press) assesses all these manuals correctly when they say, "a year of read-ing about how the archaeologist works will teach a person *less than a week* [italics added] at an archaeological site putting these techniques into practice." Many of these books illustrate and advocate the use of standard forms for recording such phenomena such as burials, structure patterns, artifacts, and other data.

In their second chapter, Ashmore and Sharer, list the progression of the archaeologist's interests as follows: (1) first comes form, that is, the physical attributes of the objects recovered or observed; (2) the function or the purpose of the object or data as deduced or analyzed from the form; and finally, (3) process and the causes and manner of culture change. These interests agree with and parallel the progression Trigger observed or noted in the interpreting of archaeological data. In later chap-ters, Ashmore and Sharer briefly outline the steps the archaeologist takes in planning fieldwork, describing (1) how to recover archaeological data through survey (i.e., the search for locations where one or another pre-historic activity left physical evidence of one or more events), (2) excava-tion and recording procedures, (3) how to analyze and derive meaning from the materials recorded, and (4) the context noted during the excava-tion. In several places they emphasize that the archaeologist must *never* go to the field without a reason, a question to answer, a hypothesis to test, or a problem to solve; in other words, the fieldwork has to have a specified goal. If in the excavator's mind the hypothesis withstands the test, the question is answered or the problem solved, the goal has been reached. If none of the specific goals is reached, presumably the project has failed.

By their standards, then, I do not qualify as an archaeologist, but I have long been doing fieldwork and thinking I was doing it effectively. Why then, if I had no problems to solve, was I doing it? My answer is simply that I was curious about the past, both the American and Native American past. When in 1931 I blundered into the field there were few data and no time perspectives in American archaeology except in the relatively small area—parts of Arizona, New Mexico, Colorado, and Utah today—called the Southwestern United States. Elsewhere, although there were archaeological materials known and available for study, they were merely old and they were Indian. Little more was known about them. Therefore, in those days one dug primarily to learn whether prehistoric or historic people had once dwelled in or left evidence of their passage in whatever was one's "study" area. Any data recovered were new and therefore potentially useful to others with similar interests, whether they were antiquarian, culture historical, evolutionary, or whatever.

Asking to be forgiven for the foregoing preamble, I would now like to outline some of my own attitudes toward archaeology, indicate my thoughts about the many changes in its content and direction that have occurred since I entered the field, and finally answer the student's second question: how do I do fieldwork and possibly why I do it as I do.

I begin by describing my early field experiences. I should say at the outset that I was never at any point in my student career aware of any interest in the archaeology of any area or of any period. My first season as a student in the summer field school offered by the University of Chicago in central Illinois was not by my choice. All graduate students in the Department of Anthropology at that time were flatly ordered to contribute one summer to the field school. I much later found out that it was because we were learning something about the sequence of cultures in central Illinois. I had no interest whatever in another summer of physical labor, having already worked as a farmer and as unskilled laborer on several summer public-work jobs. Naturally, therefore, I went reluctantly; at no time did I expect to enjoy it! Once there, I found that because I had been a farmer and ditchdigger, I knew more about soils and the "art" of shoveling than anyone else, including our supervisor. Almost at once I found myself helping other students, pointing out different soil textures and colors, coaching them in the mechanics of using a shovel without early and total exhaustion and other practical matters. Being both observant and very curious, I developed an interest in the process of excavation and recovery, although at that time the reasons for doing it were never particularly clear nor obvious.

Within two or three weeks I was given a notebook and a small crew and told to supervise and record the work as we excavated a small earthen mound. Thus, I began to learn how, if not why, archaeology could be done. The one season as a reluctant student stretched into five as I moved from student to dig supervisor to camp manager and teacher for a total of four more summers. All the while I was mentally sorting out the many procedures, separating those that gave us solid perhaps useful data from the time-wasting rote or ritual steps required by the system we were using. I continuously weighed the amount of relevant information recovered against the amount of time required to recover that information. As an example, I cite the discovery of a small cache of glass trade beads while we were excavating with shallow shovel cuts in the fill of the mound. There were about one hundred beads in the cache. Immediately, a trowel and sieve were substituted for the shovel, and the area adjacent to the find was carefully searched for several hours; four more beads were recovered. I thought that four more beads were scant reward for many more hours of work. The important fact was that an isolated and intrusive cache of European trade beads occurred in an otherwise pre-European collection of objects. The first one hundred beads made the point; it was made no stronger with four more beads.

On another occasion, as a thin midden zone was being removed, a couple of charred corncobs were discovered. For the next two days the midden area was slowly eroded away with trowels. Five more cobs were discovered at a cost of thirty-two hours (two men, two days) of effort, but the excavator already knew, because of the first two cobs, that corn was an item of diet. Did a total of seven cobs make it any clearer that the site's inhabitants had known about maize? At that point I began to balance cost against data recovery, that is, relevant new data as opposed to redundancy. In short, I was long ago in agreement with an author of a recent paper who phrased it so aptly saying, "*precision* is not [italics added] synonymous with accuracy or relevance," since I, forty years earlier, had inveighed in a site report against "spurious meticulousness."

Nor do I see any reason for slavishly sifting many cubic yards of midden fill through a three-eighths inch or smaller screen in order to recover most of the discarded materials included in the fill. Larger objects are noted and saved during excavation. Smaller pieces, usually of the same material (e.g., flint scrap, pottery, fragments of bone or plants) do not add materially to the inventory, unless they represent different classes of material. The periodic sifting of samples taken at regular or random intervals from the several strata or local deposits will provide an adequate collection of the microrefuse. In the same vein, I decided early on that a dragnet approach was better than a dip net. Digging alertly with coarse tools such as small mattocks and shovels, leads to the recovery of perhaps 90 percent or more of the *range* of cultural objects and recovers them with full provenience control. The laws of chance militate against failing to find at least *one* specimen of everything at the site, and much more of the site can thus be explored. The dip net approach requires the slow erosion of a small part of the deposit with trowels and brushes and the mapping of every item in order to discover the same discarded objects, but many fewer of them. I hasten to say the sentences above *do not* contend that trowels, brushes and other fine tools or fine screens should never be used; the argument is only to use them where coarse tools would be destructive; structural phenomena, a burial, a firepit containing charcoal, and dozens of other evidences of past activities, *should* be done with all care. I argue merely for realistic cost- and time-conscious selection of tools and a rate of digging that matches the nature of the phenomena being uncovered.

Throughout my sixty-plus years of experience, the procedures used in the recovery, recording of archaeological data, and the kinds of material saved during the excavation process have become increasingly complex. Although from the beginning one was always concerned with site history and the associations, context, and sequences observed and preserved (in the record) during excavation, my understanding and interpretations were improved, extended, and expanded as ancillary sciences, new interests, and concepts were introduced throughout the 1960s, 1970s, and 1980s. In my view the discipline owes much more to the improved, and more detailed insights into the prehistoric cultures provided by the many ancillary additions to the arsenal of field procedures and general concepts than to either theory or "science."

In order to discuss the changes I have noticed, I suspect a chronological approach would be appropriate. As I have indicated in the beginning there was very little background so far as I knew. In the east, where we were working, in Illinois, there was not then more than a glimmering of awareness of cultural succession or of any significant chronology. It was simply a matter of "let's see what's there." If the site proved to be stratified, then there was sequence, but it was local. It stood more or less unique with no regional matrix into which the data from a single site could be fitted. However, beginning in 1934, there were many—some very extensive—WPA and TVA excavation programs which, by the 1940s, had yielded regional sequences (sometime incomplete) over most of the Southeast, from Louisiana to Kentucky and the areas in between; nowhere else except in the Southwest was a significant, tight chronology existent. In 1940 two authors, James Ford and Gordon Willey, were able to build a reasonably complete chronology for the Southeast, drawing their data from the wPA digs. Many of the wPA digs were never reported, but by means of the Southeastern Archaeological Conference and, of course, personal correspondence, the general sequence was known. Its age, however, was then grossly underestimated.

World War II, of course, brought fieldwork to a halt, but after the war two things happened. Perhaps because of the G.I. awareness of other places and other cultures, departments of anthropology were established in a number of universities west of the Mississippi, and archaeological work began in many essentially unknown areas. However, even more important, were the new river-basin archaeological programs which began in 1945–46 and in some areas continued for nearly twenty years. The largest of the programs was in the Missouri River Basin, where some hitherto unknown and undescribed cultures were discovered, from the Paleo-Indian on up until essentially modern times. To a lesser degree the same thing happened as well in the Northwest, the Great Basin, and the Southeast.

In any case, by 1960, there were quite accurate cultural sequences established for every region including parts of Alaska. And thanks to radiocarbon or C-14 dating, which was introduced late in 1948, a chronology based on actual time spans could be allotted to the successive assemblages wherever they were known. Thus, with regional sequences established and generally understood, it was possible to recognize a general continent-wide progression from Paleo-Indian to the simple hunter-gatherer cultures, usually called Archaic, to the complex, so-called higher cultures which would include the Hopewellian, the Mississippian, and the several Southwestern cultures. This succession was documented for most of the continent with the result that research interest shifted to questions of why, when, and how. The new interests, I believe, were conceived as being likely to "flesh out" the bare bones of the culture history that was available in most places.

In the 1960s, there was also introduced the New Archaeology, and the interest of many young scholars swung to the more exciting (in their view) concerns with science, theory, and speculation. Speculation is really fun, because little or no data are required. These interests became dominant and the mundane interest I and many others had in culture history was regarded either as a waste of time or merely the interest of senile old men. In fact, I would say that for a time the term *culture history* not only fell into disuse but also was almost an obscenity, not to be mentioned in mixed company. I, at least, was untouched by the interest in theory because in the '50s I had already read the logical positivists' views and they seemed to me too sterile, too remote to engage anyone interested in the past as such. It was too remote for those of us who thought of prehistory as a human activity, as human behavior, rather than events acting in response to obscure and unidentified scientific laws. The discipline survived the New Archaeology era quite well; many of its most ardent practitioners are now concerned with other, perhaps more mundane, aspects of archaeology. There came, however, in 1972 and 1973, a totally new concept—Cultural Resource Management (CRM)—which was born and has flourished ever since. The goals of CRM are different, being neither culture history nor theory. They will be discussed later.

In order to learn my own attitude toward all this, I will revert to the '50s and try to isolate the events that enlarged, expanded, improved, and helped focus the archaeology I know and have practiced.

The most important concept introduced in the 1950s was the general notion of cultural ecology. That simple concept—cultural ecology—led to a number of lesser interests, all of which were focused on the general matter of human adaptation to environment. Among them, of course, were the paleoenvironment and subsistence patterning, both of which singly and together began to establish the natural theater where prehistoric peoples pursued their livelihood. The two studies continuously increased and refined our knowledge of the climate and the inventory of plants and animals characteristic of any given period of time. The sourcing of lithic and metal materials used in prehistoric tools and handicrafts began in turn to give insights into trade and commerce, and to some extent they testified to the more ephemeral social influence of the ideas and beliefs that were recognized as possible social concomitants of the exchange of material goods.

Also early, and of perhaps importance equal to that of cultural ecology, was the formal awareness of, and attempts to define, the significance of settlement patterning. Although field archaeologists had long known that sites were not randomly distributed but were purposefully situated and that an experienced surveyor could predict where sites would be found, the elaboration, definition, and formalization of the idea greatly expanded access to some of the details of the functioning of the prehistoric cultures. It provided hitherto unrecognized clues to resource exploitation, evidence of social systems and social ordering, trade, social stratification, and perhaps even politics.

About the same time, and diametrically opposed to the interpretive advantages of settlement patterning, was the introduction of the idea of sampling. It was argued that a "scientifically" designed sampling program would give an accurate inventory of the kinds (and the ratio among them) of all the sites in any given study area. It was based on the ill-starred notion that archaeological sites are evenly distributed across any area large or small. It was asserted that a 1 or 2 or 10 or 20 percent sample would provide an adequate or accurate estimate of the cultures within a study area. The fallacy of such procedures slowly, far too slowly, became apparent; so far as I know sampling in order to establish a site inventory is rarely used today. Searching for sites in areas where there are reasons to suspect there are some is today, I believe, called "intuitive" survey. However, I must also say that combining a uniform sampling procedure with the settlement pattern concept, that is, sampling where cultural evidence is known to exist—in order to learn the range of prehistoric remains represented in the study area—is both valid and useful.

Also, a few students began to use the optimal foraging concept (sometimes called evolutionary biology) as an explanatory tool. That approach basically means that the caloric input of the known foodstuffs is weighed against the costs of time and effort of procuring, transporting, and preparing dietary items. Optimal foraging is no more than the long-known minimum-effort–maximum-gain economic theory as it is applicable to the study of subsistence.

During this same period, another concept developed. Labeled "spatial analysis" (it could be called "microarchaeology"), it was a study concerned with how prehistoric peoples allocated space for domestic and village activities. The concern with spatial use is connected with a concern a few scholars have with the patterning of discard of debris from eating and food preparation and manufacturing activities. A *primary* deposit was one where waste materials lay where they fell during manufacture or during eating, with *secondary* deposits occurring where waste materials were redeposited outside the activity area—in short, were picked up and tossed or scraped together and placed somewhere else. The question of primary versus secondary discard is important in that it helps establish the associational validity of any objects found together; if the waste were generated at the location where it was found—that is, a primary deposit—the interpretation of the materials would be quite different from that for materials fortuitously associated after being collected and redeposited in a spot different from the one where they had been generated.

Some of the spatial studies are actually quite amusing. In a recent *American Antiquity* there was an article reporting spatial analysis of the microdebitage of items less than fifty millimeters in diameter found on a prehistoric house floor. After literally hundreds of hours of trowel cleaning, collecting, sifting, flotation, and sorting of tiny scraps of bone, plant parts, and flint chips, the authors quietly concluded that the flint knapper sat indoors on the south side of and close to the central fireplace. In all fairness, the authors somewhat plaintively note that the interpretive insights gained by the exercise may not have repaid the hundreds of hours of effort expended. To the objective observer, it certainly seems to be another case of "much threshing for little grain."

There are other fine-focused areas of study that seem to be rewarding in providing knowledge of prehistoric behaviors. One is the replication by modern flint knappers of artifact forms recovered during archaeological study, followed by the use of those same stone tools on various materials (bone, wood, hide) in an attempt to understand use wear and, in this way, perhaps determine how such tools were actually originally used. Other interesting and quite rewarding detailed studies concern the many variations in the ways ceramic vessels are created. Such analyses help in determining the probable uses for which various vessels were destined— dry storage of foods, cooking, transporting water or other liquid, or liquid storage. Both subsistence and domestic tasks can be thus inferred from ceramic fabric.

One of the most unexpected contributions to the study of subsistence or diet was the discovery that the ratio of C-13 to C-14 in human bone reflected a diet heavy with maize or lacking it. Although all plants take up and use carbon, the tropical plants, including maize, utilize more C-13 and less C-14, while plants grown in the temperate zones utilize more C-14. This discovery, which was made by physical anthropologists, was extremely important in that it settled a long-standing debate as to just when the several aboriginal American groups began to use maize, a plant that originated in Mexico, in their diet. The availability of maize in a culture thus became detectable through the analysis of human bone even though no maize parts were found at the site. In any case, the search for trace elements has established the timing of the distribution of maize across the continent for all areas where agriculture was practiced. As mentioned earlier, both environmental and dietary data have also been recovered from pollen grains and phytoliths.

Although several new avenues of study aimed at deeper understanding of prehistoric behavior exist, the ones cited above exemplify the changes in the direction of the study of prehistoric cultures in the decades after 1960. Fieldwork, of course, became increasingly complex as the newer areas of interest required the excavator to notice and recover more varied data. There was a concomitant loss of interest in culture history as such. But by the late 1980s culture history was no longer a dirty word, and we see a resumption of interest in that area of archaeological endeavor.

Up until the 1970s, with the exception of the large emergency projects in the river basins of the '40s and '50s, most archaeological research was done by individuals based in universities or museums, rarely involving many people either in the laboratory or in the field. The drastic change that occurred in the 1970s was Cultural Resource Management (CRM), mentioned earlier. Because of CRM and those involved in it, American archaeology has undergone significant, and I think probably permanent, change. The change came because CRM has neither science nor culture history as its major goal, but aims instead at preservation of the past. It is an outgrowth of the Environmental Protection Act and is currently nurtured by huge sums of federal money. As a result, CRM has come to dominate the American archaeological profession.

It is not possible to describe the CRM juggernaut quickly nor simply. There is, of course, a huge federal component, especially among the land-holding agencies, these being primarily the National Park Service, the Bureau of Land Management, the Bureau of Reclamation, the Corps of Engineers, the Forest Service, and to some extent the Soil Conservation Service, where the interest is in preservation and "outreach." *Outreach* is a trendy term that translates to public education about and heightened appreciation of the American archaeological past, whether it be Native American or the past 500 years of European presence. There are numerous catch phrases: "Save the Past for the Present," "The Past is Key to the

Future," "Make the Past Live Again"—all of which are aimed at increasing public awareness of the American heritage. That heritage would include, of course, all of the Native American material, although few Americans today can claim to be connected genetically to that history.

The explanation of the interest in archaeology, I believe, is simpler than heritage, genetic or otherwise. The effectiveness of the "outreach" is rooted, I think, in the more deeply seated interest all people seem to have in the human past. If it is ancient and leaves its evidence, it is interesting. CRM has become so important to the federal government that there is a journal called *CRM* which was in its sixteenth year in 1993. Published by the National Parks Service, it is devoted exclusively to government activity in the archaeological and archaeological education fields. By 1993, according to the publication, at least twenty-two states held "Archaeology Weeks." During these Weeks there are local lectures, flint-chipping demonstrations, visits to operating digs (if available), and other events over the state that attract thousands of visitors. As would be expected, many grade and high school students attend the events. The Weeks are sponsored by federal agencies, historical societies, various professional groups, even private companies, or a combination of such groups.

So, as a result of federal interest in preserving the American heritage, and as a result of salvaging archaeological data from locations where such material is threatened by highway, airport, gas-, oil-, and water-pipelines, and other construction, the demand in the 1970s for trained archaeologists far exceeded the supply of skilled field personnel then available from museums, colleges, or universities. In the face of heavy demand, therefore, many private firms appeared overnight and began contracting for CRM excavation jobs. Rarely were the firms headed by experienced people; many were clearly incompetent. Contracts were simply let to the low bidders, with no apparent effort by the agencies involved to weigh the experience, reputation, or competence of the contracting firm or its members. As a result, many of the projects of the '70s were criminally inept and the results without value. Moreover, the contracting agencies prescribed in great detail the kinds of data to be included in the reports and even the form and sequence of presentation. The result is a vast backlog of gray literature often prolix and repetitive, containing material irrelevant in the reporting of the phenomena observed or recorded and the conclusions derived from the evidence. As one author so succinctly puts it, "[CRM] is increasingly standardized and regulated."

Beginning in the 1980s, however, private firms began to hire better qualified personnel, who bid higher so that more money and time were made available for laboratory study and analysis, and, importantly, better and more complete data were generated. However, the reports of large informative projects are still dull and boring as a result of being forced into a straightjacket of prescribed report format. Although reams could be written (both good and bad) about CRM archaeology, the fact is that it has changed the nature of American archaeology. Today, probably half of the several thousand identified American archaeologists are employed in CRM work, whereas in the early '70s almost all, perhaps 90 percent, or more, of the qualified people had academic or museum affiliations. Along with the tendency of contractors to use personnel who meet higher professional standards, there is a marked improvement in the quality of final reports despite the bureaucratic emphasis on form over content.

Regardless of anyone's reaction to it, CRM is an exceedingly powerful force today, and will be for the foreseeable future. One can only hope that more of the well-prepared reports find their way out of the gray and into the professional journals and scholarly journals.

Now, IN A DIFFERENT vein I will attempt to answer the question: "How do you do archaeology?" by attempting to describe briefly and directly how I approach the excavation of a single site.

In the account which follows, it is assumed that the site location is known, and the tools, labor, and all the resources needed, including money for a few weeks of operation, are at hand. The question then is how does one approach the site one intends to excavate? Very early in my experience as an excavator, I developed a few procedures that allowed me to attack a site more or less confidently, and I use the work *attack* advisedly in that I came early to regard a site as a skilled opponent against whom I was competing in a complicated game—one moreover, where the opponent sets the rules. (Is the site stratified? Are the strata clear or blurred? Were the soils brought in by humans or deposited by water or wind? Have animals or later humans modified the site after an initial abandonment? Does it contain complex structures? The list of possible complications to be encountered in any site is endless). And I, the excavator working back through time, must learn the rules before I can begin to learn, in spite of the conditions set by both humans and nature, the natural and cultural history of that location. Cultural history, of course, equates with human activity at the site. Natural history includes the effects of erosion, deposition, animal depredations (badgers, rabbits, gophers, and other animals who make tunnels or dens), whatever has gone on at the site since its abandonment. I learned early that each site is unique and guards its secrets in its own way. Therefore, to bring a theory to be tested or a preconception of what the site contains is to impose upon oneself a set of real handicaps.

Instead, I begin each game with my mind a blank. (Some friends have told me that beginning with my mind blank should require almost no effort on my part). The site is unique as is its history, and I can unravel it only by observing and pondering (possibly understanding) all the countless bits of evidence of both the natural and human events that have occurred. I learn them one by one as work progresses shovelful by shovelful. As I slowly learn the internal details of the site and the conditions under which the contest is being waged, with luck I can also learn the history, the story of human behavior that it tells, and the purpose or purposes for which the site was long ago utilized.

To excavate successfully requires the excavator to have curiosity, patience and a high tolerance for hours of boredom and an awareness that he or she may miss one or another key piece of evidence. However, he or she is protected by a stance of vigilance and what I should perhaps call concentration. I do not mean the concentration and instantaneous response time of an Indy race-car driver or a basketball superstar, but an almost subconscious sensitivity to detail, detecting the slightest changes in soil texture or color, which may herald a change in the conditions of the game. In short, the excavator is constantly honing his or her observational skills and recording what is seen. Although the laborers, whether hired help or students or volunteers, are an extension of the excavator's eyes and tactile nerves, he or she must be continuously on the move, visiting each location within the site where work is going on. For me, an excavator who spends hours personally working at, let us say, cleaning a burial, or carefully uncovering a floor and doing nothing else, will inevitably lose some elusive bit of evidence elsewhere in the site because the helpers didn't see it and he or she was not there to see it. At the end of the dig, terminated by physical constraints, time limitations, weather, total eradication of the site, or whatever else, with luck the site can be re-created descriptively and, to some degree, interpreted from the record created during its destruction.

As for the record itself, the system I have long favored evolved over a series of digs, with record keeping continuously modified toward simplicity. Several kinds of record are required. Among them are, importantly, the point of origin or the provenience of all artifacts (these data are easiest to tabulate on standard forms). Photographs, as well as what they purport to show, can also most easily be tabulated. Accurate maps and cross sections are a crucial part of the record, as are quick sketches showing physical relationship. Such records are all necessary, but they only support the written notes, which are the most important, representing, perhaps, minute-by-minute observations being made by the excavator. The excavator, whose decisions are final, is always in complete control.

The recordation system I use is (1) simple, (2) as nearly automatic and foolproof as possible, and (3) organized in a way that facilitates later use of the notes. The system rests, as do almost all others, on the "feature" concept, but with a fundamental difference from most. For me, the feature is *not* seen as something special, but as *any* phenomenon that may require comment or description. Robert Heizer long ago said it best: "A feature is anything you need to know about the site, but can't bring back with you." For example, the site itself becomes Feature 1. Entries under F1 actually constitute a daily log of activity at the site, being essentially a day-by-day diary. Features numbered from 2 to infinity (numbers, of course, being cheap) include everything else that requires recording, the Feature being merely a noninterpretive designator, or a noncommittal label for any data recorded. Features are not sacred and are discarded or closed out when no longer needed; that number is never, never reissued again. For example, if Feature 2 were the exploratory trench (which I always use), it will likely be closed out within a day or two or less because it would conceivably have led to the discovery that at the edge of the site there are four distinct strata. These strata would, in order of discovery, become Features 3, 4, 5, and 6. Feature 2 would then be closed because the concern now is not with the trench, but with the four strata which were discovered by means of it. There might be a discoloration in Feature 6 which would become Feature 7 and which should be described as Feature 7, not as part of Feature 6. The relationship between the two, however, would be clear in both the F6 and F7 notes.

To simplify later use even more, the notes are kept in loose-leaf note-book form so that all observations about any feature can be held together on sequenced sheets kept current with dated entries covering any period of time, possibly even for the full duration of the dig or for as little as a couple of hours. Thus, everything noted about F7 would be together in chronological order as discovered, as the phenomenon was thoroughly investigated and, finally, one hopes, understood. When work on a Fea-ture is discontinued, it must be closed out by means of a summarizing statement that closes the notes on that Feature; to repeat, the number is *never* reused.

This system of note keeping results in two or three or ten times as many observations as are perhaps necessary for finally understanding of the site, but one hopes nothing which eventually became important and, moreover, no relationship or relevant detail passed unnoticed and unre-corded. Accompanying the written notes there are, of course, daily tabu-lations of artifacts and photographs on forms designed for the purpose. And at the close of each day one perhaps records in the site diary, F1, a summary of the day's progress. There, too, I sometimes included plans for the next day, reminding myself about unclear relationships and so on. With the notes as described above, a full excavation report can be written with all the associations and physical relationships succinctly stated.

While I slowly evolved this simple notation system, I learned to avoid certain situations. Among the things I have consciously avoided was the development of different blank forms to be filled out when one is uncovering one or another structure, such as a house pattern. No matter how lengthy or elaborate the form, not all the observations called for by particular phenomenon will have a space provided on the form. Fitting a house pattern or burial or anything else into a preconceived printed form forces one's observations into a Procrustean bed and perhaps does not touch on the most interesting or significant item visible. Another thing I have always, always avoided was having too many diggers in one place. I have seen many digs where the laborers were almost touching each other, leaving no room for using tools, particularly a shovel, thus increasing costs while efficiency was reduced. I have always attempted to have only one or two people working in any project area. As result, injuries have been exceedingly rare on my digs.

The field part of the dig is completed when the operation is stopped for whatever reason. The second phase of dealing with the material is done in the laboratory, where artifacts are sorted and classified, their functions determined and described (sometimes correctly) and perhaps their cultural affiliations established. The tedium of lab work is real, but it is often broken when one detects an unusual or unsuspected relationship or significance in one or more of the items in the collection. Laboratory procedures vary so much from lab to lab that they cannot be briefly described. Suffice it to say that throughout the analysis great care must be devoted to preserving the provenience controls established in the field by the excavator because an object whose origin is unknown has lost most of its value for cultural historic purposes. While an artifact may be beautiful, its interpretive potency is almost nil unless the provenience is preserved and the object is used as part of the evidence. Although many artifacts are aesthetically stimulating for me, at the level of analysis they are *merely* documents—often eloquent, but still only documents.

When laboratory analyses are completed, one moves into the final phase, or the reason for doing the dig in the first place: the writing of the report that adds one more bit of knowledge about the past. Normally a report contains a section devoted to the structure of the site, its contents and their physical relationship to each other, and anything else relevant to the sequence of events recorded by the excavation. This section can be written from the notes at almost any time after the fieldwork ends. Other sections, almost entirely descriptive, summarize the laboratory findings, artifacts, dietary evidence, environmentally relevant items, and any other data generated during excavation or analysis. Another section highlights the similarities or differences between the site being reported and any other reported site geographically near or distant. This much done, the archaeologist summarizes the exercise, assigning the newly acquired data to its proper niche in the region's cultural history as he or she understands it.

Only when all the descriptive or "factual" material is written and recorded in final form, then and only then should the author's own thoughts be included. (I have not always kept the facts separate from speculation in the report, but I always tried.) It is at this point that the excavator can bring out a hypothesis for testing or develop this or that theory about culture change. Presumably the theory or hypothesis is tested against the evidence contained in the body of the report. With the speculations thus kept separate, readers may utilize the data in whatever way they wish, ignoring the speculation.

I find that many reports, particularly in recent years, dealing with CRM materials are rendered difficult to use and very boring because the author does not take the time to collate and redefine all the items labeled as "features." Any reader can recall reports where the author lists, with what seems to be a sense of wonder, that the site contained seven or seventeen or twenty-seven or any other number of "features." The impression is given that the site was crowded with many structural components. Excited, the reader forges on, ultimately to discover that the features were refuse pits, areas of stained or disturbed soil, or other nondescript and well-nigh uninformative phenomena. It must be remembered that the "feature" is merely a field convenience to simplify and organize the notes. It has no reality of its own, but by the time each feature is done, dug away and fully explored and left exposed or abandoned as irrelevant, the excavator has always applied a name. For example, Feature 9 when fully exposed was perhaps called a house pattern, or a granary, or a residence, structure, or dwelling. It can now be labeled "house" or "structure" or "dwelling number 1." Possibly within it was a round, raised-rim fire pit labeled "Feature 10" upon discovery before it was cleared and fully identified. But in the final report it should *not* be referred to as Feature 10 because it, a fireplace, has become *the* fireplace in house number 1. In the same way, Feature 3, the topmost stratum first encountered in the digging is perhaps reported as humus or sod; Feature 4 has become a midden zone, as is Feature 5. Feature 6 bears the label "undisturbed subsoil" that extends under the site. With all field convenience labels deleted, the report becomes a coherent account of the structures, soils, burials, midden pits, log tombs, and whatever else was found, but identified by their correct names—not as numbered "features." This is what I mean by interpreting the notes, thus benefiting the reader, who will be forever grateful to the author.

Given all the above, I mention now what is to me the most important aspect of field recordation. All notes should be descriptive, only descriptive. Few people are aware of what Stuart Chase long ago labeled the "tyranny of words"; words color and affect our perceptions of the world and our reactions to it. The culprits are often nouns, because they identify/classify the material world, calling up one or another mental image which may not accurately categorize the object or phenomenon being observed. As an example, during digging, a thin streak or zone of brick-red earth is encountered. The excavator suspects it is the edge of an area reddened by fire. But until the entire extent of the red zone and associated phenomena (ashes, charcoal, calcified bone) is cleaned and can be observed in its entirety, it should only be labeled a fire-reddened zone. However, if the excavator calls it a fireplace or a hearth or the remains of an ancient bonfire, he or she already knows what it is and has already labeled it; subconsciously his or her vigilance is relaxed and evidence may be missed. It may be a small one-time fire for smoking hides, or it might have been a large, quick one-time fire for cooking cactus pads—not a hearth (which implies continuous use) or a carefully constructed fire pit or a pottery kiln.

Obviously, when all the evidence of the prehistoric event is gathered and recorded, then and only then, should the excavator give a name to the discovery—fireplace or hide-smoking pit or cactus pad steamer. The nouns are, in fact, clues to cultural behavior—subsistence, technology, or even sacred rituals—and should be applied only when all the data are available.

Another example comes to mind. During my excavation of a Mississippian village, one workman encountered three or four dark circular stains in the floor of a trench. They resembled the stains left when vertical posts decayed, which were called post molds and were characteristic evidence of the Mississippian dwellings at the site. Instructed to follow the stains, which he called a house wall, he proceeded, and in a week had discovered scores of the stains in a linear arrangement, which he followed for 200 or 300 feet. Ultimately the line of post molds was labeled "stockade or fort." Of course, calling it a house wall did no harm, but the excavation was delayed while the workman attempted for several hours to discover the floor zone which would have begun along one side or the other of the posts. In this case, the only cost was wasted labor; the phenomenon was eventually correctly identified.

To summarize, field notes should remain descriptive until any phenomenon is fully exposed, the details of its construction understood, and the relationship of any associated material is clear—then apply a label.

As the paragraphs above indicate, I feel that fieldwork is no more than the beginning of the flow that ends with a useful and reliable published summation (i.e., report) of data uncovered during the excavation of a site. The quality of all archaeological interpretation, including any theorizing or speculation the author wishes to indulge in, rests entirely on the quality of the fieldwork and the quality of the record of that fieldwork. Of course, one could dig an entire site without making a single note and probably write something resembling the truth from memory; but the thousand and one little things not remembered which give the report its validity and usefulness would be missing.

I recognize that my approach is labor intensive and up to a point puts the entire burden on the excavator who is also the recorder. In practice, however, it is possible to delegate many of the tasks. The recorder need not make the maps; he merely tells his mapper what he wants recorded. He need not sketch the cross section, but it is his interpretation, his identification of strata and phenomena within the cross section that are to be sketched. It is not left up to the artist or mapper to "read" the section; the observer does that. Similarly, if trained help is available, one can tell an experienced individual or an assistant to take the notes at a particular section of the dig. Often you show him or her what it is he or she specifically is to excavate and to follow through, to explore and note what he or she sees. Thus, at no point have I implied that the excavator did all the work that was to be done. I meant simply that one individual is responsible for what goes into the record whether by personal effort or by delegation. In my view, then, the quality of fieldwork and any use made of the data reported thereafter continues to rest with the excavator and an extensive series of notes collected under his or her guidance.

Through the years the demands facing the excavator and the records created have increased in number and perhaps in complexity. At one time the digger saved artifacts, potsherds, flint scrap, bones, possibly charcoal, and that was it. In modern excavations, however, if one plans to utilize all the ancillary assistance that is available, soil samples are collected, ash and charcoal from the fireplaces are collected, pollen samples (i.e., small amounts of soil) must be collected from bottom to top of the excavation, there must be batches of soil saved for sifting and/or flotation in order that microdebitage such as seeds or plant parts may be saved and provenienced, and so on. At the same time, the basic relational material, the sequence of events, as always must be carefully recorded.

I conclude by suggesting that these last few pages seem to set forth fairly well my position on the growth and changes in archaeological thought and procedures as well as my philosophy of fieldwork.

Aₛ I REVIEW WHAT I have written these past months about my life, I have slowly realized that part of what I have called being a "loner" could perhaps be more accurately described, in the jargon of the '80s and '90s, as being a "private person." Almost never do I talk about what I am thinking or planning; my conversation is not studded with "Imagonnas." As an example, it took several years for me to write the first edition of the *Prehistory of North America,* which I started in Evanston while I was at Northwestern. Several secretaries transformed my handwriting into typescript, but I did not at first discuss with them my hope to create a textbook.

The "private person" notion may in part explain why I sought counsel or advice on only three of the research reports I have prepared. The first time was the manuscript I prepared after my archaeological testing of several sites in northeastern Mississippi. I sought critiques from J. B. Griffin and two or three associates on the Natchez Trace Parkway. Another was when I asked F. H. H. Roberts to react to my 1955 summary of Plains archaeology. He approved the summary, but was critical, even disdainful, of the Plains Research Center idea, saying that no one could direct such a center. The reaction, I thought, told me more about Roberts than my proposal, so I left it unchanged and, as mentioned earlier, used it as a guide for setting up the Glen Canyon project, where it worked well.

Even earlier, I had requested Robert Heizer, then the best-known Great Basin scholar, to review my 1953 preliminary account of our Danger Cave data. While accepting the data, he was critical of, even upset by, my suggestion that there existed a widespread early culture over most of the West, even hinting that I didn't know enough to correctly interpret my own data. Of course, I ignored his advice to modify my remarks. Thereafter, I have never asked anyone to review or comment on anything I have written. (However, as mentioned, I did ask Melvin Aikens to review this manuscript.)

I am not sure I know why I never sought advice on my reports. One reason does come easily to mind: I, like most people, do not like criticism. Even more important is the fact that I knew my own data better than anyone else; I trusted my own reaction to that data, and what I thought about it, more than anyone else's. And my conclusions were based entirely on what I had seen in the field, in the laboratory, and what I had found in the comparative literature I always consulted. In any case,

I fully trusted my conclusions, which I always tried to phrase conservatively and matter-of-factly. As I think more about it, I realize that many of my conclusions or snap decisions were quick hunches—or, to phrase it more elegantly, they were flashes of intuition or intuitive insights, not the result of careful thought. As everyone knows, intuitive responses result from a subconscious weighing, evaluating, and ordering of thousands of scattered observations of random and apparently unrelated events and impressions that unbidden become conscious and useful, serving when needed as guides to action or solution to problems.

Despite my "private person" behavior in most aspects of my life, I emphatically did not shun my colleagues in social situations. At the many conferences and meetings I attended I greatly enjoyed and profited from the bull sessions, the barroom hilarity, and the quiet sessions by three or four of us in hotel rooms. At those times and places I must admit that my wisecracking style, laced with sometimes barbed comments about both present and absent colleagues, could well have been misinterpreted. Indeed, I suspect it was those remarks in those contexts that gave rise to the many stories about my "feuds" with this or that colleague. All I can do in the face of the "feud" rumors is to categorically deny all of them. Actually, over the years I have known scores, if not hundreds, of my colleagues personally, and I enjoyed and respected most of them. I must also admit to respecting and enjoying alert, intelligent people more than slow-witted dullards. I regret that today I only know many of the bright younger scholars through their published work; I would much prefer to know them personally as well.

My use of the literature to determine whether I could see any relationship(s) between my own findings and those of other researchers who had excavated similar materials, led me to think of North American prehistory as resembling a vast tapestry of many threads and subtle colors, in which intricate designs could be observed, some being visible over much of the fabric. Many of those designs appear first in the Archaic, and are stronger in the later high cultures of the Christian era. In short, I came to see the 11,000 years of American prehistory as a period of interrelated growth and change, not as 1,001 single sites, each discrete and unique.

As already mentioned, my other reason for believing my own conclusions was that I consciously tried to undertake all research with my mind empty. Whether in the field, laboratory, or library. I never had a hypothesis to test, a point to prove, nor an opinion to support. I have always felt that to enter any research project with a specified goal (other than to finish by preparing a publishable report) will influence all the observations recorded during the research. I am emphatically *not* implying that such observers are dishonest. Rather, I think that, subconsciously they minimize, or even don't see, any evidence that fails to support their notions of the truth. Perhaps I am suggesting that the TV series *Dragnet* of long ago was right after all. The star of the show, Sergeant Joe Friday, always found the truth as he urged the witnesses to "Give us the facts, ma'am. Just give us the facts." Certainly, in archaeological research, facts are more valuable than preconceptions.

ALTHOUGH IN MY life I have written many words, I have yet to find a graceful way to end a piece. Usually, I merely stop when I seem to be done. This time, however, I stop because I think I've said enough even though I could probably string out the account for many more pages. I close by saying I have enjoyed making this "stream-of-consciousness" effort, and hope readers will enjoy it half as much.

The Learning Process

THROUGHOUT THIS ACCOUNT I have mentioned that being an archaeologist involved continuous learning; I also recognize that, even though excavating complex sites is a highly educational experience, one learns mostly from other people. Thus, when I was asked to present an address for the fiftieth anniversary of the Society for American Archaeology on the topic "A Personal Perspective on the Development of American Archaeology," my awareness of my debt to others led me to list, decade by decade, what I had learned and from whom I learned it, beginning in the 1930s. Titled simply *American Archaeology, 1930–1985,** it is reprinted here, except for a couple of the introductory paragraphs. (Several points related in earlier passages in this volume are touched upon in the address.)

AMERICAN ARCHAEOLOGY, 1930–1985

Since 1930–1931 my major activities have been directed toward archaeological study. I have been privileged to do research in Illinois, North Carolina, Florida, Tennessee, Mississippi, New Mexico, Utah, Nevada, Georgia, the Plains states, Guatemala, and lately in Western Samoa. It is a point of great satisfaction that I have no project unfinished or unreported; every piece of research for which I was personally responsible, no matter how trivial, has been reported, mistakes and all.

---

* Published by permission of the Society for American Archaeology from *American Archaeology: Past and Future,* by David J. Meltzer, Don D. Fowler, and Jeremy A. Sabloff, editors, 1986, pp. 53–61.

My adventures in archaeology began quite accidentally as a part of graduate work at the University of Chicago. The primary concern, it seemed to me, in my first field experience, was with technique, not with time nor history nor science nor adaptation nor other lofty goals. The aim was to record the phenomena and their relationships and the truth would be revealed—to someone. To this end, there were mandatory, rote, and often mindless procedures to be observed during excavation. But I profited greatly from this experience because, being new and unwilling at the job, I was perhaps overcritical. I attempted to assess the validity of each procedure at any given time; my conception of technique derives from this experience in that I learned to apply any given procedure *only* as it was appropriate, not because it appeared in a sequence of ritual acts to be performed. There I developed many of my professional stances (including a respect for detail), such supervisory/administrative skills as I have, and a flexible arsenal of field techniques.

In none of my learnings was I hampered by classes in American archaeology. During my seven years (1929–1936) as intermittently a graduate student, there was offered one class in European prehistory (I remember the instructor's disdain for L. S. B. Leakey and his extravagant claims of the early 1930s!!), and one sketchy seminar in field techniques. A few BAE annual reports and the lavish works of C. B. Moore gave me the limited insights into American archaeology I acquired during my graduate work. Then, as today, we learned by reading. My own reading was guided by curiosity or by whatever my fieldwork required for comprehension of the data I was uncovering. In all my research, except the Southwest, I was extremely fortunate in that most of the projects were located in blank spots on the archaeological map. Of course, most of the map was blank in the 1930s. That meant that any reported data were new and therefore comprised slight increments or contributions to knowledge. But archaeologists were then few in number. One was alone; the stimuli of discussion, pooling of ideas, debate, and argument were never available. Except for rare, informal meetings and correspondence with colleagues, there were no exchanges. Thus, I largely made my own mistakes and reached my own conclusions, with little blame attaching to others.

What was it like to develop along with a discipline? It was, and remains, a continuous learning and unlearning process. By unlearning I mean the necessity of mentally replacing incomplete, even false, data learned earlier, with this year's more complete or corrected findings. The shape of the reconstructed prehistoric landscape was forever changing. Thanks to the society and its bulletin, *American Antiquity*, there became available a series of once-manageable annual meetings and a flow of current data and interpretation. *American Antiquity* was read avidly. Then, as now, some of its content was trivial, but through its pages one began to perceive a patterning of American prehistory that all of you here today can learn with much less effort than I did.

Perhaps the most efficient way to give a personal "perspective on the development of American archaeology" is to list the events that, so far as I recall, expanded and enriched the discipline for me.

The first step toward understanding the Eastern Culture Sequence was through the McKern classificatory system. Devoid of chronological intent, its aim was Linnean; it was to establish prehistoric cultural relationships by comparing attributes (traits), and thus group, in ever larger clusters, the chaotic but numerous archaeological data of the East and Midwest. While the groupings accumulated, excavations continued, so that a relative chronology was established for many clusters of sites as these were grouped or separated by traits alone. Soon regional cultures and subcultures and sequences were recognized. Once that occurred, the usefulness of the McKern system ended and its use largely discontinued. Introduced about 1933, it helped order the data of half a continent and disappeared within a few years. Few ideas succeed so well. Its use was flawed because many did not fully understand its goals.

The 1930s were marked by other methodological matters. Trait lists dominated reports and the resultant cultural ascriptions. Comparisons were paramount; they remain in use today and are evidently a basic tool in doing culture history. And pottery types dominated thinking. Both trait lists and ceramic types were, and are, useful in many ways. They are important aids in cultural classification, but they tended in the 1930s to become ends in themselves and thus stultified thought. Their interpretive limitations still haunt us; many reports of that day are well-nigh useless for other than ceramic study.

During those years dendrochronology was much refined in the Southwest. The technique was also introduced into Southeast studies and showed great promise in several areas. Its abandonment there was lamentable, in that a valuable tool was denied to eastern archaeologists.

At this same time excavations in the Great Basin and Plains brought many new claims of association of extinct Pleistocene fauna with distinctive flint artifacts. All over the West small bands of men sought the oldest and finest of these objects. The basic scaffolding of the Early Man (or Paleo-Indian) chronology and content was erected during this decade; in fact, the Clovis site had provided a complete stratigraphic yardstick by 1933. Those terminal Pleistocene remains of the Plains forced the discarding of the constricting 3,000 to 4,000 years Holmes, Hrdlička, Kidder, and others had allowed for human occupancy of the New World. Before 1940 Luther Cressman in Oregon had discovered, and correctly interpreted, an early level of what came to be called the Western Archaic. His claim of an ancient era of habitation of the Great Basin was dismissed, flatly rejected, by Smithsonian scholars.

And in considering the 1930s, one must emphasize the tremendous impact of the Works Progress Administration (wpa) and Tennessee Valley Authority (tva) dragnet, those vast archaeological programs that revealed the variety, richness, and depth of Southeastern prehistory. But the true time depth of the sequence was not realized because there was still the straitjacket of the Southwestern calendar. At that time the Southwest's high cultures were acknowledged to be precedent and ancestral to all other North American cultural developments. There were also extensive wpa programs in the Plains during these years.

As one involved at three separate times in wpa-tva excavation programs, where large crews, unskilled assistants, and bureaucratic obstructionism created an optimal atmosphere for frustration, I look back on those years affectionately but somewhat sadly. I survived only because of my legendary patience and optimism. Many wpa excavations, no doubt including my own, were criminally inept. Many deeply stratified sites were dug and reported as if they were the debris of only a moment in time. Many more were not reported at all, or in some cases years later, when the skimpy notes were cold and the excavator no longer available. I will not dwell on this aspect of wpa research because it has been dealt with before. But one is compelled to mention Maj. William S. Webb, physicist *cum* archaeologist, who, acting in response to pressure from the Smithsonian (si) and later this society, was the prime visible force in creating government awareness of its responsibility for preservation of cultural resources as he directed the tva program.

One would be even more remiss in failing to mention that the era ended with a masterly synthesis by James Ford and Gordon Willey of the decade of Southeastern WPA-TVA research. That study, spectacularly wrong in some ways but enduringly correct in most things, is truly a benchmark in establishing a regional cultural sequence where there had been but a vacuum. Even earlier, Duncan Strong produced a synthesis of the scattered data of the Plains so brilliantly that Plains scholars stood in his shadow for twenty years.

After World War II the tempo of archaeological life was permanently changed. There came the River Basin Surveys. The Missouri River Basin and many other river basins were soon populated by archaeologists; my involvement was first with the Missouri River Basin and was relatively early and richly rewarding. I was assigned to the Midwest Region of the National Park Service (NPS) in Omaha, but no one knew what I was expected to do. Because the NPS took the lead in the basin program, justifying and defending the budget for the operation and then transferring the funds to the SI, which reluctantly undertook the research, I was assigned as liaison between the SI, NPS, and all institutions of higher learning in the Missouri River Basin. I worked as closely as possible with the administrative hierarchy of the SI (F. H. H. Roberts, W. Wedel, and P. S. Cooper) as consultant, gadfly, and co-conspirator. (Wedel once took written notice of my efforts as "helpful and stimulating," a most charitable description.) But my most useful activity was persuading the archaeologists of the Missouri Basin to divert their research funds, field schools, etc., to sites jeopardized by the dam/reservoir construction. That kind of cooperation of course was built into the River Basin Surveys design from the beginning. The cooperative program I helped establish soon evolved into the NPS contract system, a system still operating. The River Basin Surveys ultimately involved some 200 reservoirs. The research resulted in extraordinary gains in knowledge, the ordering of the major cultures in all major river valleys from Washington State to North Florida. Serendipitously, the salvage operation crystallized the conservation ethic as a governmental obligation so far as archaeological data are concerned.

In 1948, before my stint on the Plains was over, two major events led to almost catastrophic changes in the already unstable landscape of archaeological fact. First was Antevs's reconstruction of Holocene climate of the continent westward from the Mississippi River. He provided an environmental framework that both stimulated and restricted research. The reasoning went thus: if the archaeological record of the region was apparently locally blank, from 5000 to 3000 B.C., the explanation was ready at hand. That period was the height of the Antevs Altithermal, and humans had left the region in order to survive. It offered instant explanation and was invoked daily in the Great Basin, the Southwest, and the Plains. Very soon, the Antevs sequence of environments became dogma and served to delay the acceptance of any data that ran counter to Antevs's scheme. Interestingly, Antevs himself did not postulate anything but climate! It was the archaeologists who created the equation: Altithermal = too hot for humans = abandonment. Most of the problems that grew out of Antevs's contribution have been survived; his findings are still valid and are still used, but with more restraint.

Then, again in 1947, the results of Libby's experiments with C-14 on dated organic artifacts (whose ages were already known by other means) were available by word of mouth. Long before the publication of his famous paper the revisions of chronological perspective had begun. Suddenly, the true time depth of the Southeast was known, outmoding all previous wisdom; the true relationship of Adena to Hopewell became apparent; the extreme age of the Tennessee River shell mounds was established. Cressman's insistence that the desert cultures of the West were ancient was instantly confirmed. There are scores of other examples of changes in then-current belief because of the availability of C-14 dates. The importance of C-14 to the discipline today need not be examined, being universally recognized. A third event, ignored by many and therefore largely futile, was W. W. Taylor's essay in which a somewhat new view of the nature of archaeology was proposed. Although ignored for a time, its essence was reissued serially by many authors in the 1960s as the "New Archaeology."

In retrospect, the 1950s were no more tranquil than the last half of the 1940s, because other methodological breakthroughs occurred. That decade was one of consolidation of data, expansion of field research, and the quiet reintroduction of at least one idea—human ecology—that was highly attractive to many of us. (The step to systems, made by Clarke in the 1960s, intensified the concern with ecology). Several Paleo-Indian sites were excavated and lucidly reported. The most outstanding events, however, were a series of seminal publications that gave new vitality to field archaeology by opening new avenues of interpretation. One was Willey's Viru Valley study and its use of settlement patterns to gain new perspectives on prehistoric cultures; another was Spaulding's first article on statistics, which was not the first by any means but had the greatest impact; the Willey and Phillips volume on method and theory brought a pseudotheoretical base, a classificatory scheme, and the phrase "archaeology is anthropology or it is nothing," thus expanding the scope of archaeological interpretations. And, diffidently, I mention Danger Cave, which suggested a different interpretation of Great Basin prehistory. The study of American prehistory has not yet outgrown the concepts of that decade. Salvage projects—I prefer to say "emergency archaeology"—have continued. One long-term project, the Glen Canyon program under my direction, marks the first explicit and continual use of multidiscipline research teams. Soon thereafter the much more tightly organized and widely reported Tehuacan Project firmly established the value of such field teams and their ecological findings in expanding the scope of archaeological understanding.

The stimulation of the 1950s was shattered in the 1960s by an effort, by a few vocal zealots (who had read and varyingly understood Binford's 1962 seminal article, "Archeology as Anthropology") to confine archaeological endeavor within the sterile boundaries established by the logical positivists and the philosophers of science. Having discovered, studied, and discarded the philosophers of science at least a decade earlier, I was dismayed, but relatively untouched and unscarred by the storm of preachment and polemic that confused and polarized the then-younger students of prehistory. Many have since recovered. To characterize the decade of the 1960s and into the 1970s, I paraphrase the felicitous words of the prominent British scholar and see it as a time of polemic, the decline of literacy, and the denigration of fieldwork. There also arose a temporary contempt for culture history as being intellectually barren and wasteful or as being a humanistic interest for which there was no room in the science archaeology was to become. Throughout this phase the dominant theme was a demand for theory and the discovering of laws. Of more lasting value was the concern with culture change and its causes. If the causes are indeed discoverable, the search is taking far longer than was predicted.

When the stifling polemic dust subsided and polarization diminished, a series of important, useful, if not powerful, ideas from geography, ecology, statistics, and biology, among others, can be identified as having survived. Archaeologists of the 1980s routinely invoke a series of conceptual tools, most of which can be subsumed under the single rubric of human ecology. I refer, of course, to concerns (from different conceptual spheres) with such things as paleoenvironments, subsistence, paleobotany (which involves both macrofossils and palynology), faunal analysis, ethnoarchaeology, central place theory and trade/exchange networks, settlement pattern and locational analysis, and other concepts that enrich and refine our interpretations of prehistoric human behavior. All these concepts can best be recognized as powerful technical and methodological refinements in both data collection and manipulation.

Even while I recognize the value of these new ways of looking at archaeological data, I truly deplore the trend toward the narrowing of scholarly focus. Careers can now be built on flint technology or use-wear studies, what happens to an archaeological deposit after abandonment, the uses and abuses of sampling in archaeological research, taphonomy, bone tool industries, and the like. With such narrow interests I see many archaeologists becoming terribly parochial, losing the holistic view that has made archaeological synthesis the lifeblood of the discipline. Here I mention with pleasure that there has been a call of late by some young scholars for a "return to basics." There is no problem for those of us who tried never to leave them.

I mention the last convulsive event merely in passing, because all of you know much about it. It is the traumatic refocusing or unfocusing of archaeological effort in the early 1970s on what is called Cultural Resource Management. This I can conservatively label as a mixed blessing, which has often led to grave mistakes and has had costs far beyond its scientific rewards; while there are a few bright spots in the record, on balance CRM has generally harmed our discipline.

One important last positive continuing force in shaping our discipline must be identified. I have already mentioned those times in the past when huge quantities of new data were being generated, but were not always understood by isolated researchers new to the region. Here the regional working conference has time and again been a powerful force in the consolidation and synthesis of those newly discovered regional data. I have been privileged to have been active in three such conferences: the Southeastern Archaeological Conference in the 1930s, the Plains Conference in the 1940s and 1950s, and the Great Basin Conference in the 1950s. All three have broadened to become Anthropological conferences; two sponsor journals. The importance of these informal, lightly structured voluntary associations of scholars in facilitating the early ordering of widely divergent data cannot be overstressed even today.

An encouraging trend that began in the late 1970s continues today. That was the appearance of several summaries of regional culture sequences: volumes dealing with New England, the Great Lakes area, Florida, the Southeast, the Southwest, and California by regional authorities are some examples. As might be expected, they vary in excellence. Their very existence is an important comment upon the increasingly complete knowledge of regional culture histories now available and the continuing need for the careful building of such histories.

As for the twenty years' effects of the "revolution" of the 1960s, I still see, along with Dunnell, (1) a lack of any comprehensive theory; (2) the continuing conflicts in CRM archaeology; (3) parochialism characterizing the discipline; and (4) loss of faith in the new archaeology.

Although this account is an undocumented highly personal one, I think I have identified most of the breakthroughs and some of the residual constraints of our discipline in what has been a progression from gathering data to attempts at explanations. Certainly I have listed the events that required me continuously to rearrange and replace ideas and data, and, therefore, have contributed to my own ever-broadening conception of what archaeology is and is not to the changing pattern of American culture history over the years.

In order to terminate these nostalgic ramblings, I recapitulate. I have been both a participant and observer as the society grew from a few dozen forlorn, but courageous, souls to several thousand members. To the corpus of data and concepts that comprise American archaeology today I have contributed energy, mistakes, and a few scattered ideas. So, perforce, I have been *in seriatum* involved in gathering, classifying, ordering, sequencing, and synthesizing data; proselyting, sympathizing, and even agonizing as I learned and passed on to students and others what I know about American prehistory. And in recent decades I witnessed wrangling and jangling, and division, prostitution, and even moral destitution of some segments of our profession. More lately, I have seen the healing of psychic wounds and a return to fieldwork.

Those who know me best know that throughout fifty of the fifty-five years of my professional life I have enjoyed the moral support of my wife, Jane. Therefore, this year brought me another anniversary of a more personal and valued kind. As Jane and I shared those years, the love and respect we hold for each other grows ever stronger.

Thus, I have experienced more than fifty years of excitement, spent much time with collections, journals, and books, and have enjoyed great intellectual and emotional satisfaction. As I always have, I see archaeology as rooted in anthropology, the humanities, and in certain aspects of science. Further, I see culture history as the core of the discipline, a core much enriched by today's concern with human ecology and culture as a system. Despite some pessimism in the remarks above, I feel that archaeology is today in ferment and therefore healthy. It is much more interesting than ever before.

APPENDIX II

Résumé

1980–1994   Adjunct Professor, University of Oregon, Eugene

1986   Distinguished Professor of Anthropology Emeritus, University of Utah, Salt Lake City

1975   Distinguished Professor of Anthropology, University of Utah, Salt Lake City

1963–1973   Director, Utah Museum of Natural History, Salt Lake City

1952–1960   Professor and Head, Department of Anthropology, University of Utah, Salt Lake City

1948–1975   Professor of Anthropology, University of Utah, Salt Lake City
1947–1948   Regional Archaeologist, Region II, National Park Service, Omaha, Nebraska

1945–1946   Archaeologist, Natchez Trace Parkway, National Park Service,
1938–1942   Tupelo, Mississippi

1938–1939   Acting Superintendent, Ocmulgee National Monument, National Park Service, Macon, Georgia

1937–1938   Ranger, Montezuma Castle National Monument, National Park Service, Camp Verde, Arizona

SELECTED PROFESSIONAL ACTIVITIES AND HONORS

Jesse D. Jennings Prize for Excellence, established by the Great Basin Anthropological Conference, 1990
Plenary address, 50th Anniversary Meeting, Society for American Archaeology, 1985.
Distinguished Service Award, Society for American Archaeology, 1982.
Distinguished Service Award, Society for Conservation Archaeology, 1982.

Doctor of Science, University of Utah, 1980.
Member, National Academy of Sciences, 1977.
Fulbright-Hayes Lecturer, University of Auckland, New Zealand, 1979.
Distinguished Professor of Anthropology as of January 1, 1974.
Distinguished Research Professor, University of Utah, 1970–1971.
Director, Glen Canyon Archaeological Salvage Project, 1957–1965.
Vice-President, American Association for the Advancement of Science; Chairman, Section H, 1961, 1971.
President, Society for American Archaeology, 1959–1960.
Viking Medalist in Archaeology, 1958.
Executive Board Member, American Anthropological Association, 1953–1956.

EDITORSHIPS

1950–1953   Editor, University of Utah Anthropological Papers
1963–1985

1950–1954   Editor, *American Antiquity*, vols. 16, 17, 18, 19. Bulletin of the Society for American Archaeology

1947–1950   Editor, *Plains Archeological Conference Newsletter*

SELECTED PUBLICATIONS

1994   *Accidental Archaeologist: Memoirs of Jesse D. Jennings.* University of Utah Press, Salt Lake City.

1989   *Prehistory of North America.* Third Edition. Mayfield Publishing Company, Mountain View, California.

1986   American Archaeology 1930–1985: One Person's View. In *American Archaeology: Past and Future. A Celebration of the Society for American Archaeology, 1935–1985*, edited by David J. Meltzer, Don D. Fowler, and Jeremy A. Sabloff. Smithsonian Institution Press, Washington, D.C.

1986   *Handbook of American Indians*, Volume 11, *Great Basin.* Washington, D.C. Smithsonian Institution (subeditor and contributor).

1985   River Basin Surveys: Origins, Operations, and Results, 1945–1969. *American Antiquity*, Vol. 50, No. 2, pp. 281–296.

1983   Samoan Village Patterns: Four Examples (with Richard Holmer and Gregory Jackmond). *Journal of Polynesian Society*, Vol. 91, No. 1, pp. 81–102.

1983   *Ancient North Americans*, and *Ancient South Americans* (editor and contributor). W. H. Freeman and Co., San Francisco.

1981   *Bull Creek.* University of Utah Anthropological Papers, No. 105. University of Utah Press, Salt Lake City.

1980   *Cowboy Cave.* University of Utah Anthropological Papers, No. 104. University of Utah Press, Salt Lake City.

1980   *Sudden Shelter* (with Alan Schroedl, Richard Holmer). University of Utah Anthropological Papers, No. 103. University of Utah Press, Salt Lake City.

1980   *Archaeological Excavations in Western Samoa* (with Richard Holmer, and sections by Nancy Hewitt, Gregory Jackmond, Joel Janetski, Ernest Lohse). Pacific Anthropological Records, No. 32, Department of Anthropology, Bernice P. Bishop Museum, Honolulu, Hawaii.

1979   *Polynesian Prehistory* (editor and contributor). Harvard University Press, Cambridge.

1978   *Prehistory of Utah and Eastern Great Basin.* University of Utah Anthropological Papers, No. 98. University of Utah Press, Salt Lake City.

1978   *Ancient Native Americans* (editor and contributor). W. H. Freeman and Company, San Francisco.

1977   *The Native Americans* (with Robert F. Spencer). Second Edition. Harper and Rowe, Inc., New York.

1976   *Excavations on Upolu, Western Samoa* (with R. Holmer, J. Janetski, and H. Smith). Pacific Anthropological Records, No. 25, Bernice P. Bishop Museum, Honolulu, Hawaii.

1974   Across an Arctic Bridge. In *The World of the American Indian.* National Geographic Society, Washington, D.C.

1974   *Prehistory of North America.* Second Edition. McGraw-Hill Book Co., New York.

1973   The Short Useful Life of a Simple Hypothesis. *Tebiwa,* Vol. 16, No. 1, pp. 1–9.

1973   *The Social Uses of Archaeology.* Addison-Wesley Module in Anthropology, No. 41, Reading, Mass.

1972   *Readings in Anthropology,* Third Edition. McGraw-Hill Book Co., New York.

1968   *Prehistory of North America.* McGraw-Hill Book Co., Inc., New York.

1966   Early Man in the Desert West. *Quaternaria,* Vol. 8, pp. 81–89.

1966   *Glen Canyon: A Summary.* University of Utah Anthropological Papers, No. 81, *Glen Canyon Series,* No. 31. Reprinted 1974. University of Utah Press, Salt Lake City.

1966   *Readings in Anthropology.* Second Edition. McGraw-Hill Book Co., New York.

1965   The Glen Canyon: A Multidiscipline Project (with Floyd W. Sharrock). *Utah Historical Quarterly,* Vol. 33, No. 1.

1965   *Native Americans* (edited with Robert F. Spencer). Harper and Row, Inc., New York.

1964   *Prehistoric Man in the New World* (edited with Edward Norbeck). Rice University Semicentenntial Publications. University of Chicago Press, Chicago.

1963   Educational Functions. In *The Teaching of Archaeological Anthropology.* American Anthropological Association Memoir, No. 94, pp. 247–252. Washington, D.C.

1963   Administration of Contract Emergency Archaeological Programs. *American Antiquity,* Vol. 28, No. 3, pp. 282–285.

1960   Aboriginal Peoples. *Utah Historical Quarterly,* Vol. 28, No. 3, pp. 211–221.

1960   Early Man in Utah. *Utah Historical Quarterly,* Vol. 28, No. 1, pp. 3–27.

1959   *The Glen Canyon Archeological Survey,* parts I and II. University of Utah Anthropological Papers, No. 39. *Glen Canyon Series,* No, 6, pp. iv–13, 677–707. University of Utah Press, Salt Lake City.

1957   *Danger Cave.* University of Utah Anthropological Papers, No. 27. (Also published as Memoirs of the Society for American Archaeology, No. 14). Reprinted 1973. University of Utah Press, Salt Lake City.

1957   *The Ormond Beach Mound, East Central Florida* (with G. R. Willey and M. T. Newman). Bureau of American Ethnology Bulletin, No. 164, Anthropological Papers, No. 49. Washington, D.C.

1956   Editor, The American Southwest: A Problem in Cultural Isolation. In *Seminars in Archaeology: 1955,* Robert Wauchope, ed. Memoirs of the Society for American Archaeology, Vol. 22, No. 2, pp. 81–127. Washington, D.C.

1955   *Readings in Anthropology* (with E. A. Hoebel and E. R. Smith). McGraw-Hill Book Co., Inc., New York.

1952   Prehistory of the Lower Mississippi Valley. In *Archaeology of Eastern United States,* J. B. Griffin, ed., pp. 256–271. University of Chicago Press, Chicago.

1950   Table Top Archaeology. *Archaeology,* Vol. 3, No. 3, pp. 174–178.

1950   On the Validity of Tepexpan Man. *Texas Archeological and Paleontological Society Bulletin,* Vol. 21, pp. 105–110.

1949   Proceedings of the Fifth Conference for Plains Archeology (associate editor). *University of Nebraska Anthropology Notebook Series,* No. 1.

1946   *Excavations at Kaminal Juyu, Guatemala* (with A. V. Kidder and E. M. Shook). Carnegie Institution of Washington Publication, No. 561. Washington, D.C.

1944   Archaeological Survey of Natchez Trace. *American Antiquity,* Vol. 9, No. 4, pp. 408–414.

1943   The Site Kaminal Juyu and its Contribution in Certain Chronological Problems of Middle America. Ph.D. dissertation, University of Chicago (microfilmed).

1941   Chickasaw and Earlier Indian Cultures of Northeast Mississippi. *Journal of Mississippi History,* Vol. 3, No. 3, pp. 158–226.

1941   *Peachtree Mound and Village Site, Cherokee County, N.D.* (with F. M. Setzler). Bureau of American Ethnology Bulletin, No. 131. Washington, D.C.

1939   Recent Excavations at the Lamar Site, Ocmulgee National Monument, Macon, Georgia. In *Proceedings of the Society for Georgia Archeology,* pp. 45–55.

1934   The Importance of Scientific Method in Excavation. In *Bulletin of the Archaeological Society of North Carolina,* Vol. 1, No. 1, pp. 13–15.

INDEX

303